SEMIOTICS
THE BASICS

Following the success of the first edition, *Semiotics: the Basics* has been revised to include new material on the development of semiotics from Saussure to contemporary socio-semiotics. This second edition is fully updated with an extended index, glossary, and further reading section. Using jargon-free language and lively up-to-date examples, this book demystifies this highly interdisciplinary subject and addresses questions such as:

- What is a sign?
- Which codes do we take for granted?
- What is a text?
- How can semiotics be used in textual analysis?
- Who are Saussure, Peirce, Barthes and Jakobson – and why are they important?

The new edition of *Semiotics: the Basics* provides an interesting and accessible introduction to this field of study, and is a must-have for anyone coming to semiotics for the first time.

Daniel Chandler is a Lecturer in the department of Theatre, Film and Television Studies at the University of Wales, Aberystwyth.

SEMIOTICS
THE BASICS

SECOND EDITION

Daniel Chandler

Routledge
Taylor & Francis Group

LONDON AND NEW YORK

First published 2002 by Routledge
2 Park Square, Milton Park, Abingdon,
Oxon OX14 4RN

Simultaneously published in the USA and Canada
by Routledge
270 Madison Ave, New York, NY 10016

Reprinted 2002, 2004 (twice), 2005, 2007, 2008 (twice)

Routledge is an imprint of the Taylor & Francis Group, an informa business

Second edition 2007

© 2002, 2007 Daniel Chandler

Typeset in Times New Roman and Scala Sans by
Florence Production, Stoodleigh, Devon
Printed and bound in Great Britain by
The Cromwell Press, Trowbridge, Wiltshire

British Library Cataloguing in Publication Data
A catalogue record for this book is available from the British Library

Library of Congress Cataloging in Publication Data
Chandler, Daniel.
 Semiotics: the basics/Daniel Chandler. – 2nd ed.
  p. cm.
 Includes bibliographical references and index.
  1. Semiotics. I. Title.
 P99.C463 2007 302.2–dc22

                        2006024738

ISBN10: 0–415–36376–4 (hbk)
ISBN10: 0–415–36375–6 (pbk)
ISBN10: 0–203–01493–6 (ebk)

ISBN13: 978–0–415–36376–1 (hbk)
ISBN13: 978–0–415–36375–4 (pbk)
ISBN13: 978–0–203–01493–6 (ebk)

For Jem

'The subtlety of nature is greater many times
over than the subtlety of argument'
Francis Bacon, *Novum Organum*
(1620) Aphorism XXIV

CONTENTS

ILLUSTRATIONS

PREFACE

The first version of this book was written in 1994 as an online hypertext document. No comparable introductory text on the subject was available at the time so I rashly attempted to create one which suited my own purposes and those of my media studies students. It was partly a way of advancing and clarifying my own understanding of the subject. Like many other readers driven by a fascination with meaning-making, my forays into semiotics had been frustrated by many of the existing books on the subject which seemed to make it confusing, dull and deeply obscure. So much of what is written about semiotics is written as if to keep out those who are not already 'members of the club'. This text is intended to be a 'reader's companion' in approaching more difficult semiotic texts, which so often assume knowledge of much of the jargon.

One of the things that attracted me to semiotics was the way in which it supports my own enjoyment of crossing the 'boundaries' of academic disciplines, and of making connections between apparently disparate phenomena. However, I am not a polymath, so there are inevitably many subjects which are neglected here. In this text I have confined myself to *human* semiosis, so that this is not the place to find an introduction to such branches of semiotics as *zoosemiotics* (the study of the behaviour and communication of animals) or *biosemiotics* (the study of the semiotics of biology and of the biological basis of signs). My focus is on the humanities and so there is no mathematical or computer semiotics here either. Even within the humanities, I did not feel competent to cover topics such as musical or architectural semiotics. I know that students of some of these subjects are among those who have consulted the text, which lends me some hope that they will find the exploration of general principles of some relevance to their own priorities. To support the needs of such readers, the current edition does include suggestions for further reading in some of the subject areas not explicitly covered within the text. The exclusion of certain subjects is not, of course, to suggest that they are any less important to the semiotic enterprise. The unavoidable selectivity of the text invites the productivity of the reader in its deconstruction. Driven by their own purposes, readers will no doubt be alert to 'what is conspicuous by its absence'.

Semiotics is a huge field, and no treatment of it can claim to be comprehensive. My attempt to offer a coherent account of some key concepts is in some ways misleading: there are divergent schools of thought in semiotics, and there is remarkably little consensus among contemporary theorists regarding the scope of the subject, core concepts or methodological tools. In part through terminology such as *signifier*, *signified* and *code*, this account reflects the influence of European 'semiology'; however, it goes beyond the Saussurean legacy of 'bracketing the referent' and draws upon the Peircean tradition in recognizing that meanings depend on referential contexts as well as systemic codes. Indeed, in this second edition, I have given more emphasis to the theories of Roman Jakobson precisely because his version of structuralism, while both building upon and reacting against some of Saussure's tenets, also adopted Peircean concepts. Indeed, Jakobson even co-opted Peirce as 'one of the greatest pioneers of structural linguistic analysis' (Jakobson 1952b, 555). Nevertheless, readers seeking an introduction to specifically Peircean semiotics (as opposed to how Peircean concepts have been incorporated into the European structuralist tradition) are referred elsewhere (Merrell 1995b, Zeman 1997, Deledalle 2000, Merrell 2001).

The lengthy treatment of structuralist semiotics in this book is intended to be of particular value to readers who wish to use semiotics as an approach to textual analysis. However, semiotics is far more than a method of analysing texts, and I hope I will also inspire the reader's enthusiasm for exploring some of the fascinating philosophical issues raised by semioticians. In case it is not obvious to readers, I should declare a social constructionist bias, which is not shared by all semioticians. For semioticians who are (in contrast) drawn towards philosophical realism, reality is wholly external to and independent of how we conceptualize the world. Social constructionism does not entail denying the existence of all external reality but it does assume that our sign-systems (language and other media) play a major part in 'the social construction of reality' (or at least 'the construction of social reality') and that realities cannot be separated from the sign-systems in which they are experienced. It is hardly surprising when social constructionists are drawn to semiotics, but readers may of course insist on being philosophical realists without abandoning semiotics (many semioticians are indeed realists). Note that I make reference here to an opposition between idealism and realism, and those who are already well-read in philosophy may object that this sometimes involves a common conflation of two pairings, namely:

1. *idealism* vs. *epistemological realism* (stances on the issue of whether or not the reality of a physical world is dependent on our minds or language);
2. *nominalism* vs. *conceptual realism* (stances on the issue of whether or not the reality of abstract universals is dependent on our minds or language).

Though I may be blamed for oversimplification, such conflation should be taken to refer to what these pairings have in common: namely, the issue of whether we have any access to what is real apart from the mind and language. A potential problem is that I refer to Peirce (as do most commentators, and as did Peirce himself) as a 'realist' (by which I mean an epistemological realist), but he can *also* be labelled a 'conceptual idealist' (Sebeok 1994a, 14–15; cf. Merrell 1997, Chapter 4, on Peirce's 'objective idealism').

In quoting from the text of Saussure's *Course in General Linguistics*, the translation used is that of Roy Harris (Saussure 1983), although, following the practice of John Sturrock in using this translation (Sturrock 1986, 31, 32), I have retained the terms 'signifier' and 'signified' rather than use Harris's translation of *signifiant* as 'signal' and *signifié* as 'signification'. Citations from Peirce's *Collected Papers* (Peirce 1931–58) follow the standard practice of listing the volume number and section number thus: (2.227). Wherever I include quotations within the current text it may be assumed that any italicization was that of the original author except where I add the note – '*my emphasis*'.

A Korean translation of the first edition of this book is currently in progress. If there is a demand for translations into other languages, please approach my British publishers.

At the time of writing, the online version of this text was at:

http://www.aber.ac.uk/media/Documents/S4B/

URLs change periodically, so, if necessary, you could use a search engine to locate it.

ACKNOWLEDGEMENTS

The original online text might not have found its way into print if it were not for the unsolicited encouragement to publish which I received from the philosopher Anthony C. Grayling of Birkbeck College, University of London, to whcm I am particularly grateful. Special thanks go to my linguist colleagues Bob Morris Jones and Marilyn Martin-Jones for their continued support and encouragement throughout the evolution of this text and of its author. I would also like to thank Vanessa Hogan Vega and Iván Rodrigo Mendizábal for producing a Spanish translation of an early online version (Chandler 1998), and Maria Constantopoulou of the Athens University of Economics and Business for the Greek translation of the online version and for several invitations to teach summer schools in Greece for MSc students of Marketing and Communication. The development of both editions of the book has benefited from the useful comments of a number of reviewers (although it was not always possible to address all of their sometimes conflicting points). Special thanks for helpful reviews are due to Juan A. Prieto-Pablos of the University of Seville, to Ernest W. B. Hess-Lüttich of the University of Berne, to Edward McDonald of the University of Auckland, and to Guy Cook of the Open University.

For specific assistance with the first edition I would like to repeat my thanks to Winfried Nöth of the University of Kassel for his useful comments on articulation and empty signifiers and to David Glen Mick of the University of Wisconsin-Madison, who kept me updated on the semiotics of advertising. For the second edition, thanks to Roderick Munday, Osama Ammar and Tommi Turunen (all of whom have studied with me) for their helpful comments and to Jo B. Paoletti of the University of Maryland for tracking down for me the original source of the widely misattributed 'pink and blue' quotation in Chapter 5. Martin Ryder of the University of Colorado at Denver suggested weblinks. Figure 4.4 was adapted from diagrams ©2001 Software Usability Research Laboratory, Wichita State University. The image from the plaque on Pioneer 10 shown in Figure 6.1 was produced by the Pioneer Project at NASA Ames Research Center and obtained from NASA's National Space Science Data Center with the kind assistance of John F. Cooper.

INTRODUCTION

If you go into a bookshop and ask an assistant where to find a book on semiotics, you are likely to meet with a blank look. Even worse, you might be asked to define what semiotics is – which would be a bit tricky if you were looking for a beginner's guide. It's worse still if you do know a bit about semiotics, because it can be hard to offer a simple definition which is of much use in the bookshop. If you've ever been in such a situation, you'll probably agree that it's wise not to ask. Semiotics could be anywhere. The shortest definition is that it is *the study of signs*. But that doesn't leave enquirers much wiser. 'What do you mean by a sign?' people usually ask next. The kinds of signs that are likely to spring immediately to mind are those which we routinely refer to as 'signs' in everyday life, such as road signs, pub signs and star signs. If you were to agree with them that semi-otics can include the study of all these and more, people will probably assume that semiotics is about 'visual signs'. You would confirm their hunch if you said that signs can also be drawings, paintings and photographs, and by now they'd be keen to direct you to the art and photography sections. But if you are thick-skinned and tell them that it also includes words, sounds and 'body language', they may reasonably wonder what all these things have in common and how anyone could possibly study such disparate phenomena. If you get this far, they've probably already 'read the signs' which suggest that you are either eccentric or insane and communication may have ceased.

DEFINITIONS

Beyond the most basic definition as 'the study of signs', there is considerable variation among leading semioticians as to what semiotics involves. One of the broadest definitions is that of Umberto Eco, who states that 'semiotics is concerned with everything that can be taken as a sign' (Eco 1976, 7). Semiotics involves the study not only of what we refer to as 'signs' in everyday speech, but of anything which 'stands for' something else. In a semiotic sense, signs take the form of words, images, sounds, gestures and objects. Contemporary semioticians study signs not in isolation but as part of semiotic 'sign-systems' (such as a medium or genre). They study how meanings are made and how reality is represented.

Theories of signs (or 'symbols') appear throughout the history of philosophy from ancient times onwards (see Todorov 1982), the first explicit reference to semiotics as a branch of philosophy appearing in John Locke's *Essay Concerning Human Understanding* (1690). However, the two primary traditions in contemporary semiotics stem respectively from the Swiss linguist Ferdinand de Saussure (1857–1913) and the American philosopher Charles Sanders Peirce (pronounced 'purse') (1839–1914). Saussure's term *sémiologie* dates from a manuscript of 1894. The first edition of his *Course in General Linguistics*, published posthumously in 1916, contains the declaration that:

> It is . . . possible to conceive of a science *which studies the role of signs as part of social life*. It would form part of social psychology, and hence of general psychology. We shall call it

semiology (from the Greek *sēmeîon*, 'sign'). It would investigate the nature of signs and the laws governing them. Since it does not yet exist, one cannot say for certain that it will exist. But it has a right to exist, a place ready for it in advance. Linguistics is only one branch of this general science. The laws which semiology will discover will be laws applicable in linguistics, and linguistics will thus be assigned to a clearly defined place in the field of human knowledge.

(Saussure 1983, 15–16)

While for the linguist Saussure 'semiology' was 'a science which studies the role of signs as part of social life', to the philosopher Charles Peirce the field of study which he called 'semeiotic' (or 'semiotic') was the 'formal doctrine of signs', which was closely related to logic (Peirce 1931–58, 2.227). Working quite independently from Saussure across the Atlantic, Peirce borrowed his term from Locke, declaring that:

Logic, in its general sense, is . . . only another name for semiotic (sémeiötiké), the quasi-necessary, or formal, doctrine of signs. By describing the doctrine as 'quasi-necessary', or formal, I mean that we observe the characters of such signs as we know, and . . . by a process which I will not object to naming abstraction, we are led to statements, eminently fallible, and therefore in one sense by no means necessary, as to what must be the characters of all signs used by a 'scientific' intelligence, that is to say, by an intelligence capable of learning by experience.

(Peirce 1931–58, 2.227)

Peirce and Saussure are widely regarded as the co-founders of what is now more generally known as *semiotics*. They established two major theoretical traditions. Saussure's term 'semiology' is sometimes used to refer to the Saussurean tradition while the term 'semiotics' sometimes refers to the Peircean tradition. However, nowadays the term 'semiotics' is widely used as an umbrella term to embrace the whole field (Nöth 1990, 14). We will outline and discuss both the Saussurean and Peircean models of the sign in the next chapter.

Some commentators adopt Charles W. Morris's definition of semiotics (a reductive variant of Saussure's definition) as 'the science of signs' (Morris 1938, 1–2). The term 'science' is misleading. As yet, semiotics involves no widely agreed theoretical assumptions, models or empirical methodologies. Semiotics has tended to be largely theoretical, many of its theorists seeking to establish its scope and general principles. Peirce and Saussure, for instance, were both concerned with the fundamental definition of the sign. Peirce developed logical taxonomies of types of signs. Many subsequent semioticians have sought to identify and categorize the codes or conventions according to which signs are organized. Clearly there is a need to establish a firm theoretical foundation for a subject which is currently characterized by a host of competing theoretical assumptions. As for methodologies, Saussure's theories constituted a starting point for the development of various structuralist methodologies for analysing texts and social practices. For Roman Jakobson, semiotics 'deals with those general principles which underlie the structure of all signs whatever and with the character of their utilization within messages, as well as with the specifics of the various sign systems and of the diverse messages using those different kinds of signs' (Jakobson 1968, 698). Structuralist methods have been very widely employed in the analysis of many cultural phenomena. However, they are not universally accepted: socially oriented theorists have criticized their exclusive focus on structure, and no alternative methodologies have as yet been widely adopted.

Semiotics is not widely institutionalized as an academic discipline (although it does have its own associations, conferences and journals, and it exists as a department in a handful of universities). It is a field of study involving many different theoretical stances and methodological tools. Although there are some self-styled 'semioticians', those involved in semiotics include linguists, philosophers, psychologists, sociologists, anthropologists, literary, aesthetic and media theorists, psychoanalysts and educationalists.

RELATION TO LINGUISTICS

This book concentrates on structuralist semiotics (and its poststructuralist critiques). It is difficult to disentangle European semiotics from structuralism in its origins. Linguistic structuralism derived primarily from Saussure, Hjelmslev and Jakobson. It was Jakobson who first coined the term 'structuralism' in 1929 (Jakobson 1990, 6). Structuralism is an analytical method which involves the application of the linguistic model to a much wider range of social phenomena. Jakobson wrote that 'Language is . . . a purely semiotic system . . . The study of signs, however, . . . must take into consideration also applied semiotic structures, as for instance, architecture, dress, or cuisine . . . any edifice is simultaneously some sort of refuge and a certain kind of message. Similarly, any garment responds to definitely utilitarian requirements and at the same time exhibits various semiotic properties' (1968, 703). He identified 'the cardinal functions of language' (see Chapter 6) and argued that this should lead to 'an analogous study of the other semiotic systems' (ibid.). Structuralists search for 'deep structures' underlying the 'surface features' of sign-systems: Lévi-Strauss in myth, kinship rules and totemism; Lacan in the unconscious; Barthes and Greimas in the 'grammar' of narrative. Julia Kristeva declared that 'what semiotics has discovered . . . is that the *law* governing or, if one prefers, the *major constraint* affecting any social practice lies in the fact that it signifies; i.e. that it is articulated *like* a language' (Kristeva 1973, 1249).

Saussure argued that 'nothing is more appropriate than the study of languages to bring out the nature of the semiological problem' (Saussure 1983, 16). Semiotics draws heavily on linguistic concepts, partly because of his influence, and also because linguistics is a more established discipline than the study of other sign-systems. Saussure referred to language (his model being speech) as 'the most important' of all of the systems of signs (Saussure 1983, 15). Many other theorists have regarded language as fundamental. Roman Jakobson insisted that 'language is the central and most important among all human semiotic systems' (Jakobson 1970, 455). Émile Benveniste observed that 'language is the interpreting system of all other systems, linguistic and non-linguistic' (Benveniste 1969, 239), while Claude Lévi-Strauss noted that 'language is the semiotic system *par excellence*; it cannot but signify, and exists only through signification' (Lévi-Strauss 1972, 48). Language is almost invariably regarded as the most powerful communication system by far.

One of the most powerful 'design features' of language is called *double articulation* (or 'duality of patterning'). Double articulation enables a semiotic code to form an infinite number of meaningful combinations using a small number of low-level units which in themselves are meaningless (e.g. phonemes in speech or graphemes in writing). The infinite use of finite elements is a feature which in relation to media in general has been referred to as 'semiotic economy'. Traditional definitions ascribe double articulation only to human language, for which this is regarded as a key 'design feature' (Hockett 1958). Louis Hjelmslev regarded it as an essential and defining feature of language (Hjelmslev 1961). Jakobson asserted that 'language is the only system which is composed of elements which are signifiers and yet at the same time signify nothing' (Jakobson 1976, 230). Double articulation is seen as being largely responsible for the creative economy of language. The English language, for instance, has only about forty or fifty elements of second articulation (phonemes) but these can generate hundreds of thousands of words. Similarly, from a limited vocabulary we can generate an infinite number of sentences (subject to the constraint of syntax which governs structurally valid combinations). It is by *combining* words in multiple ways that we can seek to render the particularity of experience. If we had individual words to represent every particularity, we would have to have an infinite number of them, which would exceed our capability of learning, recalling and manipulating them.

Double articulation does not seem to occur in the natural communication systems of animals other than humans. A key semiotic debate is over whether or not semiotic systems such as photography, film or painting have double articulation. The philosopher Susanne Langer argued that while visual media such as photography, painting and drawing have lines, colours, shadings, shapes, proportions and so on which are 'abstractable and combinatory', and which 'are just as capable of *articulation*, i.e. of complex combination, as words', they have no vocabulary of units with independent meanings (Langer 1951, 86–7).

> A symbolism with so many elements, such myriad relationships, cannot be broken up into basic units. It is impossible to find the smallest independent symbol, and recognize its identity when the same unit is met in other contexts . . . There is, of course, a technique of picturing objects, but the laws governing this technique cannot properly be called a 'syntax', since there are no items that might be called, metaphorically, the 'words' of portraiture.
>
> (Langer 1951, 88)

Rather than dismissing 'non-discursive' media for their limitations, however, Langer argues that they are more complex and subtle than verbal language and are 'peculiarly well-suited to the expression of ideas that defy linguistic "projection"'. She argues that we should not seek to impose linguistic models upon other media since the laws that govern their articulation 'are altogether different from the laws of syntax that govern language'. Treating them in linguistic terms leads us to 'misconceive' them: they resist 'translation' (ibid., 86–9).

Saussure saw linguistics as a branch of 'semiology':

> Linguistics is only one branch of this general science [of semiology]. The laws which semiology will discover will be laws applicable in linguistics . . . As far as we are concerned . . . the linguistic problem is first and foremost semiological . . . If one wishes to discover the true nature of language systems, one must first consider what they have in common with all other systems of the same kind . . . In this way, light will be thrown not only upon the linguistic problem. By considering rites, customs etc. as signs, it will be possible, we believe, to see them in a new perspective. The need will be felt to consider them as semiological phenomena and to explain them in terms of the laws of semiology.
>
> (Saussure 1983, 16–17)

While Roland Barthes (1967b, xi) declared that 'perhaps we must invert Saussure's formulation and assert that semiology is a branch of linguistics', most of those who call themselves semioticians at least implicitly accept Saussure's location of linguistics within semiotics. The linguist and semiotician Roman Jakobson was in no doubt that 'language is a *system of signs*, and linguistics is part and parcel of the science of signs or semiotics' (Jakobson 1949a, 50; cf. 1970, 454). However, even if we theoretically locate linguistics within semiotics it is difficult to avoid adopting the linguistic model in exploring other sign-systems. The American linguist Leonard Bloomfield asserted that 'linguistics is the chief contributor to semiotics' (Bloomfield 1939, 55). Jakobson defined semiotics as 'the general science of signs which has as its basic discipline linguistics, the science of verbal signs' (Jakobson 1963e, 289). Semioticians commonly refer to films, television and radio programmes, advertising posters and so on as 'texts', and to 'reading television' (Fiske and Hartley 1978). Media such as television and film are regarded by some semioticians as being in some respects like languages. The issue tends to revolve around whether such media are closer to what we treat as reality in the everyday world of our own experience or whether they have more in common with a symbolic system like writing. However, there is a danger of trying to force all media into a linguistic framework. Contemporary 'social semiotics' has moved beyond the structuralist focus on signifying systems as languages, seeking to explore the use of signs in specific social situations.

LANGUE AND PAROLE

We will shortly examine Saussure's highly influential model of the sign, but before doing so it is important to understand something about the general framework within which he situated it. Saussure made what is now a famous distinction between *langue* (language) and *parole* (speech). *Langue* refers to the system of rules and conventions which is independent of, and pre-exists, individual users; *parole* refers to its use in particular instances. Applying the notion to semiotic systems in general rather than simply to language, the distinction is one between *system* and *usage*, *structure* and *event* or *code* and *message*. According to the Saussurean distinction, in a semiotic system such as cinema, for instance, individual films can be seen as the *parole* of an underlying system of cinema 'language'. Saussure focused on *langue* rather than *parole*. To the Saussurean semiotician, what matters most are the underlying structures and rules of a semiotic system as a whole rather than specific performances or practices which are merely instances of its use. Saussure's approach was to study the system 'synchronically' as if it were frozen in time (like a photograph) – rather than 'diachronically' – in terms of its evolution over time (like a film). Some structuralist cultural theorists subsequently adopted this Saussurean priority, focusing on the functions of social and cultural phenomena within semiotic systems. Theorists differ over whether the system precedes and determines usage (structural determinism) or whether usage precedes and determines the system (social determinism) (although note that most structuralists argue that the system *constrains* rather than completely *determines* usage).

The structuralist dichotomy between usage and system has been criticized for its rigidity, splitting process from product, subject from structure (Coward and Ellis 1977, 4, 14; Csikszentmihalyi and Rochberg-Halton 1981, 44, 173–4). A fundamental objection is that the prioritization of structure over usage fails to account for changes in structure. Marxist theorists have been particularly critical. In the late 1920s, Valentin Voloshinov rejected Saussure's synchronic approach and his emphasis on internal relations within the system of language (Voloshinov 1973; Morris 1994). Voloshinov reversed the Saussurean priority of *langue* over *parole*: 'The sign is part of organized social intercourse and cannot exist, as such, outside it, reverting to a mere physical artifact' (Voloshinov 1973, 21). The meaning of a sign is not in its relationship to other signs within the language system but rather in the social context of its use. Saussure was criticized for ignoring historicity (ibid., 61). The Russian linguists Roman Jakobson and Yuri Tynyanov declared in 1927 that 'pure synchronism now proves to be an illusion', adding that 'every synchronic system has its past and its future as inseparable structural elements of the system' (cited in Voloshinov 1973, 166). Writing in 1929, Voloshinov observed that 'there is no real moment

in time when a synchronic system of language could be constructed
... A synchronic system may be said to exist only from the point
of view of the subjective consciousness of an individual speaker
belonging to some particular language group at some particular
moment of historical time' (Voloshinov 1973, 66). While the French
structuralist Claude Lévi-Strauss applied a synchronic approach in
the domain of anthropology, most contemporary semioticians have
sought to reprioritize historicity and social context. Language is
seldom treated as a static, closed and stable system which is inherited from preceding generations but as constantly changing. The sign,
as Voloshinov put it, is 'an arena of the class struggle' (ibid., 23).
Seeking to establish a wholeheartedly 'social semiotics', Robert
Hodge and Gunther Kress declare that 'the social dimensions of
semiotic systems are so intrinsic to their nature and function that the
systems cannot be studied in isolation' (Hodge and Kress 1988, 1).

WHY STUDY SEMIOTICS?

While Saussure may be hailed as a founder of semiotics, semiotics
has become increasingly less Saussurean since the 1970s. While the
current account of semiotics focuses primarily on its structuralist
forms, we will also explore relevant critiques and subsequent developments. But before launching on an exploration of this intriguing
subject, let us consider why we should bother: why should we study
semiotics? This is a pressing question in part because the writings
of semioticians have a reputation for being dense with jargon: one
critic wittily remarked that 'semiotics tells us things we already know
in a language we will never understand' (Paddy Whannel, cited in
Seiter 1992, 31).

  The semiotic establishment may seem to be a very exclusive
club but its concerns are not confined to members. No one with an
interest in how things are represented can afford to ignore an
approach which focuses on, and problematizes, the process of representation. While we need not accept the postmodernist stance that
there is no external reality beyond sign-systems, studying semiotics
can assist us to become more aware of the mediating role of signs
and of the roles played by ourselves and others in constructing social

realities. It can make us less likely to take reality for granted as something which is wholly independent of human interpretation. Exploring semiotic perspectives, we may come to realize that information or meaning is not 'contained' in the world or in books, computers or audio-visual media. Meaning is not 'transmitted' to us – we actively create it according to a complex interplay of codes or conventions of which we are normally unaware. Becoming aware of such codes is both inherently fascinating and intellectually empowering. We learn from semiotics that we live in a world of signs and we have no way of understanding anything except through signs and the codes into which they are organized. Through the study of semiotics, we become aware that these signs and codes are normally transparent and disguise our task in reading them. Living in a world of increasingly visual signs, we need to learn that even the most realistic signs are not what they appear to be. By making more explicit the codes by which signs are interpreted, we may perform the valuable semiotic function of denaturalizing signs. This is not to suggest that all representations of reality are of equal status – quite the contrary. In defining realities signs serve ideological functions. Deconstructing and contesting the realities of signs can reveal whose realities are privileged and whose are suppressed. Such a study involves investigating the construction and maintenance of reality by particular social groups. To decline the study of signs is to leave to others the control of the world of meanings which we inhabit.

MODELS OF THE SIGN

We seem as a species to be driven by a desire to make meanings: above all, we are surely *homo significans* – meaning-makers. Distinctively, we make meanings through our creation and interpretation of 'signs'. Indeed, according to Peirce, 'we think only in signs' (Peirce 1931–58, 2.302). Signs take the form of words, images, sounds, odours, flavours, acts or objects, but such things have no intrinsic meaning and become signs only when we invest them with meaning. 'Nothing is a sign unless it is interpreted as a sign', declares Peirce (ibid., 2.172). Anything can be a sign as long as someone interprets it as 'signifying' something – referring to or *standing for* something other than itself. We interpret things as signs largely unconsciously by relating them to familiar systems of conventions. It is this meaningful use of signs which is at the heart of the concerns of semiotics.

The two dominant contemporary models of what constitutes a sign are those of the Swiss linguist Ferdinand de Saussure and the American philosopher Charles Sanders Peirce. These will be discussed in turn.

THE SAUSSUREAN MODEL

Saussure's model of the sign is in the dyadic tradition. Prior advocates of dyadic models, in which the two parts of a sign consist of a 'sign vehicle' and its meaning, included Augustine (397), Albertus Magnus and the Scholastics (13th century), Hobbes (1640) and Locke (1690) (see Nöth 1990, 88). Focusing on *linguistic* signs (such as words), Saussure defined a sign as being composed of a 'signifier' (*signifiant*) and a 'signified' (*signifié*) (see Figure 1.1). Contemporary commentators tend to describe the signifier as the form that the sign takes and the signified as the concept to which it refers. Saussure makes the distinction in these terms:

> A linguistic sign is not a link between a thing and a name, but between a concept [*signified*] and a sound pattern [*signifier*]. The sound pattern is not actually a sound; for a sound is something physical. A sound pattern is the hearer's psychological impression of a sound, as given to him by the evidence of his senses. This sound pattern may be called a 'material' element only in that it is the representation of our sensory impressions. The sound pattern may thus be distinguished from the other element associated with it in a linguistic sign. This other element is generally of a more abstract kind: the concept.
>
> (Saussure 1983, 66)

For Saussure, both the signifier (the 'sound pattern') and the signified (the concept) were purely 'psychological' (ibid., 12, 14–15, 66).

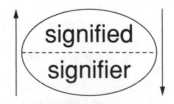

FIGURE 1.1 Saussure's model of the sign

Source: Based on Saussure 1967, 158

Both were non-material *form* rather than *substance*. Figure 1.2 may help to clarify this aspect of Saussure's own model. Nowadays, while the basic 'Saussurean' model is commonly adopted, it tends to be a more materialistic model than that of Saussure himself. The *signifier* is now commonly interpreted as the *material (or physical) form* of the sign – it is something which can be seen, heard, touched, smelled or tasted – as with Roman Jakobson's *signans*, which he described as the external and perceptible part of the sign (Jakobson 1963b, 111; 1984b, 98).

Within the Saussurean model, the *sign* is the whole that results from the association of the signifier with the signified (ibid., 67). The relationship between the signifier and the signified is referred to as 'signification', and this is represented in the Saussurean diagram by the arrows. The horizontal broken line marking the two elements of the sign is referred to as 'the bar'.

If we take a linguistic example, the word 'open' (when it is invested with meaning by someone who encounters it on a shop doorway) is a *sign* consisting of:

- a *signifier*: the word 'open';
- a *signified concept*: that the shop is open for business.

A sign must have both a signifier and a signified. You cannot have a totally meaningless signifier or a completely formless signified

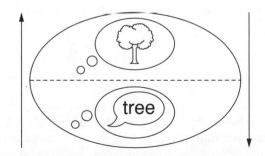

FIGURE 1.2 Concept and sound pattern

(ibid., 101). A sign is a recognizable combination of a signifier with a particular signified. The same signifier (the word 'open') could stand for a different signified (and thus be a different sign) if it were on a push-button inside a lift ('push to open door'). Similarly, many signifiers could stand for the concept 'open' (for instance, on top of a packing carton, a small outline of a box with an open flap for 'open this end') – again, with each unique pairing constituting a different sign.

Saussure focused on the linguistic sign and he 'phonocentrically' privileged the spoken word. As we have noted, he referred specifically to the signifier as a 'sound pattern' (*image acoustique*). He saw writing as a separate, secondary, dependent but comparable sign-system (ibid., 15, 24–5, 117). Within the ('separate') system of written signs, a signifier such as the written letter 't' signified a sound in the primary sign-system of language (and thus a written word would also signify a sound rather than a concept). Thus for Saussure, writing relates to speech as signifier to signified or, as Derrida puts it, for Saussure writing is 'a sign of a sign' (Derrida 1967a, 43). Most subsequent theorists who have adopted Saussure's model tend to refer to the form of linguistic signs as either spoken or written (e.g. Jakobson 1970, 455–6 and 1984b, 98). We will return later to the issue of the post-Saussurean 'rematerialization' of the sign.

As for the *signified*, Umberto Eco notes that it is somewhere between 'a mental image, a concept and a psychological reality' (Eco 1976, 14–15). Most commentators who adopt Saussure's model still treat the signified as a mental construct, although they often note that it may nevertheless refer indirectly to things in the world. Saussure's original model of the sign 'brackets the referent', excluding reference to objects existing in the world – somewhat ironically for one who defined semiotics as 'a science *which studies the role of signs as part of social life*' (Saussure 1983, 15). His *signified* is not to be identified directly with such a referent but is a *concept* in the mind – not a thing but the notion of a thing. Some people may wonder why Saussure's model of the sign refers only to a concept and not to a thing. An observation from Susanne Langer (who was not referring to Saussure's theories) may be useful here. Note that like most contemporary commentators, Langer uses the term 'symbol' to refer to the linguistic sign (a term which Saussure himself avoided): 'Symbols are not proxy for their objects but are *vehicles for the conception of objects* . . . In talking *about* things we have conceptions of them, not the things themselves; and *it is the conceptions, not the things, that symbols directly mean*. Behaviour towards conceptions is what words normally evoke; this is the typical process of thinking'. She adds that 'If I say "Napoleon", you do not bow to the conqueror of Europe as though I had introduced him, but merely think of him' (Langer 1951, 61).

Thus, for Saussure the linguistic sign is wholly immaterial – although he disliked referring to it as 'abstract' (Saussure 1983, 15). The immateriality of the Saussurean sign is a feature which tends to be neglected in many popular commentaries. If the notion seems strange, we need to remind ourselves that words have no value in themselves – that is their value. Saussure noted that it is not the metal in a coin that fixes its value (ibid., 117). Several reasons could be offered for this. For instance, if linguistic signs drew attention to their materiality this would hinder their communicative transparency. Furthermore, being immaterial, language is an extraordinarily economical medium and words are always ready to hand. Nevertheless, a principled argument can be made for the revaluation of the materiality of the sign, as we shall see in due course.

TWO SIDES OF A PAGE

Saussure stressed that sound and thought (or the signifier and the signified) were as inseparable as the two sides of a piece of paper (Saussure 1983, 111). They were 'intimately linked' in the mind 'by an associative link' – 'each triggers the other' (ibid., 66). Saussure presented these elements as wholly interdependent, neither pre-existing the other. Within the context of spoken language, a sign could not consist of sound without sense or of sense without sound. He used the two arrows in the diagram to suggest their interaction. The bar and the opposition nevertheless suggest that the signifier and the signified can be distinguished for analytical purposes. Poststructuralist theorists criticize the clear distinction which the Saussurean bar seems to suggest between the signifier and the signified; they seek to blur or erase it in order to reconfigure the sign. Common sense tends to insist that the *signified* takes precedence over, and pre-exists, the signifier: 'look after the sense', quipped Lewis Carroll, 'and the sounds will take care of themselves' (*Alice's Adventures in Wonderland*, Chapter 9). However, in dramatic contrast, post-Saussurean theorists have seen the model as implicitly granting primacy to the *signifier*, thus reversing the commonsensical position.

THE RELATIONAL SYSTEM

Saussure argued that signs only make sense as part of a formal, generalized and abstract system. His conception of meaning was purely *structural* and *relational* rather than *referential*: primacy is given to relationships rather than to things (the meaning of signs was seen as lying in their systematic relation to each other rather than deriving from any inherent features of signifiers or any reference to material things). Saussure did not define signs in terms of some essential or intrinsic nature. For Saussure, signs refer primarily to each other. Within the language system, 'everything depends on relations' (Saussure 1983, 121). No sign makes sense on its own but

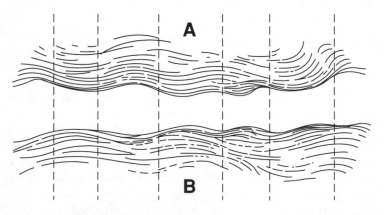

FIGURE 1.3 Planes of thought and sound

Source: Based on Saussure 1967, 156

only in relation to other signs. Both signifier and signified are purely relational entities (ibid., 118). This notion can be hard to understand since we may feel that an individual word such as 'tree' does have some meaning for us, but Saussure's argument is that its meaning depends on its relation to other words within the system (such as 'bush').

Together with the 'vertical' alignment of signifier and signified *within* each individual sign (suggesting two structural 'levels'), the emphasis on the relationship *between* signs defines what are in effect two planes – that of the signifier and the signified. Later, Louis Hjelmslev referred to the 'expression plane' and the 'content plane' (Hjelmslev 1961, 59). Saussure himself referred to *sound* and *thought* as two distinct but correlated planes (see Figure 1.3). 'We can envisage . . . the language . . . as a series of adjoining subdivisions simultaneously imprinted both on the plane of vague, amorphous thought (A), and on the equally featureless plane of sound (B)' (Saussure 1983, 110–11). The arbitrary division of the two continua into signs is suggested by the dotted lines while the wavy (rather than parallel) edges of the two 'amorphous' masses suggest the lack of any natural fit between them. The gulf and lack of fit between the two planes highlights their relative autonomy. While Saussure is careful not to refer directly to reality, the American literary theorist Fredric Jameson reads into this feature of Saussure's system that:

> it is not so much the individual word or sentence that 'stands for' or 'reflects' the individual object or event in the real world, but rather that the entire system of signs, the entire field of the *langue*, lies parallel to reality itself; that it is the totality of systematic language, in other words, which is analogous to whatever organized structures exist in the world of reality, and that our understanding proceeds from one whole or Gestalt to the other, rather than on a one-to-one basis.
>
> (Jameson 1972, 32–3)

What Saussure refers to as the 'value' of a sign depends on its relations with other signs within the system (see Figure 1.4). A sign has no 'absolute' value independent of this context (Saussure 1983, 80).

FIGURE 1.4 The relations between signs

Source: Based on Saussure 1967, 159

Saussure uses an analogy with the game of chess, noting that the value of each piece depends on its position on the chessboard (ibid., 88). The sign is more than the sum of its parts. While *signification* – what is signified – clearly depends on the relationship between the two parts of the sign, the *value* of a sign is determined by the relationships between the sign and other signs within the system as a whole (ibid., 112–13).

> The notion of value . . . shows us that it is a great mistake to consider a sign as nothing more than the combination of a certain sound and a certain concept. To think of a sign as nothing more would be to isolate it from the system to which it belongs. It would be to suppose that a start could be made with individual signs, and a system constructed by putting them together. On the contrary, the system as a united whole is the starting point, from which it becomes possible, by a process of analysis, to identify its constituent elements.
>
> (Saussure 1983, 112)

As an example of the distinction between signification and value, Saussure notes that:

> The French word *mouton* may have the same meaning as the English word *sheep*; but it does not have the same value. There are various reasons for this, but in particular the fact that the English word for the meat of this animal, as prepared and served for a meal, is not *sheep* but *mutton*. The difference in value between *sheep* and *mouton* hinges on the fact that in English

there is also another word *mutton* for the meat, whereas *mouton* in French covers both.

(Saussure 1983, 114)

Saussure's relational conception of meaning was specifically *differential*: he emphasized the differences between signs. Language for him was a system of functional differences and oppositions. 'In a language, as in every other semiological system, what distinguishes a sign is what constitutes it' (ibid., 119). It has been noted that 'a one-term language is an impossibility because its single term could be applied to everything and differentiate nothing; it requires at least one other term to give it definition' (Sturrock 1979, 10). Advertising furnishes a good example of this notion, since what matters in 'positioning' a product is *not* the relationship of advertising signifiers to real-world referents, but the differentiation of each sign from the others to which it is related. Saussure's concept of the relational identity of signs is at the heart of structuralist theory.

Saussure emphasized in particular negative, oppositional differences between signs. He argued that 'concepts . . . are defined not positively, in terms of their content, but negatively by contrast with other items in the same system. What characterizes each most exactly is *being whatever the others are not*' (Saussure 1983, 115; *my emphasis*). This notion may initially seem mystifying if not perverse, but the concept of negative differentiation becomes clearer if we consider how we might teach someone who did not share our language what we mean by the term 'red'. We would be unlikely to make our point by simply showing that person a range of different objects which all happened to be red – we would probably do better to single out a red object from a set of objects which were identical in all respects except colour. Although Saussure focuses on speech, he also noted that in writing, 'the values of the letter are purely negative and differential' – all we need to be able to do is to distinguish one letter from another (ibid., 118). As for his emphasis on negative differences, Saussure remarks that although both the signified and the signifier are purely differential and negative when considered separately, the sign in which they are combined is a *positive* term. He adds that 'the moment we compare one sign with another

as positive combinations, the term *difference* should be dropped
. . . Two signs . . . are not different from each other, but only distinct.
They are simply in *opposition* to each other. The entire mechanism
of language . . . is based on oppositions of this kind and upon the
phonic and conceptual differences they involve' (ibid., 119).

ARBITRARINESS

Although the signifier is treated by its users as 'standing for' the
signified, Saussurean semioticians emphasize that there is no necessary, intrinsic, direct or inevitable relationship between the signifier
and the signified. Saussure stressed the *arbitrariness* of the sign
(ibid., 67, 78) – more specifically the arbitrariness of the link between
the signifier and the signified (ibid., 67). He was focusing on
linguistic signs, seeing language as the most important sign-system;
for Saussure, the arbitrary nature of the sign was the first principle
of language (ibid., 67) – arbitrariness was identified later by Charles
Hockett as a key 'design feature' of language (Hockett 1958). The
feature of arbitrariness may indeed help to account for the extraordinary versatility of language (Lyons 1977, 71). In the context of
natural language, Saussure stressed that there is no inherent, essential, transparent, self-evident or natural connection between the
signifier and the signified – between the sound of a word and the
concept to which it refers (Saussure 1983, 67, 68–9, 76, 111, 117).
Note that although Saussure prioritized speech, he also stressed that
'the signs used in writing are arbitrary, The letter *t*, for instance, has
no connection with the sound it denotes' (Saussure 1983, 117).
Saussure himself avoids directly relating the principle of arbitrariness to the relationship between language and an external world, but
subsequent commentators often do. Indeed, lurking behind the purely
conceptual 'signified' one can often detect Saussure's allusion to
real-world referents, as when he notes that 'the street and the train
are real enough. Their physical existence is essential to our understanding of what they are' (ibid., 107). In language, at least, the form
of the signifier is not determined by what it signifies: there is nothing
'treeish' about the word 'tree'. Languages differ, of course, in how
they refer to the same referent. No specific signifier is naturally more

suited to a signified than any other signifier; in principle any signifier could represent any signified. Saussure observed that 'there is nothing at all to prevent the association of any idea whatsoever with any sequence of sounds whatsoever' (ibid., 76); 'the process which selects one particular sound-sequence to correspond to one particular idea is completely arbitrary' (ibid., 111).

This principle of the arbitrariness of the linguistic sign was not an original conception. In Plato's dialogue *Cratylus* this issue is debated. Although Cratylus defends the notion of a natural relationship between words and what they represent, Hermogenes declares that 'no one is able to persuade me that the correctness of names is determined by anything besides convention and agreement . . . No name belongs to a particular thing by nature' (Plato 1998, 2). While Socrates rejects the absolute arbitrariness of language proposed by Hermogenes, he does acknowledge that convention plays a part in determining meaning. In his work *On Interpretation*, Aristotle went further, asserting that there can be no natural connection between the sound of any language and the things signified. 'By a noun [or name] we mean a sound significant by convention . . . the limitation "by convention" was introduced because nothing is by nature a noun or name – it is only so when it becomes a symbol' (Aristotle 2004, 2). The issue even enters into everyday discourse via Shakespeare: 'That which we call a rose by any other name would smell as sweet'. The notion of the arbitrariness of language was thus not new; indeed, Roman Jakobson notes that Saussure 'borrowed and expanded' it from the Yale linguist Dwight Whitney (1827–94) – to whose influence Saussure did allude (Jakobson 1966, 410; Saussure 1983, 18, 26, 110). Nevertheless, the emphasis which Saussure gave to arbitrariness can be seen as highly controversial in the context of a theory which bracketed the referent.

Saussure illustrated the principle of arbitrariness at the lexical level – in relation to individual words as signs. He did not, for instance, argue that syntax is arbitrary. However, the arbitrariness principle can be applied not only to the individual sign, but to the whole sign-system. The fundamental arbitrariness of language is apparent from the observation that each language involves different distinctions between one signifier and another (e.g. 'tree' and 'free') and between one signified and another (e.g. 'tree' and 'bush'). The signified is clearly arbitrary if *reality* is perceived as a seamless continuum (which is how Saussure sees the initially undifferentiated realms of both thought and sound): where, for example, does a 'corner' end? Common sense suggests that the existence of things in the world preceded our apparently simple application of 'labels' to them (a 'nomenclaturist' notion which Saussure rejected and to which we will return in due course). Saussure noted that 'if words had the job of representing concepts fixed in advance, one would be able to find exact equivalents for them as between one language and another. But this is not the case' (ibid., 114–15). Reality is divided up into arbitrary categories by every language and the conceptual world with which each of us is familiar could have been divided up very differently. Indeed, no two languages categorize reality in the same way. As John Passmore puts it, 'Languages differ by differentiating differently' (Passmore 1985, 24). Linguistic categories are not simply a consequence of some predefined structure in the world. There are no natural concepts or categories which are simply reflected in language. Language plays a crucial role in constructing reality.

If one accepts the arbitrariness of the relationship between signifier and signified then one may argue counter-intuitively that the signified is determined by the signifier rather than vice versa. Indeed, the French psychoanalyst Jacques Lacan, in adapting Saussurean theories, sought to highlight the primacy of the signifier in the psyche by rewriting Saussure's model of the sign in the form of a quasi-algebraic sign in which a capital 'S' (representing the *signifier*) is placed over a lower-case and italicized '*s*' (representing the *signified*), these two signifiers being separated by a horizontal 'bar' (Lacan 1977, 149). This suited Lacan's purpose of emphasizing how the signified inevitably 'slips beneath' the signifier, resisting our attempts to delimit it. Lacan poetically refers to Saussure's illustration of the planes of sound and thought as 'an image resembling the wavy lines of the upper and lower waters in miniatures from manuscripts of *Genesis*; a double flux marked by streaks of rain', suggesting that this can be seen as illustrating the 'incessant sliding of the signified under the signifier' – although he argues that one should regard the dotted vertical lines not as 'segments of corre-spondence' but as 'anchoring points' (*points de capiton* – literally, the 'buttons' which anchor upholstery to furniture). However, he notes that this model is too linear, since 'there is in effect no signi-fying chain that does not have, as if attached to the punctuation of each of its units, a whole articulation of relevant contexts suspended "vertically", as it were, from that point' (ibid., 154). In the spirit of the Lacanian critique of Saussure's model, subsequent theorists have emphasized the temporary nature of the bond between signifier and signified, stressing that the 'fixing' of 'the chain of signifiers' is socially situated (Coward and Ellis 1977, 6, 13, 17, 67). Note that while the intent of Lacan in placing the signifier *over* the signified is clear enough, his representational strategy seems a little curious, since in the modelling of society orthodox Marxists routinely repre-sent the fundamental driving force of 'the [techno-economic] base' as (logically) below 'the [ideological] superstructure'.

The arbitrariness of the sign is a radical concept because it establishes the autonomy of language in relation to reality. The Saussurean model, with its emphasis on internal structures within a sign-system, can be seen as supporting the notion that language does not reflect reality but rather *constructs* it. We can use language 'to say what isn't in the world, as well as what is. And since we come to know the world through whatever language we have been born into the midst of, it is legitimate to argue that our language deter-mines reality, rather than reality our language' (Sturrock 1986, 79). In their book *The Meaning of Meaning*, Charles Ogden and Ivor Richards criticized Saussure for 'neglecting entirely the things for which signs stand' (Ogden and Richards 1923, 8). Later critics have lamented his model's detachment from social context (Gardiner 1992, 11). By 'bracketing the referent', the Saussurean model 'severs text from history' (Stam 2000, 122). We will return to this theme of the relationship between language and reality in Chapter 2.

The arbitrary aspect of signs does help to account for the scope for their interpretation (and the importance of context). There is no one-to-one link between signifier and signified; signs have multiple rather than single meanings. Within a single language, one signifier may refer to many signifieds (e.g. puns) and one signified may be referred to by many signifiers (e.g. synonyms). Some commentators are critical of the stance that the relationship of the signifier to the signified, even in language, is always completely arbitrary (e.g. Jakobson 1963a, 59, and 1966). Onomatopoeic words are often mentioned in this context, though some semioticians retort that this hardly accounts for the variability between different languages in their words for the same sounds (notably the sounds made by familiar animals) (Saussure 1983, 69).

Saussure declares that 'the entire linguistic system is founded upon the irrational principle that the sign is arbitrary'. This provocative declaration is followed immediately by the acknowledgement that 'applied without restriction, this principle would lead to utter chaos' (ibid., 131). If linguistic signs were to be *totally* arbitrary in every way language would not be a system and its communicative function would be destroyed. He concedes that 'there exists no language in which nothing at all is motivated' (ibid.). Saussure admits that 'a language is not completely arbitrary, for the system has a certain rationality' (ibid., 73). The principle of arbitrariness does not mean that the form of a word is accidental or random, of course. While the sign is not determined *extralinguistically* it is subject to *intralinguistic* determination. For instance, signifiers must constitute well-formed combinations of sounds which conform with existing patterns within the language in question. Furthermore, we can recognize that a compound noun such as 'screwdriver' is not wholly arbitrary since it is a meaningful combination of two existing signs. Saussure introduces a distinction between *degrees* of arbitrariness:

> The fundamental principle of the arbitrary nature of the linguistic sign does not prevent us from distinguishing in any language between what is intrinsically arbitrary – that is, unmotivated – and what is only relatively arbitrary. Not all signs are absolutely arbitrary. In some cases, there are factors which allow us to recognize different degrees of arbitrariness, although never to discard the notion entirely. *The sign may be motivated to a certain extent.*
>
> (Saussure 1983, 130)

Here, then, Saussure modifies his stance somewhat and refers to signs as being 'relatively arbitrary'. Some subsequent theorists (echoing Althusserian Marxist terminology) refer to the relationship between the signifier and the signified in terms of 'relative autonomy' (e.g. Tagg 1988, 167). The *relative* conventionality of relationships between signified and signifier is a point to which we will return shortly.

It should be noted that, while the relationships between signifiers and their signifieds are *ontologically* arbitrary (philosophically, it would not make any difference to the status of these entities in 'the order of things' if what we call 'black' had always been called 'white' and vice versa), this is not to suggest that signifying systems are *socially* or *historically* arbitrary. Natural languages are not, of course, arbitrarily established, unlike historical inventions such as Morse Code. Nor does the arbitrary nature of the sign make it socially 'neutral' – in Western culture 'white' has come to be a privileged (but typically 'invisible') signifier (Dyer 1997). Even in the case of the 'arbitrary' colours of traffic lights, the original choice of red for 'stop' was not entirely arbitrary, since it already carried relevant associations with danger. As Lévi-Strauss noted, the sign is arbitrary *a priori* but ceases to be arbitrary *a posteriori* – after the sign has come into historical existence it cannot be arbitrarily changed (Lévi-Strauss 1972, 91). As part of its social use within a sign-system, every sign acquires a history and connotations of its own which are familiar to members of the sign-users' culture. Saussure remarked that although the signifier 'may seem to be freely chosen', from the point of view of the linguistic community it is 'imposed rather than freely chosen' because 'a language is always an inheritance from the past' which its users have 'no choice but to accept' (Saussure 1983, 71–2). Indeed, 'it is because the linguistic sign is arbitrary that it knows no other law than that of tradition, and [it is] because it is founded upon tradition that it can be arbitrary' (ibid., 74). The arbitrariness principle does *not*, of course mean that an individual can arbitrarily choose any signifier for a given signified. The relation between a signifier and its signified is *not* a matter of individual choice; if it were, then communication would become impossible. 'The individual has no power to alter a sign in any respect once it has become established in the linguistic community' (ibid., 68). From the point of view of individual language-users, language is a 'given' – we don't create the system for ourselves. Saussure refers to the language system as a non-negotiable 'contract' into which one is born (ibid., 14) – although he later problematizes the term (ibid., 71). The ontological arbitrariness which it involves becomes invisible to us as we learn to accept it as natural. As the anthopologist Franz Boas noted, to the native speaker of a language, none of its classifications appear arbitrary (Jakobson 1943, 483).

The Saussurean legacy of the arbitrariness of signs leads semioticians to stress that the relationship between the signifier and the signified is *conventional* – dependent on social and cultural conventions which have to be learned. This is particularly clear in the case of the linguistic signs with which Saussure was concerned: a word means what it does to us only because we collectively agree to let it do so. Saussure felt that the main concern of semiotics should be 'the whole group of systems grounded in the arbitrariness of the sign'. He argued that: 'signs which are entirely arbitrary convey better than others the ideal semiological process. That is why the most complex and the most widespread of all systems of expression, which is the one we find in human languages, is also the most characteristic of all. In this sense, linguistics serves as a model for the whole of semiology, even though languages represent only one type of semiological system' (ibid., 68). He did not in fact offer many examples of sign-systems other than spoken language and writing, mentioning only: the deaf-and-dumb alphabet; social customs; etiquette; religious and other symbolic rites; legal procedures; military signals and nautical flags (ibid., 15, 17, 68, 74). Saussure added that 'any means of expression accepted in a society rests in principle upon a collective habit, or on convention – which comes to the same thing' (ibid., 68). However, while purely conventional signs such as words are quite independent of their referents, other less conventional forms of signs are often somewhat less independent of them. Nevertheless, since the arbitrary nature of linguistic signs is clear, those who have adopted the Saussurean model have tended to avoid 'the familiar mistake of assuming that signs which appear natural to those who use them have an intrinsic meaning and require no explanation' (Culler 1975, 5).

THE PEIRCEAN MODEL

At around the same time as Saussure was formulating his model of the sign and of 'semiology' (and laying the foundations of structuralist methodology), across the Atlantic closely related theoretical work was also in progress as the pragmatist philosopher and logician Charles Sanders Peirce formulated his own model of the sign, of 'semeiotic [*sic*]' and of the taxonomies of signs. In contrast to Saussure's model of the sign in the form of a 'self-contained dyad', Peirce offered a triadic (three-part) model consisting of:

1. The *representamen*: the form which the sign takes (not necessarily material, though usually interpreted as such) – called by some theorists the 'sign vehicle'.
2. An *interpretant*: not an interpreter but rather the *sense* made of the sign.
3. An *object*: something beyond the sign to which it refers (a *referent*).

In Peirce's own words:

> A sign . . . [in the form of a *representamen*] is something which stands to somebody for something in some respect or capacity. It addresses somebody, that is, creates in the mind of that person an equivalent sign, or perhaps a more developed sign. That sign which it creates I call the *interpretant* of the first sign. The sign stands for something, its *object*. It stands for that object, not in all respects, but in reference to a sort of idea, which I have sometimes called the *ground* of the representamen.
> (Peirce 1931–58, 2.228)

To qualify as a sign, all three elements are essential. The sign is a unity of what is represented (the object), how it is represented (the representamen) and how it is interpreted (the interpretant). The Peircean model is conventionally illustrated as in Figure 1.5 (e.g. Eco 1976, 59), though note that Peirce did not himself offer a visualization of it, and Floyd Merrell (who prefers to use a 'tripod' with a central node) argues that the triangular form 'evinces no genuine triadicity, but merely three-way dyadicity' (Merrell 1997, 133). The broken line at the base of the triangle is intended to indicate that there is not necessarily any observable or direct relationship between the sign vehicle and the referent. Note here that semioticians make a distinction between a sign and a 'sign vehicle' (the latter being a 'signifier' to Saussureans and a 'representamen' to Peirceans). The sign is more than just a sign vehicle. The term 'sign' is often used loosely, so that this distinction is not always preserved. In the Saussurean framework, some references to 'the sign' should be to the *signifier*, and similarly, Peirce himself frequently mentions 'the sign' when, strictly speaking, he is referring to the *representamen*. It is easy to be found guilty of such a slippage, perhaps because we are so used to 'looking beyond' the form which the sign happens to take. However, to reiterate: the *signifier* or *representamen* is the *form* in which the sign appears (such as the spoken or written form of a word) whereas the *sign* is the whole meaningful ensemble.

The interaction between the *representamen*, the *object* and the *interpretant* is referred to by Peirce as 'semeiosis' (ibid., 5.484; alternatively *semiosis*). A good explanation of how Peirce's model works is offered by one of my own students, Roderick Munday:

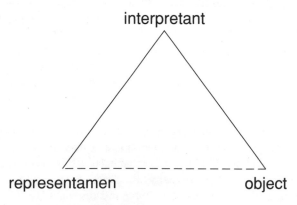

FIGURE 1.5 Peirce's semiotic triangle

The three elements that make up a sign function like a label on an opaque box that contains an object. At first the mere fact that there is a box with a label on it suggests that it contains something, and then when we read the label we discover what that something is. The process of semiosis, or decoding the sign, is as follows. The first thing that is noticed (the *representamen*) is the box and label; this prompts the realization that something is inside the box (the *object*). This realization, as well as the knowledge of what the box contains, is provided by the *interpretant*. 'Reading the label' is actually just a metaphor for the process of decoding the sign. The important point to be aware of here is that the object of a sign is always hidden. We cannot actually open the box and inspect it directly. The reason for this is simple: if the object could be known directly, there would be no need of a sign to represent it. We only know about the object from noticing the label and the box and then 'reading the label' and forming a mental picture of the object in our mind. Therefore the hidden object of a sign is only brought to realization through the interaction of the representamen, the object and the interpretant.

(personal correspondence, 14/4/2005)

The representamen is similar in meaning to Saussure's signifier while the interpretant is roughly analogous to the signified. However, the interpretant has a quality unlike that of the signified: it is itself a sign in the mind of the interpreter (see Figure 1.6). Peirce noted that 'a sign . . . addresses somebody, that is, creates in the mind of that person an equivalent sign, or perhaps a more developed sign. The sign which it creates I call the *interpretant* of the first sign' (Peirce 1931–58, 2.228). In Roman Jakobson's words, for Peirce, 'the meaning of the sign is the sign it can be translated into' (Jakobson 1952b, 566). Umberto Eco uses the phrase 'unlimited semiosis' to refer to the way in which this could lead (as Peirce was well aware) to a series of successive interpretants (potentially) *ad infinitum* (Eco 1976, 68–9; Peirce 1931–58, 1.339, 2.303). Elsewhere Peirce added that 'the meaning of a representation can be nothing but a representation' (ibid., 1.339). Any initial interpretation can be reinterpreted. That a signified can itself

play the role of a signifier is familiar from using a dictionary and find-
ing oneself going beyond the original definition to look up yet another
word which it employs. Peirce's emphasis on sense-making involves a
rejection of the equation of 'content' and meaning; the meaning of a
sign is not contained within it, but arises in its interpretation. Note that
Peirce refers to an 'interpretant' (the sense made of a sign) rather than
directly to an interpreter, though the interpreter's presence is implicit
– which arguably applies even within Saussure's model (Thibault
1997, 184). As we have seen, Saussure also emphasized the value of
a sign lying in its relation to other signs (within the relatively static
structure of the sign system) but the Peircean concept (based on the
highly dynamic process of interpretation) has a more radical potential
which was later to be developed by poststructuralist theorists. Arising
from Peirce's concept of the interpretant is the notion of *dialogical*

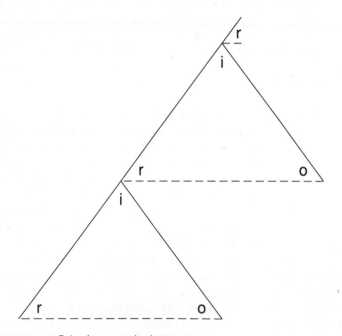

FIGURE 1.6 Peirce's successive interpretants

thought which was absent from Saussure's model. Peirce argued that 'all thinking is dialogic in form. Your self of one instant appeals to your deeper self for his assent' (Peirce 1931–58, 6.338). This notion resurfaced in a more developed form in the 1920s in the theories of Mikhail Bakhtin (1981). One important aspect of this is its characterization even of internal reflection as fundamentally social. Some writers have experienced revision as a process of arguing with themselves – as I did when I revised this text (Chandler 1995, 53).

Variants of Peirce's triad are often presented as '*the* semiotic triangle' – as if there were only one version. In fact, prior to Peirce, a triadic model of the sign was employed by Plato (*c*.400 BC), Aristotle (*c*.350 BC), the Stoics (*c*.250 BC), Boethius (*c*.500), Francis Bacon (1605) and Gottfried Wilhelm von Leibniz (*c*.1700). Triadic models were also adopted by Edmund Husserl (1900), Charles K. Ogden and Ivor A. Richards (1923) and Charles W. Morris (1938).

The most obvious difference between the Saussurean and Peircean model is of course that (being triadic rather than dyadic) Peirce's model of the sign features a third term – an *object* (or referent) beyond the sign itself. As we have seen, Saussure's *signified* is not an external referent but an abstract mental representation. Although Peirce's *object* is not confined to physical things and (like Saussure's *signified*) it can include abstract concepts and fictional entities, the Peircean model explicitly allocates a place for materiality and for reality outside the sign system which Saussure's model did not directly feature (though Peirce was not a naïve realist, and he argued that all experience is mediated by signs). For Peirce the object was not just 'another variety of "interpretant"' (Bruss 1978, 96), but was crucial to the meaning of the sign: 'meaning' within his model includes both 'reference' and (conceptual) 'sense' (or more broadly, representation and interpretation). Furthermore, Peircean semioticians argue that the triadic basis of this model enables it to operate as a more general model of the sign than a dyadic model can (ibid., 86). Nevertheless, the inclusion of a referent does not make a triadic model inherently less problematic than a dyadic one. John Lyons notes that 'there is considerable disagreement about the details of the triadic analysis even among those who accept that all three components . . . must be taken into account' (Lyons 1977, 99).

It is important in this particular account of semiotics to note how one of the foremost post-Saussurean structuralists reacted to the Peircean model of the sign, since his inflection of structuralism had important consequences for the evolution of the European semiotic tradition. Prior to his discovery of Peirce's work, Roman Jakobson, a consistent exponent of binary structures in language, had clearly adopted the Saussurean sign – despite his critique of Saussure's analytical priorities: 'The constitutive mark of any sign in general or of any linguistic sign in particular is its *twofold* character: every linguistic unit is bipartite and involves both aspects – one sensible (i.e., perceptible) and the other intelligible, or in other words, both the "signifier" and the "signified"' – his preferred terms (adopted from St Augustine) usually being *signans* (signifier) and *signatum* (signified). Jakobson added that the linguistic sign involved 'the indissoluble dualism of . . . *sound* and *meaning*' (Jakobson 1949a, 50; cf. 1949b, 396). 'Meaning' can be a slippery term in this context, since it can refer either to sense (accommodated in both the Saussurean and Peircean models) or reference (accounted for directly only in Peirce's model), but Jakobson's signified at this stage seems much the same as Saussure's. Jakobson's increasing emphasis on the importance of *meaning* represented a reaction against the attempt of 'reductionist linguists' in the USA (American structuralists and early transformational grammarians) 'to analyze linguistic structure without reference to meaning' whereas he insisted that 'everything in language is endowed with a certain significative and transmissive value' (Jakobson 1972, 42). After his encounter with Peirce's work in the early 1950s, Jakobson became and remained a key adopter and promoter of Peircean ideas, yet in 1958 he still accepted that the signified/*signatum* 'belonged to' linguistics and the referent/*designatum* to philosophy (Jakobson 1973, 320). Even when he came to emphasize the importance of *context* in the interpretation of signs he did not directly incorporate a 'referent' into his model of the sign, referring to the term as 'somewhat ambivalent' (Jakobson 1960, 353). By 1972 he had granted the referent (in the form of contextual and situational meaning) a more explicit status within linguistics (Jakobson 1973, 320), but his model of the sign still remained formally dyadic.

Nevertheless, he had come to equate the signified with Peirce's 'immediate interpretant' (Jakobson 1966, 409), and on one occasion he referred to there being 'two sets of *interpretants* . . . to interpret the sign – one [referring] to the code, and the other to the context' (Jakobson 1956, 75), despite Peirce's note that the interpretant *excluded* 'its context or circumstances of utterance' (Peirce 1931–58, 5.473). Clearly Jakobson sought to incorporate into the dyadic model the special quality of Peirce's interpretant, referring to the signified as the 'translatable' (or interpretable) part of the sign (e.g. Jakobson 1958, 261, 1963b, 111 and 1966, 408). Thus a major semiotician felt able to accommodate reference (indirectly) without abandoning a dyadic model. Indeed, he insisted that 'in spite of . . . attempts' to revise the 'necessarily twofold structure' of the sign or its constituent parts (the signifier/*signans* and the signified/*signatum*), 'this more than bimillenary model remains the soundest and safest base for the newly developing and expanding semiotic research' (Jakobson 1968, 699) – though there is some irony in the model he cites being that of the Stoics, who despite having prefigured the Saussurean distinction between signifier and signified, did so as part of a triadic rather than dyadic model (Eco 1984, 29–33). One Peircean scholar comments that: 'At base, Jakobson's semiotics is still more Saussurean than Peircean, committed to the diacritical nature of each aspect and every instance of the sign' (Bruss 1978, 93). Jakobson was a key propagator of Peircean concepts in the European semiotic tradition (Umberto Eco being the other), and although his structuralism was in many ways markedly different from that of Saussure, his stance on the sign model enabled European semiotics to absorb Peircean influences without a fundamental transformation of the dyadic model.

RELATIVITY

Whereas Saussure emphasized the arbitrary nature of the (linguistic) sign, most post-Saussurean semioticians stress that signs differ in how arbitrary/conventional (or by contrast 'transparent') they are. The relatively arbitrary 'symbolism' of the medium of verbal language reflects only one form of relationship between signifiers and their signifieds. In particular, a common-sense distinction between 'conventional signs' (the names we give to people and things) and 'natural signs' (pictures resembling what they depict) dates back to ancient Greece (Plato's *Cratylus*). St Augustine later distinguished 'natural signs' (*signa naturalia*) from conventional signs (*signa data*) on a different basis. For him, natural signs were those which were interpreted as signs by virtue of an immediate link to what they signified – even though no conscious intention had created them as such (he instanced smoke indicating fire and footprints indicating that an animal had passed by) (*On Christian Doctrine*, Book II, Chapter 1). Both of these types of 'natural' signs (respectively iconic and indexical) as well as 'conventional' (symbolic) signs feature in Charles Peirce's influential tripartite classification.

While Saussure did not offer a typology of signs, Peirce offered several (Peirce 1931–58, 1.291, 2.243). What he himself regarded as 'the most fundamental' division of signs (first outlined in 1867) has been very widely cited in subsequent semiotic studies (ibid., 2.275). Although it is often referred to as a classification of distinct 'types of signs', it is more usefully interpreted in terms of differing 'modes of relationship' between sign vehicles and what is signified (Hawkes 1977, 129). In Peircean terms they are relationships between a representamen and its object or its interpretant, but for the purpose of continuity I have continued to employ the Saussurean terms *signifier* and *signified* (cf. Jakobson 1966). Here then are the three modes:

1. **Symbol/symbolic**: a mode in which the signifier does *not* resemble the signified but which is fundamentally *arbitrary* or purely *conventional* – so that this relationship must be agreed upon and learned: e.g. language in general (plus specific languages, alphabetical letters, punctuation marks, words, phrases and sentences), numbers, morse code, traffic lights, national flags.

2. **Icon/iconic**: a mode in which the signifier is perceived as *resembling* or imitating the signified (recognizably looking, sounding, feeling, tasting or smelling like it) – being similar in possessing some of its qualities: e.g. a portrait, a cartoon,

a scale-model, onomatopoeia, metaphors, realistic sounds in 'programme music', sound effects in radio drama, a dubbed film soundtrack, imitative gestures.

3. **Index/indexical**: a mode in which the signifier is *not arbitrary* but is *directly connected* in some way (physically or causally) to the signified (regardless of intention) – this link can be observed or inferred: e.g. 'natural signs' (smoke, thunder, footprints, echoes, non-synthetic odours and flavours), medical symptoms (pain, a rash, pulse-rate), measuring instruments (weathercock, thermometer, clock, spirit-level), 'signals' (a knock on a door, a phone ringing), pointers (a pointing 'index' finger, a directional signpost), recordings (a photograph, a film, video or television shot, an audio-recorded voice), personal 'trademarks' (handwriting, catch-phrases).

These three modes arose within (and because of) Peirce's triadic model of the sign, and from a Peircean perspective it is reductive to transform a triadic relation into a dyadic one (Bruss 1978). However, our focus here is on how Peirce has been adopted and adapted within the European structuralist tradition. The widespread use of these Peircean distinctions in texts which are otherwise primarily within that tradition may suggest either the potential for (indirect) referentiality in dyadic models or merely slippage between 'sense' and 'reference' in defining the 'meaning' of the sign. Certainly, as soon as we adopt the Peircean concepts of iconicity and indexicality we need to remind ourselves that we are no longer 'bracketing the referent' and are acknowledging not only a systemic frame of reference but also some kind of referential context beyond the sign-system itself. Iconicity is based on (at least perceived) 'resemblance' and indexicality is based on (at least perceived) 'direct connection'. In other words, adopting such concepts means that – even if we are not embracing a wholly Peircean approach – we have moved beyond the formal bounds of the original Saussurean framework (as in Roman Jakobson's version of structuralism).

The three forms of relationship between signifier and signified are listed here in decreasing order of conventionality. Symbolic signs such as language are (at least) highly conventional; iconic signs always involve some degree of conventionality; indexical signs 'direct the attention to their objects by blind compulsion' (Peirce 1931–58, 2.306). *Indexical* and *iconic* signifiers can be seen as more constrained by referential *signifieds* whereas in the more conventional *symbolic* signs the *signified* can be seen as being defined to a greater extent by the *signifier*. Within each form signs also vary in their degree of conventionality. Other criteria might be applied to rank the three forms differently. For instance, Hodge and Kress suggest that indexicality is based on an act of judgement or inference whereas iconicity is closer to 'direct perception', making the highest 'modality' that of iconic signs (Hodge and Kress 1988, 26–7). Note that the terms 'motivation' (from Saussure) and 'constraint' are sometimes used to describe the extent to which the signified determines the signifier. The more a signifier is constrained by the signified, the more 'motivated' the sign is: iconic signs are highly motivated; symbolic signs are unmotivated. The less motivated the sign, the more learning of an agreed convention is required. Nevertheless, most semioticians emphasize the role of convention in relation to signs. As we shall see, even photographs and films are built on conventions which we must learn to 'read'. Such conventions are an important social dimension of semiotics.

SYMBOLIC MODE

What in popular usage are called 'symbols' would be regarded by semioticians as 'signs' of some kind but many of them would not technically be classified as purely 'symbolic'. For instance, if we joke that 'a thing is a phallic symbol if it's longer than it is wide', this would allude to *resemblance*, making it at least partly *iconic* – Jakobson suggests that such examples may be best classified as 'symbolic icons' (Jakobson 1968, 702). In the Peircean sense, *symbols* are based purely on *conventional association*. Nowadays language is generally regarded as a (predominantly) symbolic sign-system, though Saussure avoided referring to linguistic signs as 'symbols' precisely because of the danger of confusion with popular usage. He noted that symbols in the popular sense are 'never wholly arbitrary': they 'show at least a vestige of natural connection' between the signifier and the signified – a link which he later refers to as 'rational' (Saussure 1983, 68, 73). While Saussure focused on the arbitrary nature of the linguistic sign, a more obvious example of arbitrary symbolism is mathematics. Mathematics does not need to refer to an external world at all: its signifieds are indisputably *concepts* and mathematics is a system of relations (Langer 1951, 28).

For Peirce, a symbol is 'a sign which refers to the object that it denotes by virtue of a law, usually an association of general ideas, which operates to cause the symbol to be interpreted as referring to that object' (Peirce 1931–58, 2.249). We interpret symbols according to 'a rule' or 'a habitual connection' (ibid., 2.292, 2.297, 1.369). 'The symbol is connected with its object by virtue of the idea of the symbol-using mind, without which no such connection would exist' (ibid., 2.299). It 'is constituted a sign merely or mainly by the fact that it is used and understood as such' (ibid., 2.307). A symbol is 'a conventional sign, or one depending upon habit (acquired or inborn)' (ibid., 2.297). Symbols are not limited to words, although 'all words, sentences, books and other conventional signs are symbols' (ibid., 2.292). Peirce thus characterizes linguistic signs in terms of their *conventionality* in a similar way to Saussure. In a rare direct reference to the arbitrariness of symbols (which he then called 'tokens'), he noted that they 'are, for the most part, conventional or arbitrary' (ibid., 3.360). A symbol is a sign 'whose special significance or fitness to represent just what it does represent lies in nothing but the very fact of there being a habit, disposition, or other effective general rule that it will be so interpreted. Take, for example, the word "*man*". These three letters are not in the least like a man; nor is the sound with which they are associated' (ibid., 4.447). He adds elsewhere that 'a *symbol* ... fulfils its function regardless of any similarity or analogy with its object and equally regardless of any *factual* connection therewith' (ibid., 5.73). 'A genuine symbol is a symbol that has a general meaning' (ibid., 2.293), signifying a kind of thing rather than a specific thing (ibid., 2.301).

ICONIC MODE

Unfortunately, as with 'symbolic', the terms 'icon' and 'iconic' are used in a technical sense in semiotics which differs from its everyday meanings. In popular usage there are three key meanings which can lead to confusion with the semiotic terms:

- to be 'iconic' typically means that something or someone would be expected to be instantly recognized as famous by any fully fledged member of a particular culture or sub-culture;
- an 'icon' on the computer screen is a small image intended to signify a particular function to the user (to the semiotician these are 'signs' which may be variously iconic, symbolic or indexical, depending on their form and function);
- religious 'icons' are works of visual art representing sacred figures which may be venerated as holy images by devout believers.

In the Peircean sense, the defining feature of iconicity is merely *perceived resemblance*. Peirce declared that an iconic sign represents its object 'mainly by its similarity' (Peirce 1931–58, 2.276). Note that despite the name, icons are not necessarily visual. A sign is an icon 'insofar as it is like that thing and used as a sign of it' (ibid., 2.247). Indeed, Peirce originally termed such modes, 'likenesses' (e.g. ibid., 1.558). He added that 'every picture (however conventional its method)' is an icon (ibid., 2.279). Icons have qualities which 'resemble' those of the objects they represent, and they 'excite analogous sensations in the mind' (ibid., 2.299; cf. 3.362). Unlike the index, 'the icon has no dynamical connection with the object it represents' (ibid.). Just because a signifier resembles that which it depicts does not necessarily make it purely iconic. Susanne Langer argues that 'the picture is essentially a symbol, not a duplicate, of what it represents' (Langer 1951, 67). Pictures resemble what they represent only in some respects. What we tend to recognize in an image are analogous relations of parts to a whole (ibid., 67–70). For Peirce, icons included 'every diagram, even although there be no sensuous resemblance between it and its object, but only an analogy between the relations of the parts of each' (Peirce 1931–58, 2.279). 'Many diagrams resemble their objects not at all in looks; it is only in respect to the relations of their parts that their likeness consists' (ibid., 2.282). Even the most realistic image is not a replica or even a copy of what is depicted. It is not often that we mistake a representation for what it represents.

Semioticians generally maintain that there are no 'pure' icons. All artists employ stylistic conventions and these are, of course, culturally and historically variable. Peirce stated that although 'any material image' (such as a painting) may be perceived as looking like what it represents, it is 'largely conventional in its mode of representation' (Peirce 1931–58, 2.276).

> We say that the portrait of a person we have not seen is *convincing*. So far as, on the ground merely of what I see in it, I am led to form an idea of the person it represents, it is an icon. But, in fact, it is not a pure icon, because I am greatly influenced by knowing that it is an *effect*, through the artist, caused by the original's appearance . . . Besides, I know that portraits have but the slightest resemblance to their originals, except in certain conventional respects, and after a conventional scale of values, etc.
>
> (ibid., 2.92)

Iconic and indexical signs are more likely to be read as natural than symbolic signs when making the connection between signifier and signified has become habitual. Iconic signifiers can be highly evocative. Such signs do not draw our attention to their mediation, seeming to present reality more directly than symbolic signs.

An extended critique of 'iconism' can be found in Eco (1976, 191ff). The linguist John Lyons notes that iconicity is 'always dependent upon properties of the medium in which the form is manifest' (Lyons 1977, 105). He offers the example of the onomatopoeic English word *cuckoo*, noting that it is only (perceived as) iconic in the phonic medium (speech) and not in the graphic medium (writing). While the phonic medium can represent characteristic sounds (albeit in a relatively conventionalized way), the graphic medium can

represent characteristic shapes (as in the case of Egyptian hieroglyphs) (Lyons 1977, 103). We will return shortly to the importance
of the materiality of the sign.

INDEXICAL MODE

Indexicality is perhaps the most unfamiliar concept, though its links
with everyday uses of the word 'index' ought to be less misleading
than the terms for the other two modes. Indexicality is quite closely
related to the way in which the index of a book or an 'index' finger
point directly to what is being referred to. Peirce offers various criteria for what constitutes an index. An index 'indicates' something:
for example, 'a sundial or clock *indicates* the time of day' (Peirce
1931–58, 2.285). He refers to a 'genuine relation' between the 'sign'
and the *object* which does not depend purely on 'the interpreting
mind' (ibid., 2.92, 298). The *object* is 'necessarily existent' (ibid.,
2.310). The index is connected to its object 'as a matter of fact' (ibid.,
4.447). There is 'a real connection' (ibid., 5.75) which may be a
'direct physical connection' (ibid., 1.372, 2.281, 2.299). An indexical sign is like 'a fragment torn away from the object' (ibid., 2.231).
Unlike an icon (the object of which may be fictional) an index stands
'unequivocally for this or that existing thing' (ibid., 4.531). The relationship is *not* based on 'mere resemblance' (ibid.): 'indices . . . have
no significant resemblance to their objects' (ibid., 2.306). 'Similarity
or analogy' are not what define the index (ibid., 2.305). 'Anything
which focuses the attention is an index. Anything which startles us is
an index' (ibid., 2.285; cf. 3.434). Indexical signs 'direct the attention to their objects by blind compulsion' (ibid., 2.306; cf. 2.191,
2.428). Whereas iconicity is characterized by *similarity*, indexicality
is characterized by *contiguity*. 'Psychologically, the action of indices
depends upon association by contiguity, and not upon association by
resemblance or upon intellectual operations' (ibid.). Elizabeth Bruss
notes that indexicality is 'a relationship rather than a quality. Hence
the signifier need have no particular properties of its own, only a
demonstrable connection to something else. The most important of
these connections are spatial co-occurrence, temporal sequence, and
cause and effect' (Bruss 1978, 88).

While a photograph is also perceived as resembling that which
it depicts, Peirce noted that it is not only iconic but also *indexical*:
'photographs, especially instantaneous photographs, are very instructive, because we know that in certain respects they are exactly like
the objects they represent. But this resemblance is due to the
photographs having been produced under such circumstances that
they were physically forced to correspond point by point to nature.
In that aspect, then, they belong to the . . . class of signs . . . by physical connection [the indexical class]' (Peirce 1931–58, 2.281; cf.
5.554). So in this sense, since the photographic image is an index
of the effect of light, all *unedited* photographic and filmic images
are indexical (although we should remember that conventional practices are always involved in composition, focusing, developing, and
so on). Such images do of course 'resemble' what they depict, and
some commentators suggest that the power of the photographic and
filmic image derives from the iconic character of the medium.
However, while digital imaging techniques are increasingly eroding
the indexicality of photographic images, it is arguable that it is the
indexicality still routinely attributed to the medium that is primarily
responsible for interpreters treating them as objective records of
reality. Peirce, a philosophical realist, observed that 'a photograph
. . . owing to its optical connection with its object, is evidence that
that appearance corresponds to a reality' (Peirce 1931–58, 4.447).
Of the three modes, only indexicality can serve as evidence of an
object's existence. In many contexts photographs are indeed regarded
as evidence, not least in legal contexts. As for the moving image,
video-cameras are of course widely used 'in evidence'. Documentary
film and location footage in television news programmes exploit the
indexical nature of the medium (though of course they are not purely
indexical). However, in one of his essays on photographic history,
John Tagg, wary of 'the realist position', cautions that 'the existence
of a photograph is no guarantee of a corresponding pre-photographic
existent . . . The indexical nature of the photograph – the causative
link between the pre-photographic referent and the sign . . . can guarantee nothing at the level of meaning.' Even prior to digital
photography, both 'correction' and montage were practised, but Tagg
argues that *every* photograph involves 'significant distortions' (Tagg

1988, 1–3). This is an issue to which we will return in Chapter 5 when we discuss whether photography is 'a message without a code'. We may nevertheless grant the unedited photograph at least potential evidentiality.

MODES NOT TYPES

It is easy to slip into referring to Peirce's three forms as 'types of signs', but they are not necessarily mutually exclusive: a sign can be an icon, a symbol and an index, or any combination. A map is indexical in pointing to the locations of things, iconic in representing the directional relations and distances between landmarks, and symbolic in using conventional symbols (the significance of which must be learned).

As we have noted, we are dealing with symbolic, iconic and indexical modes of relationship rather than with types of signs. Thus, Jakobson observes that 'strictly speaking, the main difference . . . is rather in the hierarchy of their properties than in the properties themselves' (Jakobson 1963d, 335; cf. 1968, 700). Peirce was fully aware of this: for instance, we have already noted that he did not regard a portrait as a pure icon. A 'stylized' image might be more appropriately regarded as a 'symbolic icon' (Jakobson 1963d, 335). Such combined terms represent 'transitional varieties' (1968, 700). Peirce also insisted that 'it would be difficult if not impossible to instance an absolutely pure index, or to find any sign absolutely devoid of the indexical quality' (Peirce 1931–58, 2.306). Jakobson points out that many deliberate indexes also have a symbolic or indexical quality, instancing traffic lights as being both indexical and symbolic and noting that even the pointing gesture is not always interpreted purely indexically in different cultural contexts (Jakobson 1968, 700–1). Nor are words always purely symbolic – they can be 'iconic symbols' (such as onomatopoeic words) or 'indexical symbols' (such as 'that', 'this', 'here', 'there') (see Jakobson 1966 on iconicity and indexicality in language).

Jakobson notes that Peirce's three modes co-exist in a 'relative hierarchy' in which one mode is dominant, with dominance determined by context (Jakobson 1966, 411). Whether a sign is symbolic, iconic or indexical depends primarily on the way in which the sign is used, so textbook examples chosen to illustrate the various modes can be misleading. The same signifier may be used iconically in one context and symbolically in another: a photograph of a woman may stand for some broad category such as 'women' or may more specifically represent only the particular woman who is depicted. Signs cannot be classified in terms of the three modes without reference to the purposes of their users within particular contexts. A sign may consequently be treated as symbolic by one person, as iconic by another and as indexical by a third. Signs may also shift in mode over time. For instance, a Rolls-Royce is an index of wealth because one must be wealthy to own one, but social usage has led to its becoming a conventional symbol of wealth (Culler 1975, 17).

Consistently with his advocacy of binary relations, Jakobson boldly asserts that Peirce's three modes of relations are 'actually based on two substantial dichotomies' (Jakobson 1968, 700) – an assertion which understandably irritates a Peircean scholar (Bruss 1978, 92). Combining four terms used by Peirce, Jakobson proposes a matrix of his own with *contiguity* and *similarity* on one axis and the qualities of being either 'imputed' or 'factual' on the other. Within this scheme, the index is based on 'factual contiguity', the icon on 'factual similarity' and the symbol on 'imputed contiguity' – leaving an initially empty category of 'imputed similarity' to which Jakobson assigns ostensibly non-referential signs which nevertheless generate emotional connotations – such as music and non-representational visual art (ibid., 700–5).

CHANGING RELATIONS

Despite his emphasis on studying 'the language-state' 'synchronically' (as if it were frozen at one moment in time) rather than 'diachronically' (studying its evolution), Saussure was well aware that the relationship between the signified and the signifier in language was subject to change over time (Saussure 1983, 74ff.). However, this was not the focus of his concern. Critics emphasize that the relation between signifier and signified is subject to dynamic change: any 'fixing' of 'the chain of signifiers' is seen as both temporary and socially determined (Coward and Ellis 1977, 6, 8, 13).

In terms of Peirce's three modes, a historical shift from one mode to another tends to occur. Although Peirce made far more allowance for non-linguistic signs than did Saussure, like Saussure, he too granted greater status to *symbolic* signs: 'they are the only general signs; and generality is essential to reasoning' (Peirce 1931–58, 3.363; cf. 4.448, 4.531). Saussure's emphasis on the importance of the principle of arbitrariness reflects his prioritizing of symbolic signs while Peirce privileges 'the symbol-using mind' (Peirce 1931–58, 2.299). The idea of the evolution of sign-systems towards the symbolic mode is consistent with such a perspective. Peirce speculates 'whether there be a life in signs, so that – the requisite vehicle being present – they will go through a certain order of development'. Interestingly, he does not present this as *necessarily* a matter of progress towards the 'ideal' of symbolic form since he allows for the theoretical possibility that 'the same round of changes of form is described over and over again' (ibid., 2.111). While granting such a possibility, he nevertheless notes that 'a regular progression . . . may be remarked in the three orders of signs, Icon, Index, Symbol' (ibid., 2.299). Peirce posits iconicity as the original default mode of signification, declaring the icon to be 'an originalian sign' (ibid., 2.92), defining this as 'the most primitive, simple and original of the categories' (ibid., 2.90). Compared to the 'genuine sign . . . or symbol', an index is 'degenerate in the lesser degree' while an icon is 'degenerate in the greater degree'. Peirce noted that signs were 'originally in part iconic, in part indexical' (ibid., 2.92). He adds that 'in all primitive writing, such as the Egyptian hieroglyphics, there are icons of a non-logical kind, the ideographs' and he speculates that 'in the earliest form of speech there probably was a large element of mimicry' (ibid., 2.280). However, over time, linguistic signs developed a more symbolic and conventional character (ibid., 2.92, 2.280). 'Symbols come into being by development out of other signs, particularly from icons' (ibid., 2.302).

The historical evidence does indicate a tendency of linguistic signs to evolve from indexical and iconic forms towards symbolic forms. Alphabets were not initially based on the substitution of conventional symbols for sounds. Some of the letters in the Greek and Latin alphabets, of course, derive from iconic signs in Egyptian hieroglyphs. The early scripts of the Mediterranean civilizations used pictographs, ideographs and hieroglyphs. Many of these were iconic signs resembling the objects and actions to which they referred either directly or metaphorically. Over time, picture writing became more symbolic and less iconic (Gelb 1963). This shift from the iconic to the symbolic may have been 'dictated by the economy of using a chisel or a reed brush' (Cherry 1966, 33); in general, symbols are semiotically more flexible and efficient (Lyons 1977, 103). The anthropologist Claude Lévi-Strauss identified a similar general movement from motivation to arbitrariness within the conceptual schemes employed by particular cultures (Lévi-Strauss 1962, 156).

DIGITAL AND ANALOGUE

A distinction is sometimes made between *digital* and *analogical* signs. Anthony Wilden, a Canadian communication theorist, declared that 'no two categories, and no two kinds of experience are more fundamental in human life and thought than continuity and discontinuity' (Wilden 1987, 222). While we experience time as a continuum, we may represent it in either analogue or digital form. A watch with an analogue display (with hour, minute and second hands) has the advantage of dividing an hour up like a cake (so that, in a lecture, for instance, we can 'see' how much time is left). A watch with a digital display (displaying the current time as a changing number) has the advantage of precision, so that we can easily see exactly what time it is 'now'. Even an analogue display is now simulated on some digital watches.

We have a deep attachment to analogical modes and we have often tended to regard digital representations as less real or less authentic – at least initially (as in the case of the audio CD compared to the vinyl LP). The analogue–digital distinction is frequently represented as natural versus artificial – a logical extension of Claude Lévi-Strauss's argument that continuous is to discrete is as nature is to culture (Lévi-Strauss 1969, 28). The privileging of the analogical may be linked with the defiance of rationality in romantic ideology (which still dominates our conception of ourselves as 'individuals'). The deliberate intention to communicate tends to be dominant in digital codes, while in analogue codes 'it is almost impossible . . . *not* to communicate' (Wilden 1987, 225). Beyond any conscious intention, we communicate through gesture, posture, facial expression, intonation and so on. Analogical codes unavoidably 'give us away', revealing such things as our moods, attitudes, intentions and truthfulness (or otherwise). However, although the appearance of the 'digital watch' in 1971 and the subsequent 'digital revolution' in audio- and video-recording have led us to associate the digital mode with electronic technologies, digital codes have existed since the earliest forms of language – and writing is a 'digital technology'. Signifying systems impose digital order on what we often experience as a dynamic and seamless flux. The very definition of something as a sign involves reducing the continuous to the discrete. As we shall see later, binary (either/or) distinctions are a fundamental process in the creation of signifying structures. Digital signs involve discrete units such as words and 'whole numbers' and depend on the categorization of what is signified.

Analogical signs (such as visual images, gestures, textures, tastes and smells) involve graded relationships on a continuum. They can signify infinite subtleties which seem 'beyond words'. Emotions and feelings are analogical signifieds. Unlike symbolic signifiers, motivated signifiers (and their signifieds) blend into one another. There can be no comprehensive catalogue of such dynamic analogue signs as smiles or laughs. Analogue signs can of course be digitally reproduced (as is demonstrated by the digital recording of sounds and of both still and moving images) but they cannot be directly related to a standard 'dictionary' and syntax in the way that linguistic signs can. The North American film theorist Bill Nichols notes that 'the graded quality of analogue codes may make them rich in meaning but it also renders them somewhat impoverished in syntactical complexity or semantic precision. By contrast the discrete units of digital codes may be somewhat impoverished in meaning but capable of much greater complexity or semantic signification' (Nichols 1981, 47; cf. Wilden 1987, 138, 224). The art historian Ernst Gombrich insisted that 'statements cannot be translated into images' and that 'pictures cannot assert' – a contention also found in Peirce (Gombrich 1982, 138, 175; Peirce 1931–58, 2.291). Such stances are adopted in relation to images unattached to verbal texts – such commentators would acknowledge that a simple verbal caption may be sufficient to enable an image to be used in the service of an assertion. While images serving such communicative purposes may be more 'open to interpretation', contemporary visual advertisements are a powerful example of how images may be used to make implicit claims which advertisers often prefer not to make more openly in words.

TYPES AND TOKENS

The Italian semiotician Umberto Eco offers another distinction between sign vehicles; this relates to the concept of *tokens* and *types* which derives from Peirce (Eco 1976, 178ff.; Peirce 1931–58, 4.537). In relation to words in a spoken utterance or written text, a count of the tokens would be a count of the total number of words used (regardless of type), while a count of the types would be a count of the *different* words used, ignoring repetitions. In the language of semantics, tokens *instantiate* (are instances of) their type. Eco notes that 'grouping manifold tokens under a single type is the way in which language . . . works' (Eco 1999, 146). Language and thought depend on categorization: without categories we would be 'slaves to the particular' (Bruner et al. 1956, 1).

John Lyons notes that whether something is counted as a token of a type is relative to one's purposes – for instance:

- Are tokens to include words with different meanings which happen to be spelt or pronounced in the same way?
- Does a capital letter instantiate the same type as the corresponding lower-case letter?
- Does a word printed in italics instantiate the same type as a word printed in Roman?
- Is a word handwritten by X ever the same as a word handwritten by Y?

(Lyons 1977, 13–15)

From a semiotic point of view, such questions could only be answered by considering in each case whether the different forms signified something of any consequence to the relevant sign-users in the context of the specific signifying practice being studied.

Eco lists three kinds of sign vehicles, and it is notable that the distinction relates in part at least to material form:

- signs in which there may be any number of tokens (replicas) of the same type (e.g. a printed word, or exactly the same model of car in the same colour);
- 'signs whose tokens, even though produced according to a type, possess a certain quality of material uniqueness' (e.g. a word which someone speaks or which is handwritten);
- 'signs whose token is their type, or signs in which type and token are identical' (e.g. a unique original oil-painting or Princess Diana's wedding dress).

(Eco 1976, 178ff.)

The type–token distinction may influence the way in which a text is interpreted. In his influential essay on 'The work of art in the age of mechanical reproduction', written in 1935, the literary–philosophical theorist Walter Benjamin noted that technological society is dominated by reproductions of original works – tokens of the original type (Benjamin 1992, 211–44). Indeed, even if we do see, for instance, 'the original' of a famous oil-painting, we are highly likely to have seen it first in the form of innumerable reproductions (books, postcards, posters – sometimes even in the form of pastiches or variations on the theme) and we may only be able to 'see' the original in the light of the judgements shaped by the copies or versions which we have encountered. In the postmodern era, the bulk of our texts are indeed 'copies without originals'.

The type–token distinction in relation to signs is important in social semiotic terms not as an absolute property of the sign vehicle but only insofar as it matters on any given occasion (for particular purposes) to those involved in using the sign. Minute differences in a pattern could be a matter of life and death for gamblers in relation to variations in the pattern on the backs of playing-cards within the same pack, but stylistic differences in the design of each type of card (such as the ace of spades), are much appreciated by collectors as a distinctive feature of different packs of playing cards.

REMATERIALIZING THE SIGN

As already indicated, Saussure saw both the signifier and the signified as non-material 'psychological' forms; language itself is 'a form, not a substance' (Saussure 1983, 111, 120). He uses several examples to reinforce his point. For instance, in one of several chess analogies, he notes that 'if pieces made of ivory are substituted for pieces made of wood, the change makes no difference to the system' (ibid., 23). Pursuing this functional approach, he notes elsewhere that the 8.25 p.m. Geneva–Paris train is referred to as 'the same train' even though the combinations of locomotive, carriages and personnel may change. Similarly, he asks why a street which is completely rebuilt can still be 'the same street'. He suggests that this is 'because it is not a purely material structure' (ibid., 107). Saussure insists that this is not to say that such entities are 'abstract' since we cannot conceive of a street or train outside of their material realization (ibid.). This can be related to the type–token distinction. Since Saussure sees language in terms of formal function rather than material substance, then whatever performs the same function within the system can be regarded as just another token of the same type. With regard to language, Saussure observes that 'sound, as a material element . . . is merely ancillary, a material the language uses' (ibid., 116). Linguistic signifiers are 'not physical in any way. They are constituted solely by differences which distinguish one such sound pattern from another' (ibid., 117). He admits at one point, with some apparent reluctance, that 'linguistic signs are, so to speak, tangible: writing can fix them in conventional images' (ibid., 15). However, referring to written signs, he comments that 'the actual mode of inscription is irrelevant, because it does not affect the system . . . Whether I write in black or white, in incised characters or in relief, with a pen or a chisel – none of that is of any importance for the meaning' (ibid.). One can understand how a linguist would tend to focus on form and function within language and to regard the material manifestations of language as of peripheral interest. 'The linguist . . . is interested in types, not tokens' (Lyons 1977, 28).

This was not only the attitude of the linguist Saussure, but also of the philosopher Peirce: 'The word "*man*" . . . does not consist of three films of ink. If the word "man" occurs hundreds of times in a book of which myriads of copies are printed, all those millions of triplets of patches of ink are embodiments of one and the same word . . . each of those embodiments a *replica* of the symbol. This shows that the word is not a thing' (Peirce 1931–58, 4.447). Peirce did allude to the materiality of the sign: 'since a sign is not identical with the thing signified, but differs from the latter in some respects, it must plainly have some characters which belong to it in itself . . . These I call the *material* qualities of the sign.' He granted that materiality is a property of the sign which is 'of great importance in the theory of cognition'. However, materiality had 'nothing to do with its representative function' and it did not feature in his classificatory schemes (ibid., 5.287).

While Saussure chose to ignore the materiality of the linguistic sign, most subsequent theorists who have adopted his model have chosen to reclaim the materiality of the sign (or more strictly of the signifier). Semioticians must take seriously any factors to which sign-users ascribe significance, and the material form of a sign does sometimes make a difference. Contemporary theorists tend to acknowledge that the material form of the sign may generate connotations of its own. As early as 1929 Valentin Voloshinov published *Marxism and the Philosophy of Language* which included a materialist critique of Saussure's psychological and implicitly idealist model of the sign. Voloshinov described Saussure's ideas as 'the most striking expression' of 'abstract objectivism' (Voloshinov 1973, 58). He insisted that 'a sign is a phenomenon of the external world' and that 'signs . . . are particular, material things'. Every sign 'has some kind of material embodiment, whether in sound, physical mass, colour, movements of the body, or the like' (ibid., 10–11; cf. 28). For Voloshinov, all signs, including language, have 'concrete material reality' and the physical properties of the sign matter (ibid., 65). Though a structuralist theorist himself, Roman Jakobson also rejected Saussure's notion of the immateriality of language, declaring that 'since the sound matter of language is a matter organized and formed to serve as a semiotic instrument, not only the significative function of the distinctive features but even their phonic essence is a cultural artifact' (Jakobson 1949c, 423). Furthermore, although he accepted the traditional view that 'writing . . . is – both ontologically and phylogenetically a secondary and optional acquisition' (Jakobson 1970, 455–6) and that the written word 'as a rule' functions as a signifier for the spoken word, he regarded it as not only 'the most important transposition' of speech into another medium (Jakobson 1968, 706) but also as characterized by 'autonomous properties' (Jakobson 1971d, 718). He expressed his concern that 'written language [is] often underrated by linguists' and referred the reader to Derrida's reversal of this tradition (Jakobson 1970, 455–6).

Psychoanalytic theory also contributed to the revaluation of the signifier – in Freudian dream theory the sound of the signifier could be regarded as a better guide to its possible signified than any conventional 'decoding' might have suggested (Freud 1938, 319). For instance, Freud reported that the dream of a young woman engaged to be married featured flowers – including lilies-of-the-valley and violets. Popular symbolism suggested that the lilies were a symbol of chastity and the woman agreed that she associated them with purity. However, Freud was surprised to discover that she associated the word 'violet' phonetically with the English word 'violate', suggesting her fear of the violence of 'defloration' (another word alluding to flowers) (Freud 1938, 382–3). As the psychoanalytical theorist Jacques Lacan emphasized (originally in 1957), the Freudian concepts of *condensation* and *displacement* illustrate the determination of the signified by the signifier in dreams (Lacan 1977, 159ff.). In *condensation*, several thoughts are condensed into one symbol, while in *displacement* unconscious desire is displaced into an apparently trivial symbol (to avoid dream censorship).

Although widely criticized as idealists, poststructuralist theorists have sought to revalorize the signifier. The phonocentrism which was allied with Saussure's suppression of the materiality of the linguistic sign was challenged in 1967, when the French poststructuralist Jacques Derrida, in his book *Of Grammatology*, attacked the privileging of speech over writing which is found in Saussure (as well as in the work of many other previous and subsequent linguists) (Derrida 1967a/1976). From Plato to Lévi-Strauss, the spoken word had held a privileged position in the Western worldview, being regarded as intimately involved in our sense of self and constituting a sign of truth and authenticity. Speech had become so thoroughly naturalized that 'not only do the signifier and the signified seem to unite, but also, in this confusion, the signifier seems to erase itself or to become transparent' (Derrida 1981, 22). Writing had traditionally been relegated to a secondary position. The deconstructive enterprise marked 'the return of the repressed' (Derrida 1967b, 197). In seeking to establish 'grammatology' or the study of textuality, Derrida championed the primacy of the material word. He noted that the specificity of words is itself a material dimension. 'The materiality of a word cannot be translated or carried over into another language. Materiality is precisely that which translation relinquishes' (ibid., 210). Some readers may note a degree of (characteristically postmodern) irony in such a stance being adopted by a theorist who also attacks Western materialism and whom many critics regard as an extreme idealist (despite his criticisms of idealism). Derrida's ideas have nevertheless informed the perspectives of some theorists who have sought to 'rematerialize' the linguistic sign, stressing that words and texts are *things* (e.g. Coward and Ellis 1977, Silverman and Torode 1980).

Roland Barthes also sought to revalorize the role of the signifier in the act of writing. He argued that in 'classic' literary writing, the writer 'is always supposed to go from signified to signifier, from content to form, from idea to text, from passion to expression' (Barthes 1974, 174). However, this was directly opposite to the way in which Barthes characterized the act of writing. For him, writing was a matter of working with the signifiers and letting the signifieds take care of themselves – a paradoxical phenomenon which other writers have often reported (Chandler 1995, 60ff.).

Theoretical attention has thus been increasingly drawn to the material dimension of language since Voloshinov's critique of the Saussurean stance (dating from only thirteen years after the first edition of the *Course*) and this perspective became widely accepted from around the 1970s. More recently, studies have shown that material objects can themselves function directly as signs (more strictly, of course, as signifiers), not only in the form of 'status symbols' (such as expensive cars) but also (in the case of particular objects in their homes which individuals regard as having some special importance for them) as part of the repertoire of signs upon which people draw in developing and maintaining their sense of personal and social identity (Csikszentmihalyi and Rochberg-Halton 1981, Chalfen 1987). People attach 'symbolic values' to television sets, furniture and photograph albums which are not determined by the utilitarian functions of such mundane objects (see also Leeds-Hurwitz 1993, Chapter 6). The groundwork for such thinking had already been laid within structuralism. Lévi-Strauss had explored 'the logic of the concrete' – observing, for instance, that animals are 'good to think [with]' and that identity can be expressed through the manipulation of existing things (Lévi-Strauss 1962). Elsewhere, I have explored the notion that personal homepages on the web function as manipulable objects with which their authors can think about identity (Chandler 2006).

Jay David Bolter argues that 'signs are always anchored in a medium. Signs may be more or less dependent upon the characteristics of one medium – they may transfer more or less well to other media – but there is no such thing as a sign without a medium' (Bolter 1991, 195–6). The *sign* as such may not be a material entity, but it has a material dimension – the signifier (or sign vehicle). Robert Hodge and David Tripp insist that, 'fundamental to all semiotic analysis is the fact that any system of signs (semiotic code) is carried by a material medium *which has its own principles of structure*' (Hodge and Tripp 1986, 17). Furthermore, some media draw on several interacting sign-systems: television and film, for example, utilize verbal, visual, auditory and locomotive signs. The medium is not 'neutral'; each medium has its own affordances and constraints and, as Umberto Eco notes, each is already 'charged with cultural signification' (Eco 1976, 267). For instance, photographic and audio-visual media are almost invariably regarded as more real than other

forms of representation. Gunther Kress and Theo van Leeuwen argue
that 'the material expression of the text is always significant; it is a
separately variable semiotic feature' (Kress and van Leeuwen 1996,
231). Changing the signifier at the level of the form or medium may
thus influence the signified – the sense which readers make of what
is ostensibly the same 'content'. Breaking up a relationship by fax
is likely to be regarded in a different light from breaking up in a
face-to-face situation.

HJELMSLEV'S FRAMEWORK

The distinction between signifier and signified has sometimes been
equated to the familiar dualism of 'form and content' (though not
by Saussure). Within such a framework, the signifier is seen as the
form of the sign and the signified as the *content*. However, the
metaphor of form as a 'container' is problematic, tending to support
the equation of content with *meaning*, implying that meaning can be
'extracted' without an active process of interpretation and that form
is not in itself meaningful (Chandler 1995, 104–6). The linguist Louis
Hjelmslev acknowledged that 'there can be no content without an
expression, or expressionless content; neither can there be an expression without a content, or content-less expression' (Hjelmslev 1961,
49). He offered a framework which facilitated analytical distinctions
(ibid., 47ff.). While he referred to 'planes' of expression and content
(Saussure's *signifier* and *signified*), he enriched this model (ibid., 60).
His contribution was to suggest that both *expression* and *content*
have *substance* and *form* (see Table 1.7). This strategy thus avoids
the dualistic reduction of the sign to form and content.

  Within Hjelmslev's framework there are four categories:
substance of expression, form of expression, substance of content,
form of content. Various theorists such as Christian Metz have built
upon this theoretical distinction and they differ somewhat in what
they assign to the four categories (see Tudor 1974, 110; Baggaley
and Duck 1976, 149; Metz 1981). Whereas Saussure had insisted
that language is a non-material form and not a material substance,
Hjelmslev's framework allows us to analyse texts according to their

	Substance	*Form*
Signifiers: plane of **expression**	**Substance of expression:** physical materials of the medium (e.g. photographs, recorded voices, printed words on paper)	**Form of expression:** language, formal syntactic structure, technique and style
Signified: plane of **content**	**Substance of content:** 'human content' (Metz), textual world, subject matter, genre	**Form of content:** 'semantic structure' (Baggaley and Duck), 'thematic structure' (including narrative) (Metz)

TABLE 1.7 Substance and form

Source: Based on Tudor 1974

various dimensions and to grant to each of these the potential for signification. Such a matrix provides a useful framework for the systematic analysis of texts, broadens the notion of what constitutes a sign, and reminds us that the materiality of the sign may in itself signify.

2

SIGNS AND THINGS

While semiotics is often encountered in the form of textual analysis, there is far more to semiotics than this. Indeed, one cannot engage in the semiotic study of how meanings are made in texts and cultural practices without adopting a philosophical stance in relation to the nature of signs, representation and reality. We have already seen how the Saussurean and Peircean models of the sign have different philosophical implications. For those who adopt the stance that reality always involves representation and that signs are involved in the construction of reality, semiotics is unavoidably a form of philosophy. No semiotician or philosopher would be so naïve as to treat signs such as words as if they were the things for which they stand, but as we shall see, this occurs at least sometimes in the psychological phenomenology of everyday life and in the uncritical framework of casual discourse.

NAMING THINGS

To semioticians, a defining feature of signs is that they are treated by their users as 'standing for' or representing other things. Jonathan Swift's satirical account of the fictional academicians of Lagado outlined their proposal to abolish words altogether, and to carry around bundles of objects whenever they wanted to communicate. This highlights problems with the simplistic notion of signs being direct substitutes for physical things in the world around us. The academicians adopted the philosophical stance of naïve realism in assuming that words simply mirror objects in an external world. They believed that 'words are only names for things', a stance involving the assumption that 'things' necessarily exist independently of language prior to them being 'labelled' with words. According to this position there is a one-to-one correspondence between word and referent (sometimes called language–world *isomorphism*), and language is simply a *nomenclature* – an item-by-item naming of things in the world. Saussure felt that this was 'the superficial view taken by the general public' (Saussure 1983, 16, 65).

Within the lexicon of a language, it is true that most of the words are 'lexical words' (or nouns) which refer to 'things', but most of these things are abstract concepts rather than physical objects in the world. Only 'proper nouns' have specific referents in the everyday world, and only some of these refer to a unique entity (e.g. Llanfairpwllgwyngyllgogerychwyrndrobwllllantysiliogogogoch – the name of a Welsh village). Even proper names are not specific as they are imagined to be: for instance, a reference to 'Charles Sanders Peirce' begs questions such as 'Peirce at what date?', 'Peirce as a philosopher or in some other role?' or even 'whose Peirce?' (e.g. 'Jakobson's Peirce'?) Perhaps I should now hesitate to attribute to Peirce the observation that 'a symbol . . . cannot indicate any *particular* thing; it denotes a *kind* of thing' (Peirce 1931–58, 2.301; *my emphasis*). The communicative function of a fully functioning language requires the scope of reference to move beyond the particularity of the individual instance. While each leaf, cloud or smile is different from all others, effective communication requires general categories or 'universals'. Anyone who has attempted to communicate with people who do not share their language will be familiar with the limitations of simply pointing to things. You can't point to 'mind', 'culture' or 'history'; these are not 'things' at all. The vast majority of lexical words in a language exist on a high level of abstraction and refer to classes of things (such as 'buildings') or to concepts (such as 'construction'). Language depends on categorization, but as soon as we group instances into classes (tokens into types), we lose any one-to-one correspondence of word and thing (if by 'things' we mean specific objects). Furthermore, other than lexical words, the remaining elements of the lexicon of a language consist of 'function words' (or grammatical words, such as 'only' and 'under') which do not refer to objects in the world at all. The lexicon of a language consists of many kinds of signs other than nouns. Clearly, language cannot be reduced to the naming of objects.

The less naïve realists might note at this point that words do not necessarily name only physical things which exist in an objective material world but may also label imaginary things and also *concepts*. Peirce's referent, for instance, is not limited to things which exist in the physical world. However, as Saussure noted, the notion of words as labels for concepts 'assumes that ideas exist independently of words' (Saussure 1983, 65), and for him, 'no ideas are established in advance . . . before the introduction of linguistic structure' (ibid., 110; cf. 114–15, 118). It remains a rationalist and 'nomenclaturist' stance on language when words are seen as 'labels' for pre-existing ideas as well as for physical objects. It is reductionist: reducing language to the purely referential function of naming things. When we use language, its various kinds of signs relate to each other in complex ways which make nonsense of the reduction of language to a nomenclature. Referentiality may be a function of language but it is only one of its functions.

A radical response to realists is that things do not exist independently of the sign-systems that we use; reality is created by the media which seem simply to represent it. Language does not simply name pre-existing categories; categories do not exist in 'the world' (where are the boundaries of a cloud or when does a smile begin?). We may acknowledge the cautionary remarks of John Lyons, that such an emphasis on reality as invariably perceptually seamless may be an exaggeration. Lyons speculates that 'most of the phenomenal world, as we perceive it, is *not* an undifferentiated continuum'; and our referential categories do seem to bear some relationship to certain features which seem to be inherently salient (Lyons 1977, 247; *my emphasis*; cf. ibid., 260). In support of this caveat, we may note that the Gestalt psychologists reported a universal human tendency to separate a salient *figure* from what the viewer relegates to the (back)*ground*. However, such observations clearly do not demonstrate that the lexical structure of language reflects the structure of an external reality. As Saussure noted, if words were simply a nomenclature for a pre-existing set of things in the world, translation from one language to another would be easy (Saussure 1983, 114–15) whereas in fact languages differ in how they categorize the world – the signifieds in one language do not neatly correspond to those in another. Within a language, many words may refer to 'the same thing' but reflect different evaluations of it (one person's 'hovel' is another person's 'home'). Furthermore, what is signified by a word is subject to historical change. In this sense, reality or the world is created by the language we use: this argument insists on *the primacy of the signifier*. Even if we do *not* adopt the radical stance that the real world is a product of our sign-systems, we must still acknowledge that there are many things in the experiential world for which we have no words and that most words do not correspond to objects in the known world at all. Thus, all words are abstractions, and there is no direct correspondence between words and things in the world.

REFERENTIALITY

Saussure's model of the sign involves no direct reference to reality outside the sign. This was not a denial of extralinguistic reality as such but a reflection of his understanding of his own role as a linguist. Saussure accepted that in most scientific disciplines the 'objects of study' were 'given in advance' and existed independently of the observer's 'point of view'. However, he stressed that in linguistics, by contrast, 'it is the viewpoint adopted which creates the object' (Saussure 1983, 8). While such a statement might go without comment in a discipline with an acknowledged self-sufficiency (such as mathematics), in the context of human language one can understand how it might be criticized as an idealist model. In the Saussurean model the signified is only a mental concept; concepts are mental constructs, not external objects. A concept may, of course, refer to something in experiential reality but the Saussurean stance is a denial of the essentialist argument that signifieds are distinct, autonomous entities in an objective world which are definable in terms of some kind of unchanging essence. Saussurean semiotics asserts the non-essential nature of objects. Just like signifiers, signifieds are part of the sign-system; signifieds are socially constructed. According to the Whorfian stance, the signified is an arbitrary product of our culture's 'way of seeing'. The Saussurean perspective 'tends to reverse the precedence which a nomenclaturist accords to the world outside language, by proposing that far from the world determining the order of our language, our language determines the order of the world' (Sturrock 1986, 17).

In contrast to the Saussurean model, Peirce's model of the sign explicitly features the *referent* – something beyond the sign to which the sign vehicle refers (though not necessarily a material thing). However, it also features the *interpretant* which leads to an 'infinite series' of signs, so it has been provocatively suggested that Peirce's model could also be taken to suggest the relative independence of signs from any referents (Silverman 1983, 15). In any event, for Peirce, reality can only be known via signs. If representations are our only access to reality, determining their accuracy is a critical issue. Peirce adopted from logic the notion of 'modality' to refer to the truth value of a sign, acknowledging three kinds: actuality, (logical) necessity and (hypothetical) possibility (Peirce 1931–58, 2.454). Furthermore, his classification of signs in terms of the mode of relationship of the sign vehicle to its referent reflects their modality – their apparent transparency in relation to reality (the symbolic mode, for instance, having *low* modality). Peirce asserted that, logically, signification could only ever be partial; otherwise it would destroy itself by becoming identical with its object (Grayson 1998, 40; Peirce 1982–93, 1.79–80).

Theorists who veer towards the extreme position of philosophical *idealism* (for whom reality is purely subjective and is constructed in our use of signs) may see no problem with the Saussurean model, which has itself been described as idealist (e.g. Culler 1985, 117). Those drawn towards epistemological *realism* (for whom a single objective reality exists indisputably and independently outside us) would challenge it. According to this stance, reality may be distorted by the processes of mediation involved in apprehending it, but such processes play no part in constructing the world. Even those who adopt an intermediate *constructionist* (or *constructivist*) position – that language and other media play a major part in 'the social construction of reality' – may object to an apparent indifference towards social reality in Saussure's model. Those on the political left in particular would challenge its sidelining of the importance of the material conditions of existence. A system which brackets extralinguistic reality excludes truth values too. But post-Saussurean semiotics is not imprisoned within language in this way: Umberto Eco provocatively asserts that 'semiotics is in principle the discipline studying everything which can be used in order to lie' (Eco 1976, 7).

MODALITY

From the perspective of *social semiotics* the original Saussurean model is understandably problematic. Whatever our philosophical positions, in our daily behaviour we routinely act on the basis that some representations of reality are more reliable than others. And we do so in part with reference to cues within texts which semioticians (following linguists) call 'modality markers'. Such cues refer to what are variously described as the plausibility, reliability, credibility, truth, accuracy or facticity of texts within a given genre as representations of some recognizable reality. Gunther Kress and Theo van Leeuwen acknowledge that:

> A social semiotic theory of truth cannot claim to establish the absolute truth or untruth of representations. It can only show whether a given 'proposition' (visual, verbal or otherwise) is represented as true or not. From the point of view of social semiotics, truth is a construct of semiosis, and as such the truth

of a particular social group, arising from the values and beliefs
of that group.

(Kress and van Leeuwen 1996, 159)

From such a perspective, reality has authors; thus there are many
realities rather than the single reality posited by objectivists. This
stance is related to Whorfian framings of relationships between
language and reality. Constructionists insist that realities are not
limitless and unique to the individual as extreme subjectivists would
argue; rather, they are the product of social definitions and as such
far from equal in status. Realities are contested, and textual representations are thus 'sites of struggle'.

Modality refers to the reality status accorded to or claimed by
a sign, text or genre. More formally, Robert Hodge and Gunther
Kress declare that 'modality refers to the status, authority and reliability of a message, to its ontological status, or to its value as truth
or fact' (Hodge and Kress 1988, 124). In making sense of a text, its
interpreters make modality judgements about it, drawing on their
knowledge of the world and of the medium. For instance, they assign
it to fact or fiction, actuality or acting, live or recorded, and they
assess the possibility or plausibility of the events depicted or the
claims made in it. Modality judgements involve comparisons of
textual representations with models drawn from the everyday world
and with models based on the genre; they are therefore obviously
dependent on relevant experience of both the world and the medium.
Robert Hodge and David Tripp's semiotic study on children and television focuses on the development of children's modality judgements
(Hodge and Tripp 1986).

Clearly, the extent to which a text may be perceived as real
depends in part on the medium employed. Writing, for instance, generally has a lower modality than film and television. However, no rigid
ranking of media modalities is possible. John Kennedy showed children a simple line drawing featuring a group of children sitting in a
circle with a gap in their midst (Kennedy 1974). He asked them to
add to this gap a drawing of their own, and when they concentrated
on the central region of the drawing, many of them tried to pick up
the pencil which was depicted in the same style in the top right-hand

corner of the drawing! Being absorbed in the task led them to accept unconsciously the terms in which reality was constructed within the medium. This is not likely to be a phenomenon confined to children, since when absorbed in narrative (in many media) we frequently fall into a 'suspension of disbelief' without compromising our ability to distinguish representations from reality. Charles Peirce reflected that 'in contemplating a painting, there is a moment when we lose the consciousness that it is not the thing, the distinction of the real and the copy disappears' (Peirce 1931–58, 3.362).

While in a conscious comparison of a photographic image with a cartoon image of the same thing the photograph is likely to be judged as more realistic, the mental schemata involved in visual recognition may be closer to the stereotypical simplicity of cartoon images than to photographs. People can identify an image as a hand when it is drawn as a cartoon more quickly than when they are shown a photograph of a hand (Ryan and Schwartz 1956). This underlines the importance of perceptual codes in constructing reality. Umberto Eco argues that through familiarity an iconic signifier can acquire primacy over its signified. Such a sign becomes conventional 'step by step, the more its addressee becomes acquainted with it. At a certain point the iconic representation, however stylized it may be, appears to be more true than the real experience, and people begin to look at things through the glasses of iconic convention' (Eco 1976, 204–5).

Modality cues within texts include both formal features of the medium (such as flatness or motion) and content features (such as plausibility or familiarity), though it is their interaction and interpretation which is most important. The media which are typically judged to be the most realistic are photographic – especially film and television. James Monaco suggests that 'in film, the signifier and the signified are almost identical ... The power of language systems is that there is a very great difference between the signifier and the signified; the power of film is that there is not' (Monaco 1981, 127–8). This is an important part of what Christian Metz was referring to when he described the cinematic signifier as 'the imaginary signifier' (Metz 1977). In being less reliant than writing on symbolic signs, film, television and photography suggest less of an obvious gap between the signifier and its signified, which make them seem to offer reflections of reality (even in that which is imaginary). But photography does not *reproduce* its object: it 'abstracts from, and mediates, the actual' (Burgin 1982b, 61). While we do not mistake one for the other, we do need to remind ourselves that a photograph or a film does not simply record an event, but is only one of an infinite number of possible representations. All media texts, however 'realistic', are representations rather than simply recordings or reproductions of reality.

The film theorist André Bazin describes what he calls the 'reproductive fallacy' according to which the only kind of representation which can show things 'as they really are' would be one which is (or appears to be) exactly like that which it represents in every respect. Texts are almost always constructed from different materials from that which they represent, and representations cannot be replicas. For Bazin, aesthetic realism depended on a broader 'truth to reality' (Bazin 1974, 64; Lovell 1983, 81). Ien Ang (1985) argues that watching television soap operas can involve a kind of *psychological* or *emotional realism* for viewers which exists at the connotative rather than the denotative level. Viewers find some representations emotionally or psychologically 'true-to-life' (even if at the denotative level the treatment may seem 'unrealistic'). I would argue that especially with long-running soaps (which may become more real to their fans over time) what we could call *generic realism* is another factor. Viewers familiar with the characters and conventions of a particular soap opera may often judge the programme largely in its own generic terms rather than with reference to some external reality. For instance, is a character's current behaviour consistent with what we have learned over time about that character? The soap may be accepted to some extent as a world in its own right, in which slightly different rules may sometimes apply. This is of course the basis for what Coleridge called the 'willing suspension of disbelief' on which drama depends.

Robert Hodge and Gunther Kress argue that:

> Different genres, whether classified by medium (e.g. comic, cartoon, film, TV, painting) or by content (e.g. Western, Science Fiction, Romance, news) establish sets of modality markers,

and an overall value which acts as a baseline for the genre. This baseline can be different for different kinds of viewer/reader, and for different texts or moments within texts.

(Hodge and Kress 1988, 142)

What are recognized as realistic styles of representation reflect an aesthetic *code* (a concept which we will explore in detail later). Over time, certain methods of production within a medium and a genre become naturalized. The content comes to be accepted as a reflection of reality. In the case of popular television and film, for instance, the use of 'invisible editing' represents a widespread set of conventions which has come to seem natural to most viewers (as we shall see later). In realistic texts, what is foregrounded is the content rather than the form or style of production. As in the dominant mode of scientific discourse, the medium and codes are discounted as neutral and transparent and the makers of the text retreat to invisibility. Consequently, reality seems to pre-exist its representation and to 'speak for itself'; what is said thus has the aura of truth. John Tagg argues that in realist texts,

> The signifier is treated as if it were identical with a pre-existent signified and . . . the reader's role is purely that of a consumer . . . Signifier and signified appear not only to unite, but the signifier seems to become transparent so that the concept seems to present itself, and the arbitrary sign is naturalized by a spurious identity between reference and referents, between the text and the world.
>
> (Tagg 1988, 99)

Tagg adds that such a stance need not involve positing 'a closed world of codes' (ibid., 101) or the denial of the existence of what is represented outside the process which represents it (ibid., 167). However, he stresses 'the crucial relation of meaning to questions of practice and power', arguing that reality is 'a complex of dominant and dominated discourses which given texts exclude, separate or do not signify' (ibid., 101).

THE WORD IS NOT THE THING

The Belgian surrealist René Magritte painted *La Trahison des Images* (*The Treachery of Images*) in 1936. That it has become one of Magritte's most famous and widely reproduced works suggests the enduring fascination of its theme. At first glance, its subject is banal. We are offered a realistic depiction of an object which we easily recognize: a smoker's pipe (in side-on view). However, the painting also includes the text 'Ceci n'est pas une pipe' ('This is not a pipe'). The inclusion of text *within* the painting is remarkable enough, but the wording gives us cause to pause. If this were part of a language lesson or a child's 'reading book' (the style reminds me of old-fashioned *Ladybird* books for children), we might expect to see the words 'This is a pipe.' To depict a pipe and then provide a 'label' which insists that 'this is not a pipe' initially seems perverse. Is it purely irrational or is there something which we can learn from this apparent paradox? What could it mean? As our minds struggle to find a stable, meaningful interpretation we may not be too happy that there is no single, 'correct' answer to this question – although those of us who are relatively 'tolerant of ambiguity' may accept that it offers a great deal of food for thought about levels (or modes) of reality. The indexical word 'this' can be seen as a key to the interpretation of this painting: what exactly does the word 'this' refer to? Anthony Wilden suggests several alternative interpretations:

- this [pipe] is not a pipe;
- this [image of a pipe] is not a pipe;
- this [painting] is not a pipe;
- this [sentence] is not a pipe;
- [this] this is not a pipe;
- [this] is not a pipe.

(Wilden 1987, 245)

Although we habitually relate the meaning of texts to the stated or inferred purposes of their makers, Magritte's own purposes are not essential to our current concerns. It suits our purposes here to suggest that the painting could be taken as meaning that this representation (or any representation) is not that which it represents. That this image of a pipe is 'only an image' and that we can't smoke it seems obvious – nobody 'in their right mind' would be so foolish as to try to pick it up and use it as a functional pipe (although many readers will have heard by now of the unfortunate, deluded man who 'mistook his wife for a hat'). However, we do habitually refer to such realistic depictions in terms which suggest that they are nothing more nor less than what they depict. Any representation is more than merely a reproduction of that which it represents: it also contributes to the *construction* of reality. Even 'photorealism' does not depict unmediated reality. The most realistic representation may also symbolically or metaphorically 'stand for' something else entirely. Furthermore, the depiction of a pipe is no guarantee of the existence of a specific pipe in the world of which this is an accurate depiction. Indeed, it seems a fairly generalized pipe and could therefore be seen (as is frequently true of language lessons, children's encyclopedia entries and so on) as an illustration of the 'concept' of a pipe rather than of a specific pipe. The label seeks to anchor our interpretation – a concept to which we will return later – and yet at the same time the label is part of the painting itself rather than a title attached to the frame. Magritte's painting could be seen as a kind of defamiliarization: we are so used to seeing things and attaching labels to them that we seldom look deeper and do not see things in their specificity. One function of art (and of surrealistic art in particular) is 'to make the familiar strange' (as the Russian formalists put it).

Alfred Korzybski, the founder of a movement known as 'general semantics', declared that 'the map is not the territory' and that 'the word is not the thing' (Korzybski 1933; cf. Chase 1938 and Hayakawa 1941). The non-identity of sign and thing is, of course, a very basic Saussurean principle. However, while Saussure's model is anti-realist, the general semanticists adopted the realist stance that language comes 'between' us and the objective world and they sought to reform our verbal behaviour to counteract the linguistic distortion of reality. They felt that one reason for the confusion of signifiers and referential signifieds was that we sometimes allow language to

SIGNS AND THINGS   71

take us further up the 'ladder of abstraction' than we think we are. Here is a homely example of levels of verbal abstraction in relation to a cow called 'Bessie':

1. The cow known to science ultimately consists of atoms, electrons etc. according to present-day scientific inference . . .
2. The cow we perceive is not the word but the object of experience, that which our nervous system abstracts (selects) . . .
3. The word 'Bessie' (cow) is the *name* we give to the object of perception of level 2. The name is *not* the object; it merely *stands for* the object and omits reference to many characteristics of the object.
4. The word 'cow' stands for the characteristics we have abstracted as common to cow, cow, cow . . . cow. Characteristics peculiar to particular cows are left out.
5. When Bessie is referred to as 'livestock' only those characteristics she has in common with pigs, chickens, goats, etc. are referred to.
6. When Bessie is included among 'farm assets' reference is made only to what she has in common with all other saleable items on the farm.
7. When Bessie is referred to as an 'asset' still more of her characteristics are left out.
8. The word 'wealth' is an extremely high level of abstraction, omitting *almost* all reference to the characteristics of Bessie.
   (McKim 1972, 128; the origins of this example
   are in Korzybski, via Hayakawa 1941, 121ff.)

The ladder metaphor is consistent with how we routinely refer to levels of abstraction – we talk of thinkers with 'their heads in the clouds' and of 'realists' with their 'feet on the ground'. As we move up the ladder we move from the particular to the general, from concrete reality to abstract generalization. The general semanticists were of course hard-headed realists and what they wanted was for people to keep their feet firmly planted on the ground. In alerting language-users to levels of abstraction, the general semanticists sought to avoid the confusion of *higher logical types* with *lower logical types*. 'A map' is of a higher (more general) logical type than 'the territory', and linguistic representation in particular lends itself to this process of abstraction. Clearly we can learn more about a place by visiting it than by simply looking at a map of it, and we can tell more about a person by meeting that person than by merely looking at a photograph of that person. Translation from lower levels to higher levels involves an inevitable loss of specificity – like earth being filtered through a series of increasingly fine sieves or like photocopies being repeatedly made of the 'copies' that they produce. Being alert for the consequent losses, absences or exclusions is important to the semiotician as well as the 'general semanticist'. While the logician may be able to keep such levels separate, in most acts of communication some 'slippage' occurs routinely, although we are normally capable of identifying what kind of messages we are dealing with, assigning them to appropriate levels of abstraction. Semioticians observe that some kind of 'translation' is unavoidable in human communication. Claude Lévi-Strauss declared that 'understanding consists in the reduction of one type of reality to another' (Lévi-Strauss 1961, 61; cf. Leach 1976, 27). Similarly, Algirdas Greimas observed that 'signification is . . . nothing but . . . transposition from one level of language to another, from one language to a different language, and meaning is nothing but the possibility of such *transcoding*' (Greimas 1970, 13; translation by Jameson 1972, 215–16).

While it can be useful to consider abstraction in terms of levels and logical typing, the implicit filter metaphor in the general semanticists' 'ladder of abstraction' is too uni-dimensional. Any given object of perception could be categorized in a variety of ways rather than in terms of a single objective hierarchy. The categories applied depend on such factors as experience, roles and purposes. This raises issues of interpretation. For instance, looking at an advertisement featuring a woman's face, some viewers might assume that the image stood for women in general, others that she represented a particular type, role or group, and yet others might recognize her as a particular individual. Knowing the appropriate level of abstraction in relation to interpreting such an image would depend primarily on familiarity with the relevant cultural codes.

The general semanticists set themselves the therapeutic goal of 'purifying' language in order to make its relationship to reality more transparent, and from such roots sprang projects such as the development of 'Basic English' (Ogden 1930). Whatever reservations we may have about such goals, Korzybski's popularization of the principle of arbitrariness could be seen as a useful corrective to some of our habits of mind. As a caveat, Korzybski's aphorism seems unnecessary: we all know that the word 'dog' cannot bark or bite, but in some circumstances we do behave as if certain signifiers are inseparable from what they stand for. Common sense still leads us routinely to identify sign and thing, representation with what it represents. Readers who find this strange should consider how they would feel about 'mutilating' a photograph of someone for whom they care deeply.

In his massively influential book *The Interpretation of Dreams* (first published in 1900), Sigmund Freud argued that 'dream-content is, as it were, presented in hieroglyphics, whose symbols must be translated . . . It would of course be incorrect to read these symbols in accordance with their values as pictures, instead of in accordance with their meaning as symbols' (Freud 1938, 319). He also observed that 'words are often treated in dreams as things' (ibid., 330). Magritte played with our habit of identifying the signifier with the signified in a series of drawings and paintings in which objects are depicted with verbal labels which 'don't belong to them'. In an oil-painting entitled *La Clef des Songes* (*The Interpretation of Dreams*, 1930) we are confronted with images of six familiar objects together with verbal labels. Such arrangements are familiar, particularly in the language-learning context suggested by the blackboard-like background. However, we quickly realize that the words do not match the images under which they appear. If we then rearrange them in our minds, we find that the labels do not correspond to *any* of the images. The relation between the image of an object and the verbal label attached to it is thus presented as arbitrary.

The confusion of the representation with the thing represented is a feature of schizophrenia and psychosis (Wilden 1987, 201). 'In order to be able to operate with symbols it is necessary first of all to be able to distinguish between the sign and the thing it signifies' (Leach 1970, 43). However, the confusion of 'levels of reality' is also a normal feature of an early phase of cognitive development in childhood. Jerome Bruner observed that for pre-school children thought and the object of thought seem to be the same thing, but that during schooling one comes to separate word and thing (Bruner 1966). The substitution of a sign for its referent (initially in the form of gestures and imitative sounds) constitutes a crucial phase in the infant's acquisition of language. The child quickly discovers the apparently magical power of words for referring to things in their absence – this property of *displacement* being a key 'design feature' of language (Piaget 1971, 64; Hockett 1958). Helen Keller, who became blind and deaf at the age of 18 months, was gradually taught to speak by her nurse (Keller 1945). At the age of nine while playing with water she felt with her hand the motions of the nurse's throat and mouth vibrating the word 'water'. In a sudden flash of revelation she cried out words to the effect that 'everything has a name!'. It is hardly surprising that, even in mid-childhood, children sometimes appear to have difficulty in separating words from what they represent. Piaget illustrates the 'nominal realism' of young children in an interview with a child aged 9½:

> 'Could the sun have been called "moon" and the moon "sun"?' – 'No.' 'Why not?' – *'Because the sun shines brighter than the moon . . .'* 'But if everyone had called the sun "moon", and the moon "sun", would we have known it was wrong?' – *'Yes, because the sun is always bigger, it always stays like it is and so does the moon.'* 'Yes, but the sun isn't changed, only its name. Could it have been called . . . etc.?' – *'No . . . Because the moon rises in the evening, and the sun in the day.'*
>
> (Piaget 1929: 81–2)

Thus for the child, words do not seem at all arbitrary. Similarly, Sylvia Scribner and Michael Cole found that unschooled Vai people in Liberia felt that the names of sun and moon could not be changed, one of them expressing the view that these were God-given names (Scribner and Cole 1981, 141).

The anthropologist Lucien Lévy-Bruhl claimed that people in 'primitive' cultures had difficulty in distinguishing between names and the things to which they referred, regarding such signifiers as an intrinsic part of their signifieds (Olson 1994, 28). The fear of 'graven images' within the Judeo-Christian tradition and also magical practices and beliefs such as Voodoo are clearly related to such a phenomenon. Emphasizing the epistemological significance of writing, the Canadian psychologist David Olson argues that the invention (around 4,000 years ago) of 'syntactic scripts' (which superseded the use of tokens) enabled referential words to be distinguished more easily from their referents, language to be seen as more than purely referential, and words to be seen as (linguistic) entities in their own right. He suggests that such scripts marked the end of 'word magic' since referential words came to be seen as representations rather than as intrinsic properties or parts of their referents. However, in the Middle Ages words and images were still seen as having a natural connection to things (which had 'true names' given by Adam at the Creation). Words were seen as the names of things rather than as representations. As Michel Foucault has shown, only in the early modern period did scholars come to see words and other signifiers as representations which were subject to conventions rather than as copies (Foucault 1970). By the seventeenth century, clear distinctions were being made between representations (signifiers), ideas (signifieds) and things (referents). Scholars now regarded signifiers as referring to ideas rather than directly to things. Representations were conventionalized constructions which were relatively independent both of what they represented and of their authors; knowledge involved manipulating such signs. Olson notes that once such distinctions are made, the way is open to making modality judgements about the status of representations – such as their perceived truth or accuracy (Olson 1994, 68–78, 165–8, 279–80). While the seventeenth-century shift in attitudes towards signs was part of a search for 'neutrality', 'objectivity' and 'truth', in more recent times, of course, we have come to recognize that 'there is no representation without intention and interpretation' (ibid., 197).

It is said that someone once asked an astronomer how he had discovered the name of a previously unknown star! Sophisticated literates are able to joke about the notion that names belong to things. In one of Aldous Huxley's novels an old farmworker points out his pigs: 'Look at them, sir,' he said, with a motion of his hand towards the wallowing swine. 'Rightly is they called pigs' (*Chrome Yellow*, Chapter 5). Literate adults may not often seem to be prey to this sort of nominal realism. However, certain signifiers become regarded by some as far from arbitrary, acquiring almost magical power – as in relation to 'graphic' swearing and issues of prejudice – highlighting the point that signifiers are not *socially* arbitrary. Children are just as aware of this: many are far from convinced by adult advice that 'sticks and stones may break my bones, but names can never hurt me'. We may all still need some convincing that 'the word is not the thing'.

Terence Hawkes notes the 'anaesthetic function' of language by which we are numbed to the intervention of the medium (Hawkes 1977, 70). Catherine Belsey, another literary theorist, argues that:

> Language is *experienced* as a nomenclature because its existence precedes our 'understanding' of the world. Words seem to be symbols for things because things are inconceivable outside the system of differences which constitutes the language. Similarly, these very things seem to be represented in the mind, in an autonomous realm of thought, because thought is in essence symbolic, dependent on the differences brought about by the symbolic order. And so language is 'overlooked', suppressed in favour of a quest for meaning in experience and/or in the mind. The world of things and subjectivity then become the twin guarantors of truth.
>
> (Belsey 1980, 46)

Shakespeare's Hamlet refers to: 'the purpose of playing, whose end, both at the first and now, was and is, to hold, as 'twere, the mirror up to nature' (Shakespeare, *Hamlet*, III, ii), and being 'true to life' is probably still a key criterion in judgements of literary worth. However, Belsey comments:

> The claim that a literary form reflects the world is simply tautological. If by 'the world' we understand the world we

experience, the world differentiated by language, then the claim that realism reflects the world means that realism reflects the world constructed in language. This is a tautology. If discourses articulate concepts through a system of signs which signify by means of their relationship to each other rather than to entities in the world, and if literature is a signifying practice, all it can reflect is the order inscribed in particular discourses, not the nature of the world.

(Belsey 1980, 46)

The medium of language comes to acquire the illusion of transparency: this feature of the medium tends to blind its users to the part it plays in constructing their experiential worlds. Realistic texts reflect a mimetic purpose in representation – seeking to imitate so closely that which they depict that they may be experienced as virtually identical (and thus unmediated). Obviously, purely verbal signifiers cannot be mistaken for their real-world referents. While it is relatively easy for us to regard words as conventional symbols, it is more difficult to recognize the conventionality of images which resemble their signifieds. Yet even an image is not what it represents – the presence of an image marks the absence of its referent. The difference between signifier and signified is fundamental. Nevertheless, when the signifiers are experienced as highly realistic – as in the case of photography and film – it is particularly easy to slip into regarding them as identical with their signifieds. In contrast even to realistic painting and drawing, photographs seem far less obviously authored by a human being. Just as 'the word is not the thing' and 'the map is not the territory' nor is a photograph or television news footage that which it depicts. Yet in the common-sense attitude of everyday life we routinely treat high modality signifiers in this way. Indeed, many realistic filmic narratives and documentaries seem to invite this confusion of representation with reality (Nichols 1981, 21). Thus television is frequently described as a 'window on the world' and we usually assume that 'the camera never lies'. We know of course that in a film a dog can bark but it cannot bite (though, when 'absorbed', we may 'suspend disbelief' in the context of what we know to be enacted drama). However, we are frequently inclined to accept 'the evidence of our own eyes' even when events are mediated by the cameras of journalists.

Highly realistic representations in any medium always involve a point of view. Representations which claim to be real deny the unavoidable difference between map and territory. In the sense that there is always a difference between the represented and its representation, 'the camera always lies'. We do not need to adopt the 'scientific' realism of the so-called general semanticists concerning the 'distortion of reality' by our signifying systems, but may acknowledge instead that reality does not exist independently of signs, turning our critical attention to the issue of *whose* realities are privileged in particular representations – a perspective which, avoiding a retreat to subjectivism, pays due tribute to the unequal distribution of power in the social world.

EMPTY SIGNIFIERS

While Saussurean semioticians (with language as their model) have emphasized the arbitrary relationship of the signifier to the signified, some subsequent theorists have stressed 'the primacy of the signifier' – Jacques Lacan even praised Lewis Carroll's Humpty Dumpty as 'the master of the signifier' for his declaration that 'when *I* use a word, it means just what I choose it to mean – neither more nor less'. Many postmodernist theorists postulate a complete disconnection of the signifier and the signified. An 'empty' or 'floating signifier' is variously defined as a signifier with a vague, highly variable, unspecifiable or non-existent signified. Such signifiers mean different things to different people: they may stand for many or even *any* signifieds; they may mean whatever their interpreters want them to mean. In such a state of radical disconnection between signifier and signified, a sign only means that it means. Such a disconnection is perhaps clearest in literary and aesthetic texts which foreground the act and form of expression and undermine any sense of a natural or transparent connection between a signifier and a referent. However, Jonathan Culler suggests that to refer to an 'empty signifier' is an implicit acceptance of its status as a signifier and is thus 'to correlate it with a signified' even if this is not known; 'the most radical play of the signifier still requires and works through the positing of signifieds' (Culler 1985, 115). Shakespeare famously referred to 'a tale told by an idiot, full of sound and fury, signifying nothing' (*Macbeth* V, iii). As early as 1939 Jakobson referred to the 'zero-sign' in linguistics – the 'unmarked' form of a word (such as the singular form of words in which the plural involves the addition of the terminal marker -*s*) (Jakobson 1939). We will return to the notion of unmarked terms in Chapter 3. The concept of an 'empty signifier' also has some similarities with other linguistic concepts – with the notion of an 'empty category' and with Hjelmslev's *figurae* or non-signifying sign elements. The 'floating signifier' is referred to in the year 1950 in Lévi-Strauss's *Introduction to the Work of Marcel Mauss* (Lévi-Strauss 1950). For Lévi-Strauss such a signifier is like an algebraic symbol which has no immanent symbolic value but which can represent anything. Roland Barthes referred to non-linguistic signs specifically as being so open to interpretation that they constituted a 'floating chain of signifieds' (Barthes 1964, 39). The first explicit reference to an 'empty signifier' of which I am aware is that of Barthes in his essay 'Myth today' (Barthes 1957). Barthes defines an empty signifier as one with no definite signified (cf. Barthes 1982, 108).

Whereas Saussure saw the signifier and the signified (however arbitrary their relationship) as being as inseparable as the two sides of a piece of paper, poststructuralists have rejected the apparently stable and predictable relationship embedded in his model. The French psychoanalyst Jacques Lacan wrote of 'the incessant sliding of the signified under the signifier' (Lacan 1977, 154) – he argued that there could be no anchoring of particular signifiers to particular signifieds – although this in itself is hardly contentious in the context of psychoanalysis. Jacques Derrida refers (originally in the 1960s) to the 'play' or 'freeplay' of signifiers: they are not fixed to their signifieds but point beyond themselves to other signifiers in an 'indefinite referral of signifier to signified' (Derrida 1967b, 25; 'freeplay' has become the dominant English rendering of Derrida's use of the term *jeu* – see, for instance, Derrida 1967a, xix). Signs thus always refer to other signs, and there is no final sign referring only to itself. Derrida championed the 'deconstruction' of Western semiotic systems, denying that there were any ultimate determinable meanings. While for Saussure the meaning of signs derives from how they *differ* from each other, Derrida coined the term *différance* to allude also to the way in which meaning is endlessly *deferred*. There is no 'transcendent signified' (Derrida 1967b, 278–80; Derrida 1967a, 20). Endless deferral is only superficially similar to Peirce's 'unlimited semiosis': Peirce was a realist who emphasized that in practice this potentially endless process is inevitably cut short by the practical constraints of everyday life (Gallie 1952, 126), and the object is graspable at the end of such a process. Unlike Peirce, postmodernist theories grant no access to any reality outside signification. For Derrida, 'il n'y a rien hors du texte' ('there is nothing outside the text') – although this assertion need not necessarily be taken 'literally' (Derrida 1967a, 158, 163). For materialist Marxists and realists, postmodernist idealism is intolerable: 'signs cannot be permitted to swallow up their referents in a never-ending chain of signification, in which one sign always points on to another, and the circle is never broken by the intrusion of that to which the sign refers' (Lovell 1983, 16). However, an emphasis on the unavoidability of signification need not necessitate denying any external reality. Readers may be tempted to conclude from this brief review of the notion of 'the empty (or free-floating) signifier' that it has become something of an academic 'soundbite' and that the term itself is ironically in danger of being an empty signifier.

The notion of reality as degenerative is found in the Romantic mythology of a primal state of unmediatedness (referring to children before language or human beings before The Fall) (Chandler 1995, 31–2). In his book *The Image*, Daniel Boorstin charted the rise of what he called 'pseudo-events' – events which are staged for the mass media to report (Boorstin 1961). However, any 'event' is a social construction – bounded 'events' have no objective existence, and all news items are 'stories' (Galtung and Ruge 1981).

The postmodernist Jean Baudrillard interprets many representations as a means of concealing the absence of reality; he calls such representations 'simulacra' (or copies without originals) (Baudrillard 1984). He sees a degenerative evolution in modes of representation in which signs are increasingly empty of meaning:

These would be the successive phases of the image:

1. It is the reflection of a basic reality.
2. It masks and perverts a basic reality.
3. It masks the absence of a basic reality.
4. It bears no relation to any reality whatever: it is its own pure simulacrum.

(Baudrillard 1988, 170)

Baudrillard argues that when speech and writing were created, signs were invented to point to material or social reality, but the bond between signifier and signified became eroded. As advertising, propaganda and commodification set in, the sign began to hide 'basic reality'. In the postmodern age of 'hyper-reality' in which what are only illusions in the media of communication seem very real, signs hide the absence of reality and only pretend to mean something. For Baudrillard, *simulacra* – the signs that characterize late capitalism – come in three forms: *counterfeit* (imitation) – when there was still a direct link between signifiers and their signifieds; *production* (illusion) – when there was an indirect link between signifier and signified; and *simulation* (fake) – when signifiers came to stand in relation only to other signifiers and not in relation to any fixed external reality. It is hardly surprising that Douglas Kellner has criticized Baudrillard as a 'semiological idealist' who ignores the materiality of sign production. Baudrillard's claim that the Gulf War never happened is certainly provocative (Baudrillard 1995).

Such perspectives, of course, beg the fundamental question, 'What is "real"?' The semiotic stance which problematizes reality and emphasizes mediation and convention is sometimes criticized as extreme 'cultural relativism' by realists – such critics often object to an apparent sidelining of referential concerns such as 'accuracy' (e.g. Gombrich 1982, 188, 279, 286). However, even philosophical realists would accept that much of our knowledge of the world is indirect; we experience many things primarily (or even solely) as they are represented to us within our media and communication technologies. Since representations cannot be identical copies of what they represent, they can never be neutral and transparent but are instead constitutive of reality. As Judith Butler puts it, we need to ask, 'What does transparency keep obscure?' (Butler 1999, xix). Semiotics helps us to not to take representations for granted as reflections of reality, enabling us to take them apart and consider whose realities they represent. As the linguist Edward Sapir famously remarked, 'all grammars leak' (Sapir 1921, 38). Those who would learn from semiotics should search for structural leaks, seams and scaffolding as signs of the making of any representation, and also for what has been denied, hidden or excluded so that the text may seem to tell 'the whole truth'.

3

ANALYSING STRUCTURES

Semiotics is probably best known as an approach to textual analysis, and in this form it is characterized by a concern with *structural analysis*. Structuralist analysis focuses on the structural relations which are functional in the signifying system at a particular moment in history. It involves identifying the constituent units in a semiotic system (such as a text or socio-cultural practice), the structural relationships between them (oppositions, correlations and logical relations) and the relation of the parts to the whole. This is not an empty exercise since 'relations are important for what they can explain: meaningful contrasts and permitted or forbidden combinations' (Culler 1975, 14).

HORIZONTAL AND VERTICAL AXES

Saussure emphasized that meaning arises from the differences between signifiers; these differences are of two kinds: *syntagmatic* (concerning positioning) and *paradigmatic* (concerning substitution). Saussure called the latter *associative* relations (Saussure 1916/1983,

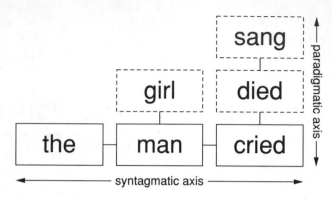

FIGURE 3.1 Syntagmatic and paradigmatic axes

121), but Roman Jakobson's term is now used. The distinction is a key one in structuralist semiotic analysis in which these two structural 'axes' (horizontal as syntagmatic and vertical as paradigmatic) are seen as applicable to all sign systems (see Figure 3.1). The plane of the syntagm is that of the combination of 'this-*and*-this-*and*-this' (as in the sentence, 'the man cried') while the plane of the paradigm is that of the selection of 'this-*or*-this-*or*-this' (e.g. the replacement of the last word in the same sentence with 'died' or 'sang'). While syntagmatic relations are possibilities of combination, paradigmatic relations are functional contrasts – they involve differentiation. Temporally, syntagmatic relations refer intratextually to other signifiers co-present within the text, while paradigmatic relations refer intertextually to signifiers which are absent from the text (ibid., 122). The 'value' of a sign is determined by both its paradigmatic and its syntagmatic relations. Syntagms and paradigms provide a structural context within which signs make sense; they are the structural forms through which signs are organized into codes.

Paradigmatic relationships can operate on the level of the signifier and on the level of the signified (ibid., 121–4; Silverman 1983, 10; Harris 1987, 124). A paradigm is a set of associated signifiers or signifieds which are all members of some defining category, but in which each is significantly different. In natural language there are grammatical paradigms such as verbs or nouns. In a given context, one member of the paradigm set is structurally replaceable with another; the choice of one excludes the choice of another. The use of one signifier (e.g. a particular word) rather than another from the same paradigm set (e.g. adjectives) shapes the preferred meaning of a text. Paradigmatic relations can thus be seen as 'contrastive'. Saussure's notion of 'associative' relations was broader and less formal than what is normally meant by 'paradigmatic' relations. He referred to 'mental association' and included perceived similarities in form (e.g. homophones) or meaning (e.g. synonyms). Such similarities were diverse and ranged from strong to slight, and might refer to only part of a word (such as a shared prefix or suffix). He noted that there was no end (or commonly agreed order) to such associations (Saussure 1983, 121–4). Jakobson rejected this conception, insisting that there is a 'hierarchical order within the paradigmatic set' (Jakobson 1962, 599; cf. 1971d, 719–20).

Paradigms are not confined to the verbal mode. In film and television, paradigms include ways of changing shot (such as cut, fade, dissolve and wipe). The medium or genre are also paradigms, and particular media texts derive meaning from the ways in which the medium and genre used differ from the alternatives. The aphorism of the Canadian media theorist Marshall McLuhan that 'the medium is the message' can thus be seen as reflecting a semiotic concern: to a semiotician the medium is not neutral.

A *syntagm* is an orderly combination of interacting signifiers which forms a meaningful whole within a text – sometimes, following Saussure, called a 'chain'. Such combinations are made within a framework of syntactic rules and conventions (both explicit and inexplicit). In language, a sentence, for instance, is a syntagm of words; so too are paragraphs and chapters. 'There are always larger units, composed of smaller units, with a relation of interdependence holding between both' (ibid., 127): syntagms can contain other syntagms. A printed advertisement is a syntagm of visual signifiers. Syntagmatic relations are the various ways in which elements within the same text may be related to each other. Syntagms are created by the linking of signifiers from paradigm sets which are chosen on the basis of whether they are conventionally regarded as appropriate or may be required by some rule system (e.g. grammar). Syntagmatic relations highlight the importance of part–whole relationships: Saussure stressed that 'the whole depends on the parts, and the parts depend on the whole' (ibid., 126).

The structure of any text or cultural practice has both syntagmatic and paradigmatic axes. Roland Barthes outlined the paradigmatic and syntagmatic elements of the 'garment system' (Barthes 1967a, 26–7). The paradigmatic elements are the items which cannot be worn at the same time on the same part of the body (such as hats, trousers, shoes). The syntagmatic dimension is the juxtaposition of different elements at the same time in a complete ensemble from hat to shoes. Within a genre, while the syntagmatic dimension is the textual structure, the paradigmatic dimension can be as broad as the choice of subject matter. In this framing, form is a syntagmatic dimension while content is a paradigmatic dimension. However, form is also subject to paradigmatic choices and content to syntagmatic arrangement. In the case of film, our interpretation of an individual shot depends on both paradigmatic analysis (comparing it, not necessarily consciously, with the use of alternative kinds of shot) and syntagmatic analysis (comparing it with preceding and following shots). The same shot used within another sequence of shots could have quite a different preferred reading. Actually, filmic syntagms are not confined to such temporal syntagms (which are manifested in *montage*: the sequencing of shots) but include the spatial syntagms found also in still photography (in *mise-en-scène*: the composition of individual frames). The determination of meaning in a narrative may seem to be primarily dependent on the syntagmatic dimension, but a recent example of a film in which the paradigmatic dimension is foregrounded is *Crash* (Paul Haggis 2004). This is a thematic film dealing with racial prejudice, and making sense of it (at least initially) requires the audience to make comparative inferences about a series of separate (and heavily cross-cut) events – only as we move towards closure does the syntagmatic dimension resume its conventional dominance.

Both syntagmatic and paradigmatic analysis treat signs as part of a system – exploring their functions within codes and sub-codes –

a topic to which we will return. Although we will discuss paradigmatic and syntagmatic relations separately, it should be emphasized that the semiotic analysis of a text or corpus has to tackle the system as a whole, and that the two dimensions cannot be considered in isolation. The description of any semiotic system involves specifying both the membership of all of the relevant paradigmatic sets and also the possible combinations of one set with another in well-formed syntagms. For the analyst, according to Saussure (who was, of course, focusing on the language system as a whole), 'the system as a united whole is the starting point, from which it becomes possible, by a process of analysis, to identify its constituent elements'; one cannot try to construct the system by working upwards from the constituent elements (Saussure 1983, 112). However, Roland Barthes argued that 'an important part of the semiological undertaking' was to divide texts 'into minimal significant units . . . then to group these units into paradigmatic classes, and finally to classify the syntagmatic relations which link these units' (Barthes 1967a, 48; cf. Leymore 1975, 21 and Lévi-Strauss 1972, 211). In practice, the analyst is likely to need to move back and forth between these two approaches as the analysis proceeds.

THE PARADIGMATIC DIMENSION

Whereas syntagmatic analysis studies the 'surface structure' of a text, paradigmatic analysis seeks to identify the various paradigms (or pre-existing sets of signifiers) which underlie the manifest content of texts. This aspect of structural analysis involves a consideration of the positive or negative connotations of each signifier (revealed through the use of one signifier rather than another), and the existence of 'underlying' thematic paradigms (e.g. binary oppositions such as public–private).

Semioticians often focus on the issue of why a particular signifier rather than a workable alternative was used in a specific context: on what they often refer to as 'absences'. Saussure noted that a characteristic of what he called 'associative' relations – what would now be called paradigmatic relations – was that (in contrast to syntagmatic relations) such relations held '*in absentia*' – in the absence from a specific text of alternative signifiers from the same paradigm (Saussure 1983, 122). He also argued that signs take their value within the linguistic system from what they are *not* (ibid., 115). The psychologist William James observed that 'the *absence of an item* is a determinant of our representations quite as positive as its presence can ever be' (James 1890, 584). We have popular sayings in English concerning two kinds of absences: we refer to 'what goes without saying' and 'what is conspicuous by its absence'. What 'goes without saying' reflects what it is assumed that you take for granted as obvious. In relation to the coverage of an issue (such as in factual genres) this is a profoundly ideological absence which helps to position the text's readers, the implication being that 'people like us already agree what we think about issues like that'. As for the second kind of absence, an item which is present in the text may flout conventional expectations, making the conventional item 'conspicuous by its absence' and the unexpected item 'a statement'. This applies no less to cultural practices. If a man wears a suit at his office it says very little other than that he is conforming to a norm. But if one day he arrives in jeans and a tee-shirt, this will be interpreted as 'making a statement'.

Paradigmatic analysis involves comparing and contrasting each of the signifiers present in the text with absent signifiers which in similar circumstances might have been chosen, and considering the significance of the choices made. It can be applied at any semiotic level, from the choice of a particular word, image or sound to the level of the choice of style, genre or medium. Figure 3.2 shows a basic paradigm set for *shot size* in photography and film. The use of one signifier rather than another from the same paradigm is based on factors such as technical constraints, code (e.g. genre), convention, connotation, style, rhetorical purpose and the limitations of the individual's own repertoire. The analysis of paradigmatic relations helps to define the 'value' of specific items in a text.

THE COMMUTATION TEST

Structuralist semioticians refer to the 'commutation test' which can be used in order to identify distinctive signifiers and to define their

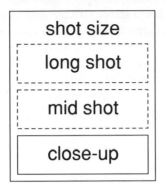

FIGURE 3.2 Paradigm set for shot size

significance – determining whether a change on the level of the signifier leads to a change on the level of the signified. Its origins lie in a linguistic test of substitution applied by the Prague school structuralists. In order to identify within a language its phonemes and their 'distinctive features', linguists experimented with changes in the phonetic structure of a word in order to see at what point it became a different word. The original commutation test has evolved into a rather more subjective form of textual analysis. Roland Barthes refers to using the commutation test to divide texts into minimal significant units, before grouping these units into paradigmatic classes (Barthes 1967a, 48). To apply this test, a particular signifier in a text is selected. Then alternatives to this signifier are considered. The effects of each substitution are evaluated in terms of how this might affect the sense made of the sign. This might involve imagining the use of a close-up rather than a mid-shot, a substitution in age, sex, class or ethnicity, substituting objects, a different caption for a photograph, etc. It could also involve swapping over two of the existing signifiers, changing their original relationship. The influence of the substitution on the meaning can help to suggest the contribution of the original signifier and also to identify syntagmatic units (Barthes 1967a, 65–7; 1967b, 19–20). The commutation test can identify the sets (paradigms) and codes to which the signifiers used belong. For instance, if changing the setting used in an advertisement contributes to changing the meaning, then 'setting' is one of the paradigms; the paradigm set for the setting would consist of all of those alternative signifiers which could have been used and which would have shifted the meaning.

The commutation test may involve any of four basic transformations, some of which involve the modification of the syntagm. However, the consideration of an alternative syntagm can itself be seen as a paradigmatic substitution.

Paradigmatic transformations
- substitution;
- transposition;

Syntagmatic transformations
- addition;
- deletion.

These four basic transformational processes were noted as features of perception and recall (Allport and Postman 1945; Newcomb 1952, 88–96). They correspond to the four general categories to which Quintilian (*c*.35–100 AD) assigned the rhetorical figures (or tropes) as 'deviations' from 'literal' language (*Institutes of Oratory* Book I, Chapter 5, 38–41).

OPPOSITIONS

Roman Jakobson argued that 'binarism is essential; without it the structure of language would be lost' (Jakobson 1973, 321). Lyons agrees that 'binary opposition is one of the most important principles governing the structure of languages' (Lyons 1977, 271). Saussure, of course, emphasized the differences between signs rather than their similarities (though he did not discuss binary oppositions). Opposites (or antonyms) clearly have a very practical function compared with synonyms: that of sorting. It was Jakobson who proposed that linguistic units are bound together by a system of binary oppositions

(Jakobson 1976). Such oppositions are essential to the generation of meaning: the meaning of 'dark' is relative to the meaning of 'light'; 'form' is inconceivable except in relation to 'content'. It is an open question whether our tendency to think in opposites is determined by the prominence of oppositions in language or whether language merely reflects a universal human characteristic. The various conventionally linked terms with which we are familiar within a culture might more appropriately be described as paired 'contrasts', since they are not always direct 'opposites' (although their use often involves polarization). Distinctions can be made between various types of 'oppositions', perhaps the most important being the following:

- *oppositions* (logical 'contradictories'): mutually exclusive terms (e.g. alive–dead, where 'not alive' can only be 'dead');
- *antonyms* (logical 'contraries'): terms which are comparatively graded on the same implicit dimension (e.g. good–bad, where 'not good' is not necessarily 'bad').

(Barthes 1967b, 162ff.; Leymore 1975, 7; Lyons 1977, 270ff.)

This is basically a distinction between digital and analogue oppositions: digital differences are 'either/or'; analogue distinctions are 'more-or-less'. Analogue oppositions clearly allow for intermediate positions. Even the apparently categorical 'black' and 'white' can of course be reconfigured as shades of grey.

Structuralists emphasize the importance of relations of paradigmatic opposition. Roman Jakobson declared that:

In an oppositive duality, if one of the terms is given, then the other, though not present, is evoked in thought. To the idea of white there is opposed only that of black, to the idea of beauty that of ugliness, to the idea of large that of small, to the idea of closed that of open, and so on. Opposites are so intimately interconnected that the appearance of one of them inevitably elicits the other.

(Jakobson 1976, 235; cf. 1973, 321)

Largely through the influence of Jakobson, the primary analytical method employed by many structuralist semioticians involves the identification of binary or polar semantic oppositions (e.g. us–them, public–private) in texts or signifying practices. Claude Lévi-Strauss described the initial steps in his own analytical procedure as being to 'define the phenomena under study as a relation between two or more terms, real or supposed' and then to 'construct a table of possible permutations between these terms' (Lévi-Strauss 1964, 16).

People have believed in the fundamental character of binary oppositions since at least classical times. For instance, in his *Metaphysics*, Aristotle advanced as primary oppositions: form–matter, natural–unnatural, active–passive, whole–part, unity–variety, before–after and being–not-being. Jakobson and Halle observe that 'the binary opposition is a child's first logical operation' (Jakobson and Halle 1956, 60). While there are no opposites in nature, the binary oppositions which we employ in our cultural practices help to generate order out of the dynamic complexity of experience. At the most basic level of individual survival humans share with other animals the need to distinguish between our own species and others, dominance and submission, sexual availability or non-availability, the edible and the inedible (Leach 1970, 39). The range of human distinctions is far more extensive than those which they share with other animals since it is supported by the elaborate system of categorization which language facilitates. The British anthropologist Edmund Leach reflects that 'a speechless ape presumably has some sort of feelings for the opposition I/other, perhaps even for its expanded version we/they, but the still more grandiose natural/supernatural (man/God) could only occur within a linguistic frame . . . The recognition of a distinction natural/supernatural (real/imaginary) is a basic marker of humanity' (Leach 1982, 108–9). So too is that between (human) culture and (animal) nature. Lévi-Strauss, who sees the opposition between nature and culture as of fundamental importance, suggests that the primary reason that human beings have employed fire since prehistoric times to transform raw into cooked food is not because this was necessary for their survival but in order to signify their otherness from beasts (Lévi-Strauss 1969).

It is a feature of culture that binary oppositions come to seem natural to members of a culture. Many pairings of concepts (such as male–female and mind–body) are familiar within a culture and may seem commonsensical distinctions for everyday communicational purposes even if some of them may be regarded as 'false dichotomies' in critical contexts. The opposition of self–other (or subject–object) is psychologically fundamental. The mind imposes some degree of constancy on the dynamic flux of experience by defining 'the self' in relation to 'the other'. The neo-Freudian psychoanalyst Jacques Lacan argued that initially, in the primal realm of 'the Real' (where there is no absence, loss or lack), the infant has no centre of identity and experiences no clear boundaries between itself and the external world. The child emerges from the real and enters 'the Imaginary' at the age of about 6 to 18 months, before the acquisition of speech. This is a private psychic realm in which the construction of the self as subject is initiated. In the realm of visual images, we find our sense of self reflected back by an other with whom we identify. Lacan describes a defining moment in the imaginary which he calls 'the mirror phase', when seeing one's mirror image (and being told by one's mother, 'That's *you*!') induces a strongly defined illusion of a coherent and self-governing personal identity. This marks the child's emergence from a matriarchal state of 'nature' into the patriarchal order of culture. As the child gains mastery within the pre-existing 'symbolic order' (the public domain of verbal language), language (which can be mentally manipulated) helps to foster the individual's sense of a conscious self residing in an 'internal world' which is distinct from 'the world outside'. However, a degree of individuality and autonomy is surrendered to the constraints of linguistic conventions, and the self becomes a more fluid and ambiguous relational signifier rather than a relatively fixed entity. Subjectivity is dynamically constructed through discourse.

MARKEDNESS

Oppositions are rarely equally weighted. The Russian linguist and semiotician Roman Jakobson introduced the theory of *markedness*: 'Every single constituent of any linguistic system is built on an opposition of two logical contradictories: the presence of an attribute ("markedness") in contraposition to its absence ("unmarkedness")' (Jakobson 1972, 42; cf. 1980a). The concept of markedness can be applied to the poles of a paradigmatic opposition: paired signs consist of an 'unmarked' and a 'marked' form. This applies, as we shall see, both at the level of the signifier and at the level of the signified. The marked signifier is distinguished by some special semiotic feature. In relation to linguistic signifiers, two characteristic features of marked forms are commonly identified: these relate to formal features and generic function. The more complex form is marked, which typically involves both of the following features:

- **Formal marking**: in morphologically related oppositions, marking is based on the presence or absence of some particular formal feature. The marked signifier is formed by adding a distinctive feature to the unmarked signifier (for instance, the marked form 'unhappy' is formed by adding the prefix *un-* to the unmarked signifier 'happy') (Greenberg 1966; Clark and Clark, 1977; Lyons 1977, 305ff.).
- **Distributional marking**: formally marked terms show a tendency to be more restricted in the range of contexts in which they occur. (Lyons 1977, 306–7)

In English, linguistically *unmarked* forms include the present tense of verbs and the singular form of nouns (Jakobson's 'zero-sign'). The active voice is normally unmarked, although in the restricted genre of traditional academic writing the passive voice is still often the unmarked form.

The markedness of linguistic signs includes semantic marking: a marked or unmarked status applies not only to signifiers but also to signifieds. With morphologically related pairings, there is an obvious relation between formal and semantic marking, and John Lyons suggests that distributional marking in oppositions is probably determined by semantic marking (Lyons 1977, 307). Jakobson reported that 'the general meaning of the marked is characterized by the conveyance of more precise, specific, and additional information than the unmarked term provides' (Jakobson 1980a, 138). The unmarked term is often used as a generic term while the marked term is used in a more specific sense. General references to humanity used to use the term 'man' (which in this sense was not intended to be sex specific), and of course the word 'he' has long been used generically. In English, the female category is generally marked in relation to the male, a point not lost on feminist theorists (Clark and Clark 1977, 524).

Where terms are paired, the pairing is rarely symmetrical but rather hierarchical. For Jakobson, hierarchy was a fundamental structural principle (Jakobson 1980a, 137): 'the entire network of language displays a hierarchical arrangement that within each level of the system follows the same dichotomous principle of marked terms superposed on the corresponding unmarked terms' (Jakobson 1972, 42). Whereas Saussure had asserted that the elements of a paradigm set have no fixed order, Jakobson argued that markedness created hierarchical relations within paradigms (Jakobson 1962, 599; 1971d, 719–20). With apologies to George Orwell we might coin the phrase that 'all signifieds are equal, but some are more equal than others'. With many of the familiarly paired terms, the two signifieds are accorded different values. The unmarked term is primary, being given precedence and priority, while the marked term is treated as secondary or even suppressed as an 'absent signifier'. While linguistic markedness may not of itself imply negativity (e.g. the unmarked term *cow* versus the marked term *bull*), morphological markers (such as *un-* or *-in*) can generate negative connotations. When morphological cues are lacking, the 'preferred sequence' or most common order of paired terms usually distinguishes the first as a semantically positive term and the second as a negative one (Lyons 1977, 276; Malkiel 1968).

'Term B' is referred to by some theorists as being produced as an 'effect' of 'Term A'. The unmarked term is presented as fundamental and originative while the marked term is conceived in relation to it as derivative, dependent, subordinate, supplemental or ancillary (Culler 1985, 112). This framing ignores the fact that the unmarked term is logically and structurally dependent on the marked term to lend it substance. Derrida demonstrated that within the oppositional logic of binarism neither of the terms (or concepts) makes sense without the other. This is what he calls 'the logic of supplementarity':

the 'secondary' term which is represented as 'marginal' and external is in fact constitutive of the 'primary' term and essential to it (Derrida 1967a). The unmarked term is defined by what it seeks to suppress.

In the pairing of oppositions or contraries, Term B is defined relationally rather than substantively. The linguistic marking of signifiers in many of these pairings is referred to as 'privative' – consisting of suffixes or prefixes signifying lack or absence – e.g. *non-*, *un-* or *-less*. In such cases, Term B is defined by negation – being everything that Term A is *not*. For example, when we refer to 'non-verbal communication', the very label defines such a mode of communication only in negative relation to 'verbal communication'. Indeed, the unmarked term is not merely neutral but implicitly positive in contrast to the negative connotations of the marked term. The association of the marked term with absence and lack is of course problematized by those who have noted the irony that the dependence of Term A on Term B can be seen as reflecting a lack on the part of the unmarked term (Fuss 1991, 3).

The unmarked form is typically dominant (e.g. statistically within a text or corpus) and therefore seems to be neutral, normal and natural. It is thus transparent – drawing no attention to its invisibly privileged status, while the deviance of the marked form is salient. Where it is not simply subsumed, the marked form is foregrounded – presented as 'different'; it is 'out of the ordinary' – an extraordinary deviational 'special case' which is something other than the standard or default form of the unmarked term. Unmarked–marked may thus be read as norm–deviation. It is notable that empirical studies have demonstrated that cognitive processing is more difficult with marked terms than with unmarked terms (Clark and Clark 1977). Marked forms take longer to recognize and process and more errors are made with these forms.

On the limited evidence from frequency counts of explicit verbal pairings in written text (online texts retrieved using the former Infoseek search engine, September 2000), while it was very common for one term in such pairings to be marked, in some instances there is not a clearly marked term (see Figure 3.3). For instance, in general usage there seemed to be no inbuilt preference for one term in a pairing such as old–young (one was just as likely to encounter

FIGURE 3.3 Markedness of some explicit oppositions in online texts

young–old). Furthermore, the extent to which a term was marked was variable. Some terms seemed to be far more clearly marked than others: in the pairing public–private, for instance, *private* was very clearly the marked term (accorded secondary status). How strongly a term is marked also depends on contextual frameworks such as genres and sociolects, and in some contexts a pairing may be very deliberately and explicitly reversed when an interest group seeks to challenge the ideological priorities which the markedness may be taken to reflect. Not all of the pairs listed will seem to be 'the right way round' to everyone – you may find it interesting to identify which ones seem counterintuitive to you and to speculate as to why this seems so.

The concept of markedness can be applied more broadly than simply to paradigmatic pairings of words or concepts. Whether in textual or social practices, the choice of a marked form 'makes a statement'. Where a text deviates from conventional expectations it is 'marked'. Conventional, or 'over-coded' text (which follows a fairly predictable formula) is unmarked whereas unconventional or 'under-coded' text is marked. Marked or under-coded text requires the interpreter to do more interpretive work. Nor is the existence of marked forms simply a structural feature of semiotic systems. The distinction between norm and deviation is fundamental in socialization (Bruner 1990). Social differentiation is constructed and maintained through the marking of differences. Unmarked forms reflect the naturalization of dominant cultural values. Binary oppositions are almost invariably weighted in favour of the male, silently signifying that the norm is to be male and to be female is to be different.

Jakobson observed in 1930 that markedness 'has a significance not only for linguistics but also for ethnology and the history of culture, and that such historico-cultural correlations as life–death, liberty–nonliberty, sin–virtue, holidays–working days, and so on are always confined to relations *a*–non-*a*, and that it is important to find out for any epoch, group, nation etc. what the marked element is' (Jakobson 1980a, 136). However natural familiar dichotomies and their markedness may seem, their historical origins or phases of dominance can often be traced. For instance, perhaps the most influential dualism in the history of Western civilization can be attributed primarily to the philosopher René Descartes (1596–1650) who divided reality into two distinct ontological substances – mind and body. This distinction insists on the separation of an external or real world from an internal or mental one, the first being material and the second non-material. It created the poles of objectivity and subjectivity and fostered the illusion that 'I' can be distinguished from my body. Furthermore, Descartes's rationalist declaration that 'I think, therefore I am' encouraged the privileging of mind over body. He presented the subject as an autonomous individual with an ontological status *prior to* social structures (a notion rejected by post-structural theorists). He established the enduring assumption of the independence of the knower from the known. Cartesian dualism also underpins a host of associated and aligned dichotomies: reason–emotion, male–female, true–false, fact–fiction, public–private, self–other and human–animal. Indeed, many feminist theorists lay a great deal of blame at Descartes's door for the orchestration of the ontological framework of patriarchal discourse. One of the most influential of theorists who have sought to study the ways in which reality is constructed and maintained within discourse by such dominant frameworks is the French historian of ideas, Michel Foucault, who focused on the analysis of 'discursive formations' in specific historical and socio-cultural contexts (Foucault 1970 and 1974).

DECONSTRUCTION

Roman Jakobson highlighted the tensions and contradictions within Saussure's *Course* (Jakobson 1984b). He had already identified the terms foregrounded by Saussure within his oppositions, such as *langue* rather than *parole*, synchrony rather than diachrony, the paradigmatic rather than the syntagmatic, linear temporality rather than spatial concurrence and the immateriality of form rather than the substance of the signifier (Jakobson 1949a, 54; 1949c, 423; 1956, 74–5; 1966; 1980b). Jakobson's own excursions beyond the formal domain of linguistics (e.g. his observations on cinema, music and fine art) began to redress Saussure's neglect of non-linguistic signs. Jakobson argued that the two sides of the Saussurean dichotomies should be regarded as complementary (Jakobson 1971d). For instance, the extralinguistic context ('bracketed' by Saussure) is as interpretively important as structural linguistic relations (Jakobson 1956, 75; 1960, 353). Subsequently Robert Hodge and Gunther Kress have outlined an explicitly social and materialist framework for semiotics based on reclaiming 'the contents of Saussure's rubbish bin' (Hodge and Kress 1988, 17) – but Jakobson had already ransacked it.

While other critical theorists have been content to 'valorize term B' in the semiotic analysis of textual representations, the work of the poststructuralist philosopher Jacques Derrida included a radical 'deconstruction' of Saussure's *Course in General Linguistics*, not only revalorizing terms which Saussure had devalorized but more radically seeking to destabilize the whole oppositional framework. In the process, he sought to expose the phonocentric privileging of speech over writing in Western culture (Derrida 1967a and 1967b). He rejected the privileging of the signified over the signifier, seeing it as a perpetuation of the traditional opposition of matter and spirit or substance and thought. He noted that within such discourse the material form is always subordinated to the less material form. Derrida sought to blur the distinction between signifier and signified, insisting that 'the signified always already functions as a signifier' (Derrida 1967a, 7). He similarly challenged other loaded oppositions such as presence over absence, nature over culture, masculine over feminine and literal over metaphorical.

ALIGNMENT

Paired signifiers are seen by structuralist theorists as part of the 'deep [or 'hidden'] structure' of texts, shaping the preferred reading. Such oppositions may appear to be resolved in favour of dominant ideologies but poststructuralists argue that tensions between them *always* remain unresolved. It is not in isolation that the rhetorical power of binary oppositions resides, but in their articulation in relation to other oppositions. Such linkages seem to become aligned in some texts and codes so that additional 'vertical' relationships (such as male–mind, female–body) acquire apparent links of their own – as feminists and queer theorists have noted (e.g. Silverman 1983, 36; Grosz 1993, 195; Butler 1999, 17). As Kaja Silverman observes, 'a cultural

code is a conceptual system which is organized around key oppositions and equations, in which a term like "woman" is defined in
opposition to a term like "man", and in which each term is aligned
with a cluster of symbolic attributes' (Silverman 1983, 36).

Applying the concept of marked forms to mass media genres,
Merris Griffiths examined the production and editing styles of television advertisements for toys. Her findings showed that the style of
advertisements aimed primarily at boys had far more in common
with those aimed at a mixed audience than with those aimed at girls,
making 'girls' advertisements' the marked category in commercials
for toys (Chandler and Griffiths 2000). Notably, the girls' ads had
significantly longer shots, significantly more dissolves (fade out/fade
in of shot over shot), fewer long shots and more close-ups, fewer
low shots, more level shots and fewer overhead shots. The gender-
differentiated use of production features which characterized these
children's commercials reflected a series of binary oppositions –
fast–slow, abrupt–gradual, excited–calm, active–passive, detached–
involved. Their close association in such ads led them to line up
consistently together as stereotypically 'masculine' vs. 'feminine'
qualities. The 'relative autonomy' of formal features in commercials
seems likely to function as a constant symbolic reaffirmation of
the broader cultural stereotypes which associate such qualities with
gender – especially when accompanied by gender-stereotyped
content. Readers may care to reflect on the way in which 'brown
goods' and 'white goods' have traditionally been sold in high-street
electrical shops (Cockburn and Ormrod 1993, Chapter 4). Brown
goods such as televisions, video-recorders, camcorders and sound-
systems were primarily targeted at men and the sales staff focused
on technical specifications. White goods such as refrigerators,
washing-machines and cookers were targeted at women and the sales
staff focused on appearance. The extent to which this particular
pattern still survives in your own locality may be checked by some
investigative 'window-shopping'.

The notion of semiotic alignment can be traced to Claude Lévi-
Strauss's discussion of analogical relationships which generate
systems of meaning within cultures. Influenced by Jakobson, Lévi-
Strauss saw certain key binary oppositions as the invariants or

universals of the human mind, cutting across cultural distinctions
(Lévi-Strauss 1972, 21). His synchronic studies of cultural practices
identified underlying semantic oppositions in relation to such
phenomena as myths, totemism and kinship rules. Individual myths
and cultural practices defy interpretation, making sense only as a
part of a system of differences and oppositions expressing fundamental reflections on the relationship of nature and culture. He
argued that binary oppositions form the basis of underlying 'classificatory systems', while myths represented a dreamlike working over
of a fundamental dilemma or contradiction within a culture,
expressed in the form of paired opposites. Apparently fundamental
oppositions such as male–female and left–right become transformed
into 'the prototype symbols of the good and the bad, the permitted
and the forbidden' (Leach 1970, 44; cf. Needham 1973).

Lévi-Strauss argued that within a culture 'analogical thought'
leads to some oppositions (such as edible–inedible) being perceived
as metaphorically resembling the 'similar differences' of other oppositions (such as native–foreign) (Lévi-Strauss 1962/1974).

This yields a series of homologous oppositions, such as *raw
is to cooked as nature is to culture* (in structuralist shorthand 'raw :
cooked :: nature : culture') (Lévi-Strauss 1969), or – in the Cartesian
dualism of the modern Western world – culture : nature :: people :
animals :: male : female :: reason : passion (Tapper 1994, 50). The
classification systems of a culture are a way of encoding differences
within society by analogy with perceived differences in the natural
world (somewhat as in Aesop's *Fables*) (Lévi-Strauss 1969, 90–1,
cf. 75–6, 96–7). They transform what are perceived as natural categories into cultural categories and serve to naturalize cultural
practices. 'The mythical system and the modes of representation
it employs serve to establish homologies between natural and
social conditions or, more accurately, it makes it possible to equate
significant contrasts found in different planes: the geographical,
meteorological, zoological, botanical, technical, economic, social,
ritual, religious and philosophical' (ibid., 93). The aggregation of
fourfold distinctions associated with Aristotle's 'four elements' and
sustained in various combinations over two millenia are of this kind
(Chandler 2002, 102–3). The alignments which develop within such

systems are not without contradictions, and Lévi-Strauss argued that the contradictions within them generate explanatory myths – such codes must 'make sense' (ibid., 228).

In his critique of Saussure, Jakobson warned that in our interpretive strategies we should beware of allowing separate dichotomies to slip into unquestioned alignments, as in the treatment of synchrony as always static and of diachrony as always dynamic. In relation to synchrony and diachrony Jakobson noted of cinematic perception:

> If a spectator is asked a question of synchronic order (for example, 'What do you see at this instant on the movie screen?'), he will inevitably give a synchronic answer, but not a static one, for at that instant he sees horses running, a clown turning somersaults, a bandit hit by bullets. In other words, these two effective oppositions, synchrony–diachrony and static–dynamic, do not coincide in reality. Synchrony contains many a dynamic element.
>
> (Jakobson 1980b, 165; cf. 1952a, 227)

Rather than Saussure's strict dichotomies, Jakobson proposed (in a quasi-poststructuralist vein) apparently oxymoronic alternative formulations such as 'permanently dynamic synchrony' (Jakobson 1981, 64). Although Lévi-Strauss's analytical approach remains formally synchronic, involving no study of the historical dimension, he does incorporate the possibility of change: oppositions are not fixed and structures are transformable. He notes that we need not regard such frameworks from a purely synchronic perspective. 'Starting from a binary opposition, which affords the simplest possible example of a system, this construction proceeds by the aggregation, at each of the two poles, of new terms, chosen because they stand in relations of opposition, correlation, or analogy to it'. In this way, structures may undergo transformation (Lévi-Strauss 1962/1974, 161).

Aesthetic 'movements' can also be interpreted in terms of paradigms of characteristic oppositions. Each movement can be loosely identified in terms of a primary focus of interest: for instance, realism tends to be primarily oriented towards the world, neo-classicism towards the text and romanticism towards the author (which is not to suggest, of course, that such goals have not been shared by other movements). Such broad goals generate and reflect associated values. Within a particular movement, various oppositions constitute a palette of possibilities for critical theorists within the movement. For instance, the codes of romanticism are built upon various implicit or explicit articulations of such oppositions as: expressive–instrumental, feeling–thought, emotion–reason, spontaneity–deliberation, passion–calculation, inspiration–effort, genius–method, intensity–reflection, intuition–judgement, impulse–intention, unconsciousness–design, creativity–construction, originality–conventionality, creation–imitation, imagination–learning, dynamism–order, sincerity–facticity, natural–artificial and organic–mechanical. The alignment of some of these pairs generates further associations: for instance, an alignment of spontaneity–deliberation with sincerity–facticity equates spontaneity with sincerity. More indirectly, it may also associate their opposites, so that deliberation reflects insincerity or untruthfulness. Romantic literary theorists often proclaimed spontaneity in expressive writing to be a mark of sincerity, of truth to feeling – even when this ran counter to their own compositional practices (Chandler 1995, 49ff.).

Even within 'the same' aesthetic movement, various theorists construct their own frameworks, as is illustrated in Abrams's study of romantic literary theory (Abrams 1971). Each opposition (or combination of oppositions) involves an implicit contrast with the priorities and values of another aesthetic movement: thus (in accord with the Saussurean principle of negative differentiation) an aesthetic movement is defined by what it is *not*. The evolution of aesthetic movements can be seen as the working-out of tensions between such oppositions.

Turning from the aesthetic to the commercial sphere, the strategic manipulation of conceptual alignments has been a common feature of the application of semiotics to marketing since British Telecom's famous advertising campaign of the 1990s – 'It's Good to Talk'. That campaign sought to increase men's willingness to use the (landline) telephone at home – avoided by many men partly because of the feminine connotations of its domestic location and its association with 'small-talk'. The traditional gender stereotypes also led men to favour 'instrumental' (and therefore short) calls rather than 'expressive' (and more expensive) uses of the medium – a state of affairs which was eventually undermined by the mobile phone's colonization of the (traditionally masculine) public sphere. Part of the research involved mapping alignments in this universe of discourse. The 'cultural norm' was a vertical alignment of female, emotional, trivial, [domestic] small-talk and male, rational, important, [public] 'big talk' (a term so unmarked that a label had to be invented) (Alexander 1995). Challenging this alignment included using gruff-voiced, 'no-nonsense' actor Bob Hoskins – a 'man's man' – to front the campaign.

More recently, the slogan for a campaign launched in 2005 for the washing powder 'Persil' in the UK was 'dirt is good'. This provocative inversion of the Christian folklore that 'cleanliness is next to godliness' can be seen as part of a deliberate strategy of conceptual realignment which has a distinctly Lévi-Straussean flavour (see in particular Lévi-Strauss 1968). For many years, the core concept had been that 'Persil washes whiter' (alluded to even by Barthes 1957, 40–2). Soap powder and detergent advertising (distinguished by Barthes in their rhetorical appeals) had long reflected conceptual frameworks in which cleanliness–dirt and godliness–evil were vertically aligned with science–nature. In other words, the vertical alignments had been of dirt with evil and with nature. This went back to the days when the advertising for many domestic products regularly featured white-coated 'scientists' – often in laboratories – 'testing' the product and representing it as a technological advance. In the new campaign, 'dirt is good' was the slogan for print ads and television commercials in which we were shown people enjoying themselves outdoors and getting dirty in the process. The company literature also refers to one of their goals being to do 'the least possible harm to the environment'. The new campaign thus challenged the traditional alignment of cleanliness, godliness and science. Within this modified mythological framework not only had dirt become explicitly good (rather than godly) but (inexplicitly) nature rather than science had become the hero. Viewers might also infer that 'dirt is fun'. This implication generates a new pairing –

namely, fun–boredom (aligning boredom with evil as in the prover-
bial wisdom that 'the devil makes work for idle hands'). This
mythological revolution was acomplished in the simplest and yet
most 'theologically' radical switch – no less than the moral inversion of good and evil. In addition to the need to position (or
reposition) the product in relation to rival brands, part of the thinking
was presumably that consumers no longer had the faith in science
(or indeed God) which they were once assumed to have. Of course,
whether this revolution in conceptual alignment generated by semiotically inspired marketing actually 'caught the public imagination'
would require empirical testing.

THE SEMIOTIC SQUARE

One analytical technique that seeks to map oppositions and their inter-
sections in texts and cultural practices involves the application of what
is known as 'the semiotic square'. This was introduced by Algirdas
Greimas as a means of analysing paired concepts more fully by mapping the logical conjunctions and disjunctions relating key semantic
features in a text (Greimas 1987, xiv, 49). The semiotic square is
adapted from the 'logical square' of scholastic philosophy and from
Jakobson's distinction between *contradiction* and *contrariety*. Fredric
Jameson notes that 'the entire mechanism . . . is capable of generating at least ten conceivable positions out of a rudimentary binary
opposition' (in Greimas 1987, xiv). While this suggests that the possibilities for signification in a semiotic system are richer than the
either/or of binary logic, they are nevertheless subject to 'semiotic
constraints' – 'deep structures' providing basic axes of signification.
In Figure 3.4, the four corners (*S1, S2, Not S1* and *Not S2*) represent
positions within the system which may be occupied by concrete or
abstract notions. The double-headed arrows represent bilateral relationships. The upper corners of the Greimasian square represent an
opposition between *S1* and *S2* (e.g. white and black). The lower corners represent positions which are not accounted for in simple binary
oppositions: *Not S2* and *Not S1* (e.g. non-white and non-black). *Not
S1* consists of more than simply *S2* (e.g. that which is not white is
not necessarily black). The horizontal relationships represent an

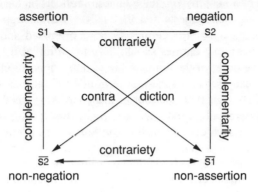

FIGURE 3.4 The semiotic square

opposition between each of the left-hand terms (*S1* and *Not S2*) and its paired right-hand term (*Not S1* and *S2*). The terms at the top (*S1*, *S2*) represent 'presences', while their companion terms (*Not S1* and *Not S2*) represent 'absences'. The vertical relationships of 'implication' offer us an alternative conceptual synthesis of *S1* with *Not S2* and of *S2* with *Not S1* (e.g. of white with not-black or of black with not-white). Greimas refers to the relationships between the four positions as: *contrariety* or opposition (*S1/S2*); *complementarity* or implication (*S1/Not S2* and *S2/Not S1*); and *contradiction* (*S1/Not S1* and *S2/Not S2*). For instance, in the case of the linked terms 'beautiful' and 'ugly', in the semiotic square the four related terms (clockwise) would be 'beautiful', 'ugly', 'not beautiful' and 'not ugly'. The initial pair is not simply a binary opposition because something which is not beautiful is not necessarily ugly and something which is not ugly is not necessarily beautiful (Leymore 1975, 29). The same framework can be productively applied to many other paired terms, such as 'thin' and 'fat'.

Occupying a position within such a framework invests a sign with meanings. The semiotic square can be used to highlight 'hidden' underlying themes in a text or practice. For instance, Fredric Jameson outlines how it might be applied to Charles Dickens's novel, *Hard Times* (Jameson 1972, 167–8). In his foreword to an English translation of a book by Greimas, Jameson reflects on his own use of the technique. He suggests that the analyst should begin by provisionally listing all of the entities to be coordinated and that even apparently marginal entities should be on this initial list. He notes that even the order of the terms in the primary opposition is crucial: we have already seen how the first term in such pairings is typically privileged. He adds that 'the four primary terms . . . need to be conceived polysemically, each one carrying within it its own range of synonyms . . . such that . . . each of the four primary terms threatens to yawn open into its own fourfold system' (in Greimas 1987, xv–xvi). Jameson suggests that *Not S2*, the negation of the negation, 'is always the most critical position and the one that remains open or empty for the longest time, for its identification completes the process and in that sense constitutes the most creative act of the construction' (ibid., xvi). Using the earlier example of aesthetic movements and their dominant focuses, the reader might find it interesting to apply the semiotic square to these.

To recap, it was suggested that realism tends to be primarily oriented towards the world, neo-classicism towards the text and romanticism towards the author. We may assign the concepts of world, text and author to three corners of the square – a fourth term is conspicuous by its absence. Jameson's caveats about the order and formulation of terms may be useful here.

Turning to other contexts, in relation to children's toys Dan Fleming offers an accessible application of the semiotic square (Fleming 1996, 147ff.). Gilles Marion has used the Greimasian square to suggest four purposes in communicating through clothing: wanting to be seen; not wanting to be seen; wanting not to be seen; and not wanting not to be seen (Marion 1994). Jean-Marie Floch has used the grid to illustrate an interesting exploration of the 'consumption values' represented by Habitat and Ikea furniture (Floch 2000, 116–44). However, the Greimasian analysis of texts in terms of the semiotic square has been criticized as easily leading to reductionist and programmatic decodings. Worse still, some theorists seem to use the square as little more than an objective-looking framework which gives the appearance of coherence and grand theory to loose argument and highly subjective opinions.

There is a delightfully ironic quip (variously attributed) that 'The world is divided into those who divide people into two types, and those who don't.' The interpretive usefulness of simple dichotomies is often challenged on the basis that life and (perhaps by a misleading realist analogy) texts are 'seamless webs' and thus better described in terms of continua. We may need to remind ourselves that any interpretive framework cuts up its material into manageable chunks; how appropriate this is can only be assessed in terms of whether it advances our understanding of the phenomenon in question. Nevertheless, useful as it may be to construct an orderly and manageable reality by slicing experience into mutually exclusive categories, cultural practices maintaining the conventional borders of what seem to be fundamental natural distinctions mask the permeability and fragility of the fabric of social reality. The ambiguous boundary zones between conceptual categories (what semiotically inspired market researchers have called areas of 'cultural contradiction') can be sacred or taboo in various cultures, and their exploration can be very revealing (Leach 1976, 33–6).

THE SYNTAGMATIC DIMENSION

Saussure, of course, emphasized the theoretical importance of the relationship of signs to each other. He also noted that 'normally we do not express ourselves by using single linguistic signs, but groups of signs, organized in complexes which themselves are signs' (Saussure 1983, 127). However, in practice he treated the individual word as the primary example of the sign. Thinking and communication depend on *discourse* rather than isolated signs. Saussure's focus on the language *system* rather than on its *use* meant that discourse was neglected within his framework. The linking together of signs was conceived solely in terms of the grammatical possibilities which the system offered. This is a key feature of the Saussurean framework which led some theorists to abandon semiotics altogether in favour of a focus on 'discourse' while leading others to seek to reformulate a more socially oriented semiotics (e.g. Hodge and Kress 1988). However, this is not to suggest that structural analysis is worthless. Analysts still engage in formal textual studies based on structuralist principles. It remains important for anyone interested in the analysis of texts to be aware of what these principles are. Structuralists study texts as *syntagmatic* structures. The syntagmatic analysis of a text (whether it is verbal or non-verbal) involves studying its structure and the relationships between its parts. Structuralist semioticians seek to identify elementary constituent *segments* within the text – its syntagms. The study of syntagmatic relations reveals the conventions or 'rules of combination' underlying the production and interpretation of texts (such as the grammar of a language). The use of one syntagmatic structure rather than another within a text influences meaning.

SPATIAL RELATIONS

Reversing Saussure's priorities, we will begin with spatial rather than temporal relations. As a result of Saussure's influence, syntagms are often defined only as 'sequential' (and thus temporal – as in speech and music). Saussure emphasized 'auditory signifiers' which 'are presented one after another' and 'form a chain'. But even in auditory signs sequential relations are not the only dimension: in music, while sequence may seem the most obvious feature, chords, polyphony and orchestration are manifestations of *simultaneity*. Furthermore, we may grant that temporal relations tend to be dominant in auditory signs, but in visual signs it is *spatial* relations that are dominant. As we have seen, the visual medium of written language for Saussure was secondary. 'Linearity', a consequence of Saussure's phonocentric stance, was the second of his two 'general principles' of the sign (Saussure 1983, 67). As Jakobson noted, we need to recognize the importance of not only temporal but also spatial syntagmatic relations (Jakobson 1956, 74–5; 1963a, 59; 1963d, 336). Spatial syntagms are important not only in the whole range of what we usually think of as visual media (such as drawing, painting and photography) but also in writing – in circumstances where specific layout contributes to the meaning (not only in relatively unusual genres such as 'shape poems' but also routinely in contexts such as notices, newspapers and magazines). Jakobson recognizes key differences between the dimensions of sequentiality and simultaneity and suggests that one important consequence is that whereas a verbal or musical sequence 'exhibits a consistently hierarchical structure and is resolvable into ultimate, discrete, strictly patterned components', in the case of a 'primarily spatial, simultaneously visible picture' there are 'no similar components . . . and even if some hierarchical arrangement appears, it is neither compulsory nor systematic' (Jakobson 1963d, 336; cf. 1967, 341 and 1968, 701). Saussure noted only in passing that visual signifiers (he instanced nautical flags) 'can exploit more than one dimension simultaneously' (Saussure 1983, 70). Of course many semiotic systems (including all audio-visual media, such as television and film) rely heavily on both spatial and temporal syntagms. In any case, what Jakobson called Saussure's 'linearity dogma' (Jakobson 1963d, 336) is clearly *not* a 'general principle' of the sign (even of linguistic signs) and any adequate semiotic framework should acknowledge this.

Unlike sequential syntagmatic relations, which are essentially about *before* and *after*, spatial syntagmatic relations include:

- above/below;
- in front/behind;
- close/distant;
- left/right (which can also have sequential significance);
- north/south/east/west; and
- inside/outside (or centre/periphery).

Such structural relationships are not semantically neutral. The 'cognitive semanticists', George Lakoff and Mark Johnson, have shown how fundamental 'orientational metaphors' are routinely linked to key concepts in a culture (Lakoff and Johnson 1980, Chapter 4). Gunther Kress and Theo van Leeuwen identify three key spatial dimensions in visual texts: left/right, top/bottom and centre/margin (Kress and van Leeuwen 1996 and 1998).

The horizontal and vertical axes are not neutral dimensions of pictorial representation. Since writing and reading in European cultures proceed primarily along a horizontal axis from left to right (as in English but unlike, for instance, Arabic, Hebrew and Chinese), the 'default' for reading a picture within such reading/writing cultures (unless attention is diverted by some salient features) is likely to be generally in the same direction. This is especially likely where pictures are embedded in written text, as in the case of magazines and newspapers. There is thus a potential sequential significance in the left-hand and right-hand elements of a visual image – a sense of 'before' and 'after'. In Western business magazines it is quite common for 'facing the future' to be signified by images of people facing or moving to the right. Kress and van Leeuwen relate the left-hand and right-hand elements to the linguistic concept of 'the Given' and 'the New'. They argue that on those occasions when pictures make significant use of the horizontal axis, positioning some elements left of centre and others right of centre, then the left-hand side is 'the side of the "already given", something the reader is assumed to know already', a familiar, well-established and agreed-upon point of departure – something which is commonsensical, assumed and self-evident, while the right-hand side is the side of the New. 'For something to be New means that it is presented as something which is not yet known, or perhaps not yet agreed upon by the viewer, hence as something to which the viewer must pay special attention' – something more surprising, problematic or contestable (Kress and van Leeuwen 1996, 186–92; cf. 1998, 189–93 and van Leeuwen 2005, 201–4).

The vertical compositional axis also carries connotations. Arguing for the fundamental significance of orientational metaphors in framing experience, Lakoff and Johnson observe that (in English usage) *up* has come to be associated with *more* and *down* with *less*. They outline further associations:

- *up* is associated with goodness, virtue, happiness, consciousness, health, life, the future, high status, having control or power, and with rationality, while
- *down* is associated with badness, depravity, sickness, death, low status, being subject to control or power, and with emotion.

(Lakoff and Johnson 1980, Chapter 4)

For one signifier to be located 'higher' than another is consequently not simply a spatial relationship but also an evaluative one in relation to the signifieds for which they stand. Erving Goffman's slim volume *Gender Advertisements* (1979) concerned the depictions of male and female figures in magazine advertisements. Although it was unsystematic and only some of his observations have been supported in subsequent empirical studies, it is widely celebrated as a classic of visual sociology. Probably the most relevant of his observations for our purposes here was that 'men tend to be located higher than women' in these ads, symbolically reflecting the routine subordination of women to men in society (Goffman 1979, 43). Offering their own speculative mapping of the connotations of top and bottom, Kress and van Leeuwen argue that, where an image is structured along a vertical axis, the upper and lower sections represent an opposition between 'the Ideal' and 'the Real' respectively. They suggest that the lower section in pictorial layouts tends to be more 'down-to-earth', concerned with practical or factual details, while the upper part tends to be concerned with abstract or generalized possibilities (a polarization between respectively 'particular/general', 'local/global', etc.). In many Western printed advertisements, for instance, 'the upper section tends to ... show us "what might be"; the lower section tends to be more informative and practical, showing us "what is"' (Kress and van Leeuwen 1996, 193–201; cf. 1998, 193–5 and van Leeuwen 2005, 204–5).

The third key spatial dimension discussed by Kress and van Leeuwen is that of centre and margin. The composition of some visual images is based primarily not on a left–right or top–bottom structure but on a dominant centre and a periphery. 'For something to be presented as Centre means that it is presented as the nucleus of the information on which all the other elements are in some sense subservient. The Margins are these ancillary, dependent elements' (Kress and van Leeuwen 1996, 206; cf. 1998, 196–8 and van Leeuwen 2005, 205–9). This is related to the fundamental perceptual distinction between *figure* and *ground*. Selective perception involves 'foregrounding' some features and 'backgrounding' others. We owe the concept of 'figure' and 'ground' in perception to the Gestalt psychologists. Confronted by a visual image, we seem to need to separate a dominant shape (a 'figure' with a definite contour) from what our current concerns relegate to 'background' (or 'ground'). In visual images, the figure tends to be located centrally.

SEQUENTIAL RELATIONS

The most obvious example of sequential relations is narrative. Some critics claim that differences between narratives and non-narratives relate to differences among media, instancing individual drawings, paintings and photographs as non-narrative forms (though see Andrews 1998); others claim that narrative is a 'deep structure' independent of the medium. Narrative theory (or narratology) is a major interdisciplinary field in its own right, and is not necessarily framed within a semiotic perspective, although the analysis of narrative is an important branch of semiotics. Semiotic narratology is concerned with narrative in any mode – literary or non-literary, fictional or non-fictional, verbal or visual – but tends to focus on minimal narrative units and the 'grammar of the plot' (some theorists refer to 'story grammars'). It follows in the tradition of the Russian formalist Vladimir Propp and the French anthropologist Claude Lévi-Strauss.

Christian Metz observed that 'a narrative has a *beginning and an ending*, a fact that simultaneously distinguishes it from the rest of the world' (Metz 1968, 17). There are no 'events' in the world (Galtung and Ruge 1981). Reality cannot be reduced objectively to discrete temporal units; what counts as an 'event' is determined by one's purposes. It is narrative form which creates events. Perhaps the most basic narrative syntagm is a linear temporal model composed of three phases – equilibrium–disruption–equilibrium – a 'chain' of events corresponding to the beginning, middle and end of a story (or, as Philip Larkin put it, describing the formula of the classic novel: 'a beginning, a *muddle* and an end'; *my emphasis*). In the orderly Aristotelian narrative form, *causation* and *goals* turn *story* (chronological events) into *plot*: events at the beginning cause those in the middle, and events in the middle cause those at the end. This is the basic formula for classic Hollywood movies in which the storyline is given priority over everything else. The film-maker Jean-Luc Godard declared that he liked a film to have a beginning, a middle and an end, but not necessarily in that order; in 'classical' (realist) narrative, events are always in that order, providing continuity and closure. Roland Barthes argued that narrative is basically translatable – 'international, transhistorical, transcultural' (Barthes 1977a, 79). It can be transposed from one medium to another (for instance, from novel to film or radio and vice versa). Some theorists argue that the translatability of narrative makes it unlike other codes and such commentators grant narrative the privileged status of a 'metacode'.

Narratives help to make the strange familiar. They provide structure, predictability and coherence. In this respect they are similar to schemas for familiar events in everyday life. Turning experience into narratives seems to be a fundamental feature of the human drive to make meaning. We are 'storytellers' with 'a readiness or predisposition to organize experience into a narrative form' which is encouraged in our socialization as we learn to adopt our culture's ways of telling (Bruner 1990, 45, 80).

Narrative coherence is no guarantee of referential correspondence. The narrative form itself has a content of its own; the medium has a message. Narrative is such an automatic choice for representing events that it seems unproblematic and natural. Robert Hodge and Gunther Kress argue that the use of a familiar narrative structure serves 'to naturalize the content of the narrative itself' (Hodge and Kress 1988, 230). Where narratives end in a return to predictable equilibrium this is referred to as narrative *closure*. Closure is often effected as the resolution of an opposition. Structural closure is regarded by many theorists as reinforcing a preferred reading, or in Hodge and Kress's terms, reinforcing the status quo. According to theorists applying the principles of Jacques Lacan, conventional narrative (in dominant forms of literature, cinema and so on) also plays a part in the constitution of the subject. While narrative appears to demonstrate unity and coherence within the text, the subject participates in the sense of closure (in part through 'identification' with characters). 'The coherence of narrative reciprocally reinscribes the coherence of the subject', returning the subject to the pre-linguistic realm of the Imaginary where the self had greater fixity and less fluidity than in the Symbolic realm of verbal language (Nichols 1981, 78).

STRUCTURAL REDUCTION

The structuralist semiotician's inductive search for underlying structural patterns highlights the similarities between what may initially seem to be very different narratives. As Barthes notes, for the structuralist analyst 'the first task is to divide up narrative and . . . define the smallest narrative units . . . Meaning must be the criterion of the unit: it is the functional nature of certain segments of the story that makes them units – hence the name "functions" immediately attributed to these first units' (Barthes 1977a, 88).

In a highly influential book, *The Morphology of the Folktale* (1928), the Russian narrative theorist Vladimir Propp reported that a hundred fairy tales which he had analysed were all based on the same basic formula. He reduced them to around thirty 'functions'. 'Function is understood as an act of character defined from the point of view of its significance for the course of the action' (Propp 1928, 21). In other words, such functions are basic units of action. As Barthes notes, structuralists avoid defining human agents in terms of 'psychological essences', and participants are defined by analysts not in terms of 'what they are' as 'characters' but in terms of 'what they do' (Barthes 1977a, 106). Propp listed seven *roles*: the *villain*, the *donor*, the *helper*, the *sought-for person (and her father)*, the *dispatcher*, the *hero* and the *false hero* and schematized the various 'functions' within the story.

This form of analysis downplays the specificity of individual texts in the interests of establishing *how* texts mean rather than *what* a particular text means. It is by definition, a 'reductive' strategy, and some literary theorists fear that it threatens to make Shakespeare indistinguishable from *Star Wars*. Even Barthes noted that 'the first analysts of narrative were attempting . . . to see all the world's stories . . . within a single structure' and that this was a task which was 'ultimately undesirable, for the text thereby loses its difference' (Barthes 1973, 3). Difference is, after all, what identifies both the sign and the text. Despite this objection, Fredric Jameson suggests that the method has redeeming features. For instance, the notion of a grammar of plots allows us to see 'the work of a generation or a period in terms of a given model (or basic plot paradigm), which is then varied and articulated in as many ways as possible until it is somehow exhausted and replaced by a new one' (Jameson 1972, 124).

Unlike Propp, both Lévi-Strauss and Greimas based their interpretations of narrative structure on underlying oppositions.

Lévi-Strauss saw the myths of a culture as variations on a limited number of basic themes built upon oppositions related to nature versus culture (note that even the traditional distinctions between signs as natural or conventional reflect this opposition). For Lévi-Strauss any myth could be reduced to a fundamental structure. He wrote that 'a compilation of known tales and myths would fill an imposing number of volumes. But they can be reduced to a small number of simple types if we abstract from among the diversity of characters a few elementary functions' (Lévi-Strauss 1972, 203–4). Myths help people to make sense of the world in which they live. Lévi-Strauss saw myths as a kind of a message from our ancestors about humankind and our relationship to nature, in particular, how we became separated from other animals. For instance, myths of the domestic fireside mediate our transition from nature to culture and from animality to humanity via the transition from the raw to the cooked (1969). However, the meaning was not to be found in any individual narrative but in the patterns underlying the myths of a given culture. Myths make sense only as part of a system. Lévi-Strauss treated the form of myths as a kind of language. He reported that his initial method of analysing the structure of myths into 'gross constituent units' or 'mythemes' involved 'breaking down its story into the shortest possible sentences' (Lévi-Strauss 1972, 211). This approach was based on an analogy with the 'morpheme', which is the smallest meaningful unit in linguistics. In order to explain the structure of a myth, Lévi-Strauss classified each mytheme in terms of its 'function' within the myth and finally related the various kinds of function to each other. He saw the possible combinations of mythemes as being governed by a kind of underlying universal grammar which was part of the deep structure of the mind itself.

A good example of the Lévi-Straussean method is provided by Victor Larrucia in his own analysis of the story of Little Red Riding-Hood (originating in the late seventeenth century in a tale by Perrault) (Larrucia 1975). According to this method the narrative is summarized in several (paradigmatic) columns, each corresponding to some unifying function or theme (see Figure 3.5). The original sequence (indicated by numbers) is preserved when the table is read (syntagmatically) row by row. Rather than offering any commentators' suggestions as to what themes these columns represent, I will avoid authorial closure and leave it to readers to speculate for themselves. Suggestions can be found in the references (Larrucia 1975; Silverman and Torode 1980, 314ff.).

The structuralist semiotician and literary theorist Algirdas Greimas (who established 'the Paris school' of semiotics) proposed a grammar of narrative which could generate any known narrative structure (Greimas 1966 and 1987). As a result of a 'semiotic reduction' of Propp's seven roles he identified three types of narrative syntagms: *syntagms performanciels* – tasks and struggles; *syntagms contractuels* – the establishment or breaking of contracts; *syntagms disjonctionnels* – departures and arrivals (Culler 1975, 213; Hawkes 1977, 94; Greimas 1987). Greimas claimed that three basic binary oppositions underlie all narrative themes, actions and character types (which he

1 Grandmother's illness causes mother to make grandmother food	2 Little Red Riding Hood (LRRH) obeys mother and goes off to wood	3 LRRH meets (wolf as) friend and talks	
4 Woodcutter's presence causes wolf to speak to LRRH	5 LRRH obeys wolf and takes long road to grandmother's	6 Grandmother admits (wolf as) LRRH	7 Wolf eats grandmother
		8 LRRH meets (wolf as) grandmother	
	9 LRRH obeys grandmother and gets into bed	10 LRRH questions (wolf as) grandmother	11 Wolf eats LRRH

FIGURE 3.5 Little Red Riding Hood

Source: Larrucia 1975, 528

collectively calls 'actants'); namely, *subject–object* (Propp's *hero* and *sought-for person*), *sender–receiver* (Propp's *dispatcher* and *hero* – again) and *helper–opponent* (conflations of Propp's *helper* and *donor*, plus the *villain* and the *false hero*) – note that Greimas argues that the hero is both *subject* and *receiver*. The *subject* is the one who seeks; the *object* is that which is sought. The *sender* sends the object and the *receiver* is its destination. The *helper* assists the action and the *opponent* blocks it. He extrapolates from the *subject–verb–object* sentence structure, proposing a fundamental, underlying 'actantial model' as the basis of story structures. He argues that in traditional syntax, 'functions' are the roles played by words – the *subject* being the one performing the action and the *object* being 'the one who suffers it' (Jameson 1972, 124). For Greimas, stories thus share a common 'grammar'. However, critics such as Jonathan Culler have not always been convinced of the validity of Greimas's methodology or of the workability or usefulness of his model (Culler 1975, 213–14, 223–4).

Syntagmatic analysis can be applied not only to verbal texts but also to audio-visual ones. In film and television, a syntagmatic analysis would involve an analysis of how each *frame, shot, scene* or *sequence* related to the others (these are the standard levels of analysis in film theory). At the lowest level is the individual *frame*. Since films are projected at a rate of twenty-four frames per second, the viewer is never conscious of individual frames, but significant frames can be isolated by the analyst. At the next level up, a *shot* is a 'single take' – an unedited sequence of frames which may include camera movement. A shot is terminated by a cut (or other transition). A *scene* consists of more than one shot set in a single place and time. A *sequence* spans more than one place and/or time but it is a logical or thematic sequence (having 'dramatic unity'). The linguistic model often leads semioticians to a search for units of analysis in audio-visual media which are analogous to those used in linguistics. In the semiotics of film, crude equivalents with written language are sometimes postulated, such as the frame as morpheme (or word), the shot as sentence, the scene as paragraph, and the sequence as chapter (suggested equivalences vary among commentators). For members of the Glasgow University Media Group the basic unit of analysis was the shot, delimited by cuts and with allowance made for camera movement within the shot and for the accompanying soundtrack (Davis and Walton 1983b, 43). However, if the basic unit is the shot, the analytical utility of this concept is highly restricted in the case of a film like Hitchcock's *Rope* (1948), in which each shot (or take) lasts up to ten minutes (the length of a reel of film at the time the film was made). Similarly, what is one to make of shots-within-shots in a film like Buster Keaton's *Sherlock Jr.* (1924), where we see a film within a film? Shots can be broken into smaller meaningful units (above the level of the frame), but theorists disagree about what these might be. Above the level of the sequence, other narrative units can also be posited.

Christian Metz offered elaborate syntagmatic categories for narrative film (Metz 1968, Chapter 5). For Metz, these syntagms were analogous to sentences in verbal language, and he argued that there were eight key filmic syntagms which were based on ways of ordering narrative space and time.

- the *autonomous shot* (e.g. establishing shot, insert);
- the *parallel syntagm* (montage of motifs);
- the *bracketing syntagm* (montage of brief shots);
- the *descriptive syntagm* (sequence describing one moment);
- the *alternating syntagm* (two sequences alternating);
- the *scene* (shots implying temporal continuity);
- the *episodic sequence* (organized discontinuity of shots);
- the *ordinary sequence* (temporal with some compression).

However, Metz's '*grande syntagmatique*' has not proved an easy system to apply to some films. In their study of children's understanding of television, Hodge and Tripp (1986, 20) divide syntagms into four kinds, based on syntagms existing in the same time *(synchronic)*, different times (*diachronic*), same space (*syntopic*), and different space *(diatopic)*.

- *synchronic/syntopic* (one place, one time: one shot);
- *diachronic/syntopic* (same place sequence over time);
- *synchronic/diatopic* (different places at same time);
- *diachronic/diatopic* (shots related only by theme).

They add that, while these are all *continuous syntagms* (single shots or successive shots), there are also *discontinuous syntagms* (related shots separated by others). Beyond the fourfold distinction between frames, shots, scenes and sequences, the interpretive frameworks of film theorists differ considerably. In this sense at least, there is no cinematic 'language'.

Semioticians have led the quest to identify and describe structural relations underlying texts and cultural practices. Sociological critics note that structural elements need not only to be related to one another and interpreted, but also to be contextualized in terms of the social systems which give rise to them. A psychologist objects that 'the question of whether categories like sacred/profane and happiness/misery are psychologically real in any meaningful sense is not posed and the internal logic of structuralism would suggest it need not be posed' (Young 1990, 184). It is also true that those who use structuralist approaches sometimes claim to be analysing the 'latent meaning' in a text – what it is 'really' about; such approaches understate the subjectivity of the interpreter's framework. Nor can it be claimed that oppositions are 'contained within' texts rather than generated by interpretation. None of these criticisms are unanswerable, however, and we would be foolish to forego the insights which may still be gained from exploring the structural analysis of texts and social practices.

4

CHALLENGING THE LITERAL

Semiotics represents a challenge to the 'literal' because it rejects the possibility that we can neutrally represent 'the way things are'. In this chapter we will explore the ways in which semioticians have problematized two key distinctions: that at the level of the signifier between the literal and the figurative and that at the level of the signified between denotation and connotation.

RHETORICAL TROPES

A sea-change in academic discourse, which has been visible in many disciplines, has been dubbed 'the rhetorical turn' or 'the discursive turn'. The central proposition of this contemporary trend is that rhetorical forms are deeply and unavoidably involved in the shaping of realities. Form and content are inseparable. Language is not a neutral medium and our choice of words matters. The North American literary theorist Stanley Fish insists that 'it is impossible to mean the same thing in two (or more) different ways' (Fish 1980,

32). To say that a glass is 'half empty' is not the same as saying that it is 'half full'. In common usage we refer dismissively to 'heated rhetoric', 'empty rhetoric' and 'mere rhetoric', but all discourse is unavoidably rhetorical.

Terence Hawkes tells us that *'figurative language* is language which doesn't mean what it says' – in contrast to *literal language* which is at least intended to be, or taken as, purely denotative (Hawkes 1972, 1). While this is a distinction which goes back to classical times, it has been problematized by poststructuralist theorists (a topic to which we will return shortly). Somewhat less problematically, tropes can be seen as offering us a variety of ways of saying '*this* is (or is *like*) *that*'. Tropes may be essential to understanding if we interpret this as a process of rendering the unfamiliar more familiar. Furthermore, however they are defined, the conventions of figurative language constitute a rhetorical code. Like other codes, figurative language is part of the reality maintenance system of a culture or sub-culture. It is a code which relates ostensibly to *how* things are represented rather than to *what* is represented. Yet such 'form' may have 'content' of its own. Occasionally in everyday life our attention is drawn to an unusual metaphor – such as the critical quip that someone is 'one voucher short of a pop-up toaster'. However, much of the time – outside of 'poetic' contexts – figures of speech retreat to 'transparency'. Such transparency tends to anaesthetize us to the way in which the culturally available stock of tropes acts as an anchor linking us to the dominant ways of thinking within our society (Lakoff and Johnson 1980). Our repeated exposure to, and use of, such figures of speech subtly sustains our tacit agreement with the shared assumptions of our society.

Once we employ a trope, our utterance becomes part of a much larger system of associations which is beyond our control. For instance when we refer metaphorically to 'putting things into words' this involves a further implicit metaphor of language as a 'container' – a particular view of language which has specific implications (Reddy 1979). Yet the use of tropes is unavoidable. We may think of figurative language as most obviously a feature of poetry and more generally of 'literary' writing, but there is more metaphor on the street corner than in Shakespeare. Roland Barthes declared that 'no sooner is a form seen than it *must* resemble something: humanity seems doomed to analogy' (Barthes 1977b, 44). The ubiquity of tropes in visual as well as verbal forms can be seen as reflecting our fundamentally *relational* understanding of reality. Reality is framed within systems of analogy. Figures of speech enable us to see one thing in terms of another. A trope such as metaphor can be regarded as a new sign formed from the signifier of one sign and the signified of another (Figure 4.1) (cf. Jakobson 1966, 417). The signifier thus stands for a different signified; the new signified replaces the usual one. As I will illustrate, the tropes differ in the nature of these substitutions.

In seventeenth-century England, the scientists of the Royal Society sought 'to separate knowledge of nature from the colours of rhetoric, the devices of the fancy, the delightful deceit of the fables' (Thomas Sprat, 1667: *The History of the Royal Society of London for the Improving of Natural Knowledge*). They saw the 'trick of metaphors' as distorting reality. An attempt to avoid figurative language became closely allied to the realist ideology of objectivism. Language and reality, thought and language, and form and content are regarded by realists as separate, or at least as separable. Realists favour the use of the 'clearest', most 'transparent' language for the accurate and truthful description of facts. However, language isn't glass (as the metaphorical references to clarity and transparency suggest), and it is unavoidably implicated in the construction of the world as we know it. Banishing metaphor is an impossible task since it is central to language. Ironically, the writings of the seventeenth-century critics of rhetoric – such as Sprat, Hobbes and Locke – are themselves richly metaphorical. Those drawn towards philosophical

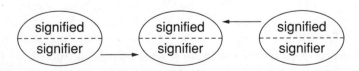

FIGURE 4.1 Substitution in tropes

idealism argue that all language is metaphor or even that reality is purely a product of metaphors. Such a stance clearly denies any referential distinction between 'literal' and 'metaphorical'.

Poststructuralists (whose own use of language is typically highly metaphorical) argue that there can be no text which 'means what it says' (which is how literal language is often defined). Constructionists might be content to insist that metaphors are pervasive and largely unrecognized within a culture or sub-culture and that highlighting them is a useful key to identifying whose realities such metaphors privilege. Identifying figurative tropes in texts and practices can help to highlight underlying thematic frameworks; semiotic textual analysis sometimes involves the identification of an 'overarching (or 'root') metaphor' or 'dominant trope'. For instance, Derrida shows how philosophers have traditionally referred to the mind and the intellect in terms of tropes based on the presence or absence of light (Derrida 1974); everyday language is rich in examples of the association of thinking with visual metaphors (bright, brilliant, dull, enlightening, illuminating, vision, clarity, reflection, etc.).

Michel Foucault adopts a stance of linguistic determinism, arguing that the dominant tropes within the discourse of a particular historical period determine what can be known – constituting the basic *episteme* of the age (Foucault 1970). 'Discursive practice' is reduced to 'a body of anonymous, historical rules, always determined by the time and space that have defined a given period, and for a given social, economic, geographical, or linguistic area, the conditions of operation of the enunciative function' (Foucault 1974, 117). Since certain metaphors have become naturalized and we do not tend to notice the ways in which they can channel our thinking about the signifieds to which they refer, deliberately using unconventional tropes can sometimes help to denaturalize taken-for-granted ways of looking at phenomena.

METAPHOR

Metaphor is so widespread that it is often used as an umbrella term (another metaphor!) to include other figures of speech (such as metonyms) which can be technically distinguished from it in its narrower usage. Similes can be seen as a form of metaphor in which the figurative status of the comparison is made explicit through the use of the word 'as' or 'like'. Much of the time we hardly notice that we are using metaphors at all and yet one study found that English speakers produced an average of 3,000 novel metaphors per week (Pollio et al. 1977). Lakoff and Johnson argue that 'the essence of metaphor is understanding and experiencing one kind of thing in terms of another' (Lakoff and Johnson 1980, 5). In semiotic terms, a metaphor involves one signified acting as a signifier referring to a different signified. In literary terms, a metaphor consists of a 'literal' primary subject (or 'tenor') expressed in terms of a 'figurative' secondary subject (or 'vehicle') (Richards 1932, 96). For instance: 'Experience is a good school, but the fees are high' (Heinrich Heine). In this case, the primary subject of *experience* is expressed in terms of the secondary subject of *school*. Typically, metaphor expresses an abstraction in terms of a more well-defined model.

The linking of a particular tenor and vehicle is normally unfamiliar: we must make an imaginative leap to recognize the resemblance to which a fresh metaphor alludes. Metaphor is initially unconventional because it apparently disregards 'literal' or denotative resemblance (though some kind of resemblance must become apparent if the metaphor is to make any sense at all to its interpreters). The basis in *resemblance* suggests that metaphor involves the *iconic* mode. However, to the extent that such a resemblance is oblique, we may also think of metaphor as *symbolic*. More interpretive effort is required in making sense of metaphors than of more literal signifiers, but this interpretive effort may be experienced as pleasurable. While metaphors may require an imaginative leap in their initial use (such as in aesthetic uses in poetry or the visual arts) many metaphors become so habitually employed that they are no longer perceived as being metaphors at all.

Metaphors need not be verbal. In film, a pair of consecutive shots is metaphorical when there is an implied comparison of the two shots. For instance, a shot of an aeroplane followed by a shot of a bird flying would be metaphorical, implying that the aeroplane is (or is like) a bird. So too would a shot of a bird landing accompanied by the sounds of an airport control tower and of a braking plane – as in an airline commercial cited by Charles Forceville (Forceville 1996, 203). In most cases the context would cue us as to which was the primary subject. An ad for an airline is more likely to suggest that an aeroplane is (like) a bird than that a bird is (like) an aeroplane. As with verbal metaphors, we are left to draw our own conclusions as to the points of comparison. Advertisers frequently use visual metaphors. Despite the frequently expressed notion that images cannot assert, metaphorical images often imply that which advertisers would not express in words.

Visual metaphor can also involve a function of 'transference', transferring certain qualities from one sign to another. In relation to advertising this has been explored by Judith Williamson in her book, *Decoding Advertisements* (Williamson 1978). It is of course the role of advertisers to differentiate similar products from each other, and they do this by associating a product with a specific set of social values – in semiotic terms, creating distinct signifieds for it. Indeed, it has been suggested that ads provide 'a kind of dictionary constantly keeping us apprised of new consumer signifieds and signifiers' (McCracken 1987, 122). One example instanced by Williamson takes the form of a photographic close-up of the head and shoulders of the glamorous French actress Catherine Deneuve (whose name appears in small type). Superimposed on the lower right-hand portion of the advertisement is the image of a bottle of perfume labelled Chanel No. 5. In this advertisement, two key signifiers are juxtaposed. The image of Catherine Deneuve richly signifies French chic, sophistication, elegance, beauty and glamour. The plain image of the bottle simply signifies Chanel No. 5 perfume. This is a rather 'empty' signifier when we cannot actually smell the perfume (though perfume ads in magazines have sometimes included a strip of paper impregnated with the scent). At the bottom of the ad, in large letters, the name of the perfume is repeated in its distinctive typographical style, making a link between the two key signifiers. The aim, of course, is for the viewer to transfer the qualities signified by the actress to the perfume, thus substituting one signified for another, and creating a new metaphorical sign which offers us the meaning that Chanel No. 5 *is* beauty and elegance (Williamson 1978, 25).

George Lakoff and Mark Johnson illustrate that underlying most of our fundamental concepts are several kinds of metaphor:

- **orientational** metaphors primarily relating to spatial organization (up/down, in/out, front/back, on/off, near/far, deep/shallow and central/peripheral);
- **ontological** metaphors which associate activities, emotions and ideas with entities and substances (most obviously, metaphors involving personification);
- **structural** metaphors: overarching metaphors (building on the other two types) which allow us to structure one concept in terms of another (e.g. rational argument is war or time is a resource).

Lakoff and Johnson note that metaphors may vary from culture to culture but argue that they are not arbitrary, being derived initially from our physical, social and cultural experience (cf. Vico 1744, 129). They argue that metaphors form systematic clusters such as that *ideas (or meanings) are objects, linguistic expressions are containers* and *communication is sending* – an example derived from Michael Reddy's discussion of 'the conduit metaphor' (Reddy 1979). Metaphors not only cluster in this way but can cohere in the extended form of cultural myths. Lakoff and Johnson argue that dominant metaphors tend both to reflect and influence values in a culture or subculture: for instance, the pervasive Western metaphors that *knowledge is power* and *science subdues nature* are involved in the maintenance of the ideology of objectivism (Lakoff and Johnson 1980). This is consistent with the Whorfian perspective that different languages impose different systems of spatial and temporal relations on experience through their figures of speech (Whorf 1956).

METONYMY

While metaphor is based on apparent unrelatedness, metonymy is a function which involves using one signified to stand for another signified which is directly related to it or closely associated with it in some way. Metonyms are based on various indexical relationships between signifieds, notably the substitution of *effect* for *cause*. The best definition I have found is that 'metonymy is *the evocation of the whole by a connection*. It consists in using for the name of a thing or a relationship, an attribute, a suggested sense, or something closely related, such as effect for cause . . . the imputed relationship being that of *contiguity*' (Wilden 1987, 198; *my emphasis*). It can be seen as based on substitution by adjuncts (things that are found together) or on functional relationships. Many of these forms notably make an abstract referent more concrete, although some theorists also include substitution in the opposite direction (e.g. *cause* for *effect*). Part–whole relationships are sometimes distinguished as a special kind of metonymy or as a separate trope, as we will see shortly. Metonymy includes the substitution of:

- *effect* for *cause* ('Don't get hot under the collar!' for 'Don't get angry!');
- *object* for *user* (or associated *institution*) ('the Crown' for the monarchy, 'the stage' for the theatre and 'the press' for journalists);
- *substance* for *form* ('plastic' for 'credit card', 'lead' for 'bullet');
- *place* for *event*: ('Chernobyl changed attitudes to nuclear power');
- *place* for *person* ('No. 10' for the British prime minister);
- *place* for *institution* ('Whitehall isn't saying anything');
- *institution* for *people* ('The government is not backing down').

Lakoff and Johnson comment on several types of metonym, including:

- *producer* for *product* ('She owns a Picasso');
- *object* for *user* ('The ham sandwich wants his check [bill]');
- *controller* for *controlled* ('Nixon bombed Hanoi').

They argue that (as with metaphor) particular kinds of metonymic substitution may influence our thoughts, attitudes and actions by focusing on certain aspects of a concept and suppressing other aspects which are inconsistent with the metonym:

> When we think of a *Picasso*, we are not just thinking of a work
> of art alone, in and of itself. We think of it in terms of its rela-
> tion to the artist, this is, his conception of art, his technique,
> his role in art history, etc. We act with reverence towards a
> *Picasso*, even a sketch he made as a teenager, because of its
> relation to the artist. Similarly, when a waitress says, 'The ham
> sandwich wants his check,' she is not interested in the person
> as a person but only as a customer, which is why the use of
> such a sentence is dehumanizing. Nixon may not himself have
> dropped the bombs on Hanoi, but via the *controller for controlled*
> metonymy we not only say 'Nixon bombed Hanoi' but also think
> of him as doing the bombing and hold him responsible for it
> ... This is possible because of the nature of the metonymic
> relationship.
>
> (Lakoff and Johnson 1980, 39)

As with metaphors, metonyms may be visual as well as verbal. In
film, which Jakobson regarded as a basically metonymic medium, a
depicted object which represents a related but non-depicted object
is a metonym. An ad for pensions in a women's magazine asked the
reader to arrange four images in order of importance: each image
was metonymic, standing for related activities (such as shopping
bags for material goods). Metonymy is common in cigarette advertising in countries where legislation prohibits depictions of the
cigarettes themselves or of people using them. The ads for Benson
and Hedges and for Silk Cut cigarettes are good examples of this.

Jakobson argues that whereas a metaphorical term is connected
with that for which it is substituted on the basis of similarity (and
contrast), metonymy is based on contiguity or proximity (Jakobson
1953, 232; 1956, 91, 95; 1963c, 309). As we have seen, Peirce noted
that contiguity is an indexical feature (Peirce 1931–58, 2.306).
Metonymy can be seen as a textual (or – as in thoughts and dreams
– quasi-textual) projection of Peirce's indexical mode. Metonyms
lack the evidential potential of Peirce's mode unless the medium is
indexical – as in photography and film. However, it is on the basis
of perceived indexicality that metonyms may be treated as 'directly
connected to' reality in contrast to the mere iconicity or symbolism

of metaphor. Metonyms seem to be more obviously 'grounded in our experience' than metaphors since they usually involve direct associations (Lakoff and Johnson 1980, 39). Metonymy does not require transposition (an imaginative leap) from one domain to another as metaphor does. This difference can lead metonymy to seem more natural than metaphors – which when still 'fresh' are stylistically foregrounded. Metonymic signifiers foreground the signified while metaphoric signifiers foreground the signifier (Lodge 1977, xiv). Jakobson suggested that the metonymic mode tends to be foregrounded in prose whereas the metaphoric mode tends to be foregrounded in poetry (Jakobson 1956, 95–6). He regarded 'so-called realistic literature' as 'intimately tied with the metonymic principle' (Jakobson 1960, 375; cf. 1956, 92). Such literature represents actions as based on cause and effect and as contiguous in time and space. While metonymy is associated with realism, metaphor is associated with romanticism and surrealism (Jakobson 1956, 92).

SYNECDOCHE

The definition of synecdoche varies from theorist to theorist (sometimes markedly). The rhetorician Richard Lanham represents the most common tendency to describe synecdoche as 'the substitution of part for whole, genus for species or vice versa' (Lanham 1969, 97). Thus one term is more comprehensive than the other. Some theorists restrict the directionality of application (e.g. part for whole but *not* whole for part). Some limit synecdoche further to cases where one element is *physically* part of the other. Here are some examples:

- *part* for *whole* ('I'm off to the smoke [London]'; 'we need to hire some more hands [workers]'; 'two heads are better than one'; 'I've got a new set of wheels', the American expression 'get your butt over here!');
- *whole* for *part* (e.g. 'I was stopped by the law' – where the law stands for a police officer, 'Wales' for 'the Welsh national rugby team' or 'the market' for customers);

- *species* for *genus* (*hypernymy*) – the use of a *member of a class* (*hyponym*) for the *class* (*superordinate*) which includes it (e.g. *a* 'mother' for 'motherhood', 'bread' for 'food', 'Hoover' for 'vacuum-cleaner');
- *genus* for *species* (*hyponymy*) – the use of a *superordinate* for a *hyponym* (e.g. 'vehicle' for 'car', or 'machine' for 'computer').

In photographic and filmic media a close-up is a simple synecdoche – a part representing the whole (Jakobson 1956, 92). Indeed, the formal frame of any visual image (painting, drawing, photograph, film or television frame) functions as a synecdoche in that it suggests that what is being offered is a 'slice-of-life', and that the world outside the frame is carrying on in the same manner as the world depicted within it. This is perhaps particularly so when the frame cuts across some of the objects depicted within it rather than enclosing them as wholly discrete entities. Synecdoche invites or expects the viewer to 'fill in the gaps' and advertisers frequently employ this trope. The goods displayed in shop windows are synecdochic signifiers of what one may expect to find for sale within.

Any attempt to represent reality can be seen as involving synecdoche, since it can only involve selection (and yet such selections serve to guide us in envisaging larger frameworks). While indexical relations in general reflect the closest link which a signifier can be seen as having with a signified, the part–whole relations of synecdoche reflect the most direct link of all. That which is seen as forming part of a larger whole to which it refers is connected existentially to what is signified – as an integral part of its being. Jakobson noted the use of 'synecdochic details' by realist authors (ibid.). In 'factual' genres a danger lies in what has been called 'the metonymic fallacy' (more accurately the 'synecdochic fallacy') whereby the represented part is taken as an accurate reflection of the whole of that which it is taken as standing for – for instance, a white, middle-class woman standing for all women (Barthes 1974, 162; Alcoff and Potter 1993, 14). Framing is of course always highly and unavoidably selective. In fictional genres, realism seeks to encourage us to treat that which is missing as 'going without saying' rather than as 'conspicuous by its absence'. In mainstream films and television dramas, for instance, we are not intended to be aware that the stage-set 'rooms' have only three walls.

Some theorists identify synecdoche as a separate trope, some see it as a special form of metonymy and others subsume its functions entirely within metonymy. Eco cites a classical distinction whereby metonymy involves 'a substitution within the framework of the conceptual content' while synecdoche involves a substitution 'with other aspects of reality with which a given thing is customarily connected' (Eco 1976, 280–1). Jakobson noted that both metonymy and synecdoche are based on *contiguity* (Jakobson 1956, 95). Synecdoche can similarly be seen as another textual form of indexicality (though once again lacking evidential potential unless the medium used is indexical). If the distinction is made as outlined above, metonymy in its narrower sense would then be confined to functional connections such as causality. Even if synecdoche is given a separate status, general usage would suggest that metonymy would remain an umbrella term for indexical links as well as having a narrower meaning of its own.

IRONY

Irony is the most radical of the four main tropes. As with metaphor, the signifier of the ironic sign seems to signify one thing but we know from another signifier that it actually signifies something very different. Where it means the *opposite* of what it says (as it usually does) it is based on binary opposition. Irony may thus reflect the opposite of the thoughts or feelings of the speaker or writer (as when you say 'I love it' when you hate it) or the opposite of the truth about external reality (as in 'There's a real crowd here' when it's deserted). It can also be seen as being based on substitution by *dissimilarity* or *disjunction*. While typically an ironic statement signifies the opposite of its literal signification, such variations as understatement and overstatement can also be regarded as ironic. At some point, exaggeration may slide into irony.

Unless the ironic sign is a spoken utterance (when a sarcastic intonation may mark the irony) the marker of its ironic status comes from beyond the literal sign. A 'knowing' smile is often offered as a cue. In Britain a fashion for 'air quotes' (gestural inverted commas) in the 1980s was followed in the 1990s by a fashion for some young people to mark spoken irony – after a pause – with the word 'Not!', as in 'he is a real hunk – not!'. However, irony is often more difficult to identify. All of the tropes involve the non-literal substitution of a new signified for the usual one, and comprehension requires a distinction between what is *said* and what is *meant*. Thus they are all, in a sense, *double* signs. Irony has indeed sometimes been referred to as a form of 'double-coding', though this formulation should not be allowed to obscure the role of *context* as well as code. Whereas the other tropes involve shifts in what is being referred to, irony involves a shift in modality. The evaluation of the ironic sign requires the retrospective assessment of its modality status. Re-evaluating an apparently literal sign for ironic cues requires reference to perceived intent and to truth status. An ironic statement is not, of course, the same as a *lie* since it is not intended to be taken as 'true'. Irony thus poses particular difficulties for the literalist stance of structuralists and formalists that meaning is immanent – that it lies *within* a text.

Irony is a marked form which foregrounds the signifier. Adolescents sometimes use it to suggest that they are sophisticated and not naïve. Limited use is usually intended as a form of humour. Frequent use may be associated with reflexiveness, detachment or scepticism. It sometimes marks a cynical stance which assumes that people never mean or do what they say. Sustained use may even reflect nihilism or relativism (nothing – or everything – is true). While irony has a long pedigree, its use has become one of the most characteristic features of postmodern texts and aesthetic practices. Where irony is used in one-to-one communication it is of course essential that it is understood as being ironic rather than literal. However, with larger audiences it constitutes a form of 'narrowcasting', since not everyone will interpret it as irony. Dramatic irony is a form whereby the reader or viewer knows something that one or more of the depicted people do not know. A British ad for the

Nissan Micra published in a women's magazine made effective use of irony. The campaign slogan was 'ask before you borrow it'. In soft focus we see a man absorbed in eating his food at a table; in sharp focus close-up we see a woman facing him, hiding behind her back an open can. As we read the label we realize that she has fed him dog-food.

MASTER TROPES

Giambattista Vico (1668–1744) is usually credited with being the first to identify metaphor, metonymy, synecdoche and irony as the four basic tropes (to which all others are reducible), although this distinction can be seen as having its roots in the *Rhetorica* of Peter Ramus (1515–72) (Vico 1744, 129–31). This reduction was popularized in the twentieth century by the American rhetorician Kenneth Burke (1897–1993), who referred to the four 'master tropes' (Burke 1969, 503–17). Figure 4.2 shows these tropes as a semiotic square (see Jameson in Greimas 1987, xix). Note that such frameworks depend on a distinction being made between metonymy and synecdoche, but that such terms are often either defined variously or not defined at all. In his book *Metahistory*, White saw the four 'master

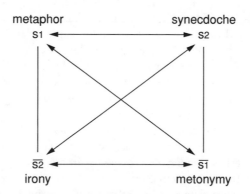

FIGURE 4.2 The four 'master tropes' as a semiotic square

Source: adapted from Jameson in Greimas 1987, xxi

tropes' as part of the 'deep structure' underlying different historio-
graphical styles (White 1973, ix). Jonathan Culler (following Hans
Kellner) even suggests that they may constitute 'a system, indeed
the system, by which the mind comes to grasp the world conceptually
in language' (Culler 1981, 65).

White argued that 'the fourfold analysis of figurative language
has the added advantage of resisting the fall into an essentially *dualistic* conception of styles'. Roman Jakobson adopted two tropes
rather than four as fundamental – metaphor and metonymy. White
felt that Jakobson's approach, when applied to nineteenth century
literature, produced the reductive dichotomy of 'a romantic–poetic–
Metaphorical tradition' and 'a realistic–prosaic–Metonymical tradition' (White 1973, 33n.). However, Jakobson's notion of two basic
axes has proved massively influential. Jakobson argued that metaphor
is a paradigmatic dimension (vertical, based on selection, substitution
and similarity) and metonymy a syntagmatic dimension (horizontal,
based on combination, contexture and contiguity) (Jakobson 1956,
90–6). Many theorists have adopted and adapted Jakobson's framework, such as Lévi-Strauss and Lacan (Lévi-Strauss 1962; Lacan
1977, 160).

DENOTATION AND CONNOTATION

While the distinction between literal and figurative language operates at the level of the signifier, that between denotation and
connotation operates at the level of the signified. We all know that
beyond its 'literal' meaning (its denotation), a particular word may
have connotations: for instance, sexual connotations. 'Is there any
such thing as a *single entendre*?' quipped the comic actor Kenneth
Williams. In semiotics, denotation and connotation are terms
describing the relationship between the signifier and its signified, and
an analytic distinction is made between two types of signifieds: a
denotative signified and a *connotative* signified. Meaning includes
both denotation and connotation.

'Denotation' tends to be described as the definitional, literal,
obvious or common-sense meaning of a sign. In the case of linguistic
signs, the denotative meaning is what the dictionary attempts to

provide. For the art historian Erwin Panofsky, the denotation of a representational visual image is what all viewers from any culture and at any time would recognize the image as depicting (Panofsky 1970, 51–3). Even such a definition raises issues – *all* viewers? One suspects that this excludes very young children and those regarded as insane, for instance. But if it really means 'culturally well-adjusted' then it is already culture specific, which takes us into the territory of connotation. The term 'connotation' is used to refer to the socio-cultural and 'personal' associations (ideological, emotional, etc.) of the sign. These are typically related to the interpreter's class, age, gender, ethnicity and so on. Connotation is thus context-dependent. Signs are more 'polysemic' – more open to interpretation – in their connotations than their denotations. Denotation is sometimes regarded as a *digital* code and connotation as an *analogue* code (Wilden 1987, 224).

As Roland Barthes noted, Saussure's model of the sign focused on denotation at the expense of connotation and it was left to subsequent theorists (notably Barthes himself – drawing on Hjelmslev) to offer an account of this important dimension of meaning (Barthes 1967a, 89ff.). In 'The photographic message' (1961) and 'The rhetoric of the image' (1964), Barthes argued that in photography connotation can be (analytically) distinguished from denotation. As John Fiske puts it 'denotation is *what* is photographed, connotation is *how* it is photographed' (Fiske 1982, 91). However, in photography, denotation is foregrounded at the expense of connotation. The photographic signifier seems to be virtually identical with its signified, and the photograph appears to be a 'natural sign' produced without the intervention of a code (Hall 1973, 132). In analysing the realist literary text Barthes came to the conclusion that connotation produces the illusion of denotation, the illusion of the medium as transparent and of the signifier and the signified as being identical (Barthes 1974, 9). Thus denotation is just another connotation. From such a perspective, denotation can be seen as no more of a natural meaning than is connotation but rather as a process of *naturalization*. Such a process leads to the powerful illusion that denotation is a purely literal and universal meaning which is not at all ideological, and indeed that those connotations which seem most obvious to individual interpreters are just as natural. According to an Althusserian reading, when we first learn denotations, we are also being positioned within ideology by learning dominant connotations at the same time (Silverman 1983, 30). Consequently, while theorists may find it analytically useful to distinguish connotation from denotation, in practice such meanings cannot be neatly separated. Most semioticians argue that no sign is purely denotative – lacking connotation. Valentin Voloshinov insisted that no strict division can be made between denotation and connotation because 'referential meaning is moulded by evaluation . . . meaning is always permeated with value judgement' (Voloshinov 1973, 105). There can be no neutral, literal description which is free of an evaluative element.

For most contemporary semioticians both denotation and connotation involve the use of codes. Structural semioticians who emphasize the relative arbitrariness of signifiers and social semioticians who emphasize diversity of interpretation and the importance of cultural and historical contexts are hardly likely to accept the notion of a literal meaning. Denotation simply involves a broader consensus. The denotational meaning of a sign would be broadly agreed upon by members of the same culture, whereas no inventory of the connotational meanings generated by any sign could ever be complete. However, there is a danger here of stressing the individual subjectivity of connotation: intersubjective responses are shared to some degree by members of a culture; with any individual example only a limited range of connotations would make any sense. Connotations are not purely personal meanings – they are determined by the codes to which the interpreter has access. Cultural codes provide a connotational framework since they are 'organized around key oppositions and equations', each term being 'aligned with a cluster of symbolic attributes' (Silverman 1983, 36). Certain connotations would be widely recognized within a culture. Most adults in Western cultures would know that a car can connote virility or freedom.

Connotation and denotation are often described in terms of levels of representation or levels of meaning. Roland Barthes adopted from Louis Hjelmslev the notion that there are different orders of signification (Barthes 1957, 124; 1961; 1967a, 89–94; 1967b, 27ff;

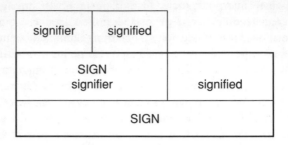

FIGURE 4.3 Orders of signification

Source: adapted from Barthes 1957, 124

Hjelmslev 1961, 114ff.). The *first order* of signification is that of denotation: at this level there is a sign consisting of a signifier and a signified. Connotation is a *second order* of signification which uses the denotative sign (signifier and signified) as its signifier and attaches to it an additional signified (Figure 4.3). In this framework, connotation is a sign which derives from the signifier of a denotative sign (so denotation leads to a chain of connotations). A signified on one level can become a signifier on another level. This is the mechanism by which signs may seem to signify one thing but are loaded with multiple meanings. Indeed, this framing of the Saussurean model of the sign is analogous to the 'infinite semiosis' of the Peircean sign in which the interpretant can become the representamen of another sign. However, it can also tend to suggest that denotation is an underlying and primary meaning – a notion which many other commentators have challenged. As we have noted, Barthes himself later gave priority to connotation, noting in 1971 that it was no longer easy to separate the signifier from the signified, the ideological from the literal (Barthes 1977a, 166).

Changing the form of the signifier while keeping the same 'literal' signified can generate different connotations. The choice of words often involves connotations, as in references to 'strikes' vs. 'disputes', 'union demands' vs. 'management offers', and so on. Tropes such as metaphor generate connotations. Subtle changes of style or tone may involve different connotations, such as changing from sharp focus to soft focus when taking a photograph or using different typefaces for exactly the same text. Indeed, the generation of connotations from typography alone demonstrates how important the material aspect of written language can be as a signifier in its own right. One study, for instance, has shown how various typefaces were rated by some computer users in the USA in terms of how 'youthful and fun' or how 'business-like' each was perceived as being (Bernard et al. 2001; see Figure 4.4).

Connotation is not a purely paradigmatic dimension, as Saussure's characterization of the paradigmatic dimension as 'associative' might suggest. While absent signifiers with which a signifier may be associated are clearly a key factor in generating connotations, so too are syntagmatic associations. The connotations of a signifier relate in part to the other signifiers with which it occurs within a particular text. However, referring to connotation entirely in terms of paradigms and syntagms confines us to the language system, and yet connotation is very much a question of how language is *used*. The Saussurean inflection of structuralism limits us to a synchronic perspective and yet both connotations and denotations are subject not only to socio-cultural variability but also to historical factors: they change over time. Signs referring to disempowered groups (such as 'woman') can be seen as having had far more negative denotations as well as negative connotations than they do now

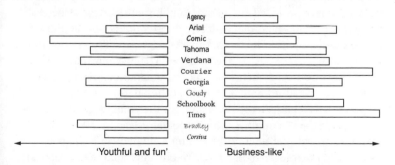

'Youthful and fun'   'Business-like'

FIGURE 4.4 Some connotations of particular fonts

Source: adapted from diagrams ©2001 Software Usability Research Laboratory, Wichita State University

because of their framing within dominant and authoritative codes of their time – including even supposedly objective scientific codes. Fiske warns that 'it is often easy to read connotative values as denotative facts' (Fiske 1982, 92). Just as dangerously seductive, however, is the tendency to accept denotation as the literal, self-evident truth. Semiotic analysis can help us to counter such habits of mind.

While the dominant methodologies in semiotic analysis are *qualitative*, semiotics is not incompatible with the use of quantitative techniques. In 1957 the psychologist Charles Osgood, together with some of his colleagues, published a book entitled *The Measurement of Meaning* (Osgood et al. 1957). In it these communication researchers outlined a technique called the *semantic differential* for the systematic mapping of *connotations* (or 'affective meanings'). The technique involves a pencil-and-paper test in which people are asked to give their impressionistic responses to a particular object, state or event by indicating specific positions in relation to at least nine pairs of bipolar adjectives on a scale of one to seven. The aim is to locate a concept in 'semantic space' in three dimensions: *evaluation* (e.g. good–bad); *potency* (e.g. strong–weak); and *activity* (e.g. active–passive). The method has proved useful in studying attitudes and emotional reactions. It has been used, for instance, to make comparisons between different cultural groups. While the technique has been used fairly widely in social science, it has not often been used by semioticians, although, as we have seen, binary oppositions have routinely provided theoretical building-blocks for structuralist semioticians. However, the semantic differential is not the only way in which quantitative methods can be used to study connotations: for instance, in a study of the kinds of personal meanings evoked by people's favourite domestic objects, quantitative data (based on ranking, correlation and statistical differences between groups) helped to reveal patterns of signification which qualitative data helped to explain (Csikszentmihalyi and Rochberg-Halton 1981). The researchers found that among the families studied (in a major city in the USA in the mid-1970s), a range of objects found in the home signified for their users various aspects of personal and social identity. For instance, some objects served partly as life-cycle markers, as reflected in 'the asymmetrical preference for stereos and photos among the youngest and oldest respondents, the curvilinear relationship of preference for TV sets with age or the importance of visual art and sculpture for the middle generation' (ibid., 94). Two major axes appeared to articulate the relationship between people and objects: action–contemplation and differentiation–integration (ibid., 112–13). While the meanings of the same kind of objects varied for individuals, television and stereos most often signified the self; photos, the immediate family; and paintings non-family (ibid., 88). From the specific objects most frequently cited the researchers noted a (stereotypical) tendency for the males to value 'objects of action', and for the females to value 'objects of contemplation'. Women also cited connotations relating to memories, associations and immediate family significantly more often than men did. Such differences reflected 'at the level of household objects', the reproduction of the traditional gender distinction between instrumental (male) and expressive (female) roles (ibid., 106).

MYTH

Discourses of gender are among the 'explanatory' cultural frameworks which have been interpreted by some cultural semioticians as myths or mythologies. We usually associate myths with classical fables about the exploits of gods and heroes, and popular usage of the term 'myth' suggests that it refers to beliefs which are demonstrably false, but the semiotic use of the term does not necessarily suggest this. Like metaphors, cultural myths help us to make sense of our experiences within a culture: they express and serve to organize shared ways of conceptualizing something within a culture (Lakoff and Johnson 1980, 185–6).

In the framework of Barthesian cultural studies, myth, like connotation, can be seen as a higher order of signification. Louis Hjelmslev had argued that above the connotative level there was 'a metasemiotic' to which belonged geographical, historical, political, sociological, psychological and religious issues relating to such concepts as 'nation, . . . region, . . . the value forms of styles, personality . . . mood, etc.' (Hjelmslev 1961, 125). For instance, an image may denote 'a child' in a context which generates the connotation of innocence; this forms part of what Roland Barthes would call a higher level (historically modern and Romantic) 'myth' of childhood which functions ideologically to justify dominant assumptions about the status of children in society. Barthes did not see the myths of contemporary culture as simply a patterned agglomeration of connotations but as ideological narratives, and, following Hjelmslev, he saw mythical form as a metalanguage (Barthes 1957, 124–6), which he defined as 'a system whose plane of content is itself constituted by a signifying system' (1967a, 90). Whereas in the case of connotation, the denotative sign becomes the *signifier* of the connotative sign, in the case of myth, 'the language (or the modes of representation which are assimilated to it) . . . which myth gets hold of in order to build its own system' becomes the *signified* of the mythical metalanguage (1957, 124; cf. Hjelmslev 1961, 114, 119–20 and Lévi-Strauss 1969, 12).

The mythological or ideological order of signification can be seen as reflecting major (culturally variable) concepts underpinning particular worldviews. For Roland Barthes, myths were the dominant ideologies of our time. *Objectivism*, for instance, is a pervasive myth in Western culture. It allies itself with scientific truth, rationality, accuracy, fairness and impartiality and is reflected in the discourse of science, law, government, journalism, morality, business, economics and scholarship (Lakoff and Johnson 1980, 188–9). Other myths or mythical discourses include those of masculinity and femininity, freedom, individualism, Englishness, success and so on. Barthes is probably most famous for his insightful analyses of some of the tacit myths of popular culture, notably in the essays represented in the anthology entitled *Mythologies* (1957). He addressed many types of contemporary cultural myths – most famously in his analysis of a cover photo in the magazine *Paris Match* depicting a young black soldier saluting the (unseen) French flag (Barthes 1957, 125–56) and of the 'Italianicity' of an advertisement for Panzani pasta (1977a). We do not have space to discuss these much-anthologized and explicated examples here but the general thrust of his analytical approach will be illustrated in the following chapter.

As we have seen, in the context of cultures other than our own Lévi-Strauss saw myths as systems of binary alignments mediating between nature and culture. Semioticians in the Saussurean tradition treat this relationship as relatively arbitrary (Lévi-Strauss 1972, 90, 95). Barthes argued that mythical signification always emerges as 'in part motivated, and unavoidably contains some analogy' (leading it to be experienced as natural) and only 'the worn-out state of a myth can be recognized by the arbitrariness of its signification' (Barthes 1957, 136). For him (as for Lévi-Strauss), myths serve the ideological function of *naturalization* (Barthes 1964, 45–6). Their function is to naturalize the cultural – in other words, to make dominant cultural and historical values, attitudes and beliefs seem entirely natural, normal, self-evident, timeless, obvious common sense – and thus objective and true reflections of 'the way things are'. Barthes saw myth as serving the ideological interests of the bourgeoisie. 'Bourgeois ideology ... turns culture into nature,' he declares (Barthes 1974, 206). Myths can function to hide the ideological function of signs. The power of such myths is that they 'go without saying' and so appear not to need to be deciphered, interpreted or demystified. The similarity to Lévi-Strauss is clear here: 'I ... claim to show, not how men think in myths, but how myths operate in men's minds without their being aware of the fact' (Lévi-Strauss 1969, 12). Barthesian semiotics demonstrates that deconstructing tropes, connotations and myths can be revealing but that they cannot be reduced to the 'literal'. Barthes excelled at this kind of analysis but the task of 'denaturalizing' the cultural assumptions embodied in such forms is problematic when the semiotician is also a product of the same culture, since membership of a culture involves taking for granted many of its dominant ideas. Barthes is a hard act to follow, but those who do try to analyse their own cultures in this way must also seek to be explicitly reflexive about their 'own' values.

Rhetoric and connotation generate complex signs, and myths are complex sign-systems which generate further ideological signs. Rather than characterizing myths simply as a cluster of tropes and connotations, Barthes argued that they function in a more integrated fashion both in their content (ideology) and in their form – as metalinguistic semiotic systems or *codes*, of which specific cultural connotations and tropes can be seen as fragments (Barthes 1957, 119–20, 145–6). It is to codes that we now turn our attention.

CODE

CODES

The concept of the 'code' is central in structuralist semiotics. While Saussure dealt only with the overall code of language (*langue*), he did of course stress that signs are not meaningful in isolation, but only when they are interpreted in relation to each other. It was another linguistic structuralist, Roman Jakobson, who emphasized that the production and interpretation of texts depends upon the existence of codes or conventions for communication (Jakobson 1960 and 1971c). Influenced by communication theorists, he substituted the distinction of code from message for the Saussurean distinction of *langue* from *parole* (Jakobson 1990, 15). Since the meaning of a sign depends on the code within which it is situated, codes provide a framework within which signs make sense. Indeed, we cannot grant something the status of a sign if it does not function within a code. Codes organize signs into meaningful systems which correlate signifiers and signifieds through the structural forms of syntagms and paradigms. If the relationship between a signifier and its signified is relatively arbitrary, then it is clear that interpreting the conventional meaning of signs requires familiarity with appropriate sets of conventions.

The conventions of codes represent a social dimension in semiotics: a code is a set of practices familiar to users of the medium operating within a broad cultural framework. Indeed, as Stuart Hall puts it, 'there is no intelligible discourse without the operation of a code' (Hall 1973, 131). Society itself depends on the existence of such signifying systems. When studying cultural practices, semioticians treat as signs any objects or actions which have meaning to members of the cultural group, seeking to identify the rules or conventions of the codes which underlie the production of meanings within that culture. Understanding such codes, their relationships and the contexts in which they are appropriate, is part of what it means to be a member of a particular culture. Codes are not simply 'conventions' of communication but rather procedural *systems* of related conventions which operate in certain domains.

Structuralists characteristically envisage such codes as in some respects analogous to verbal language. Typical in this respect is this declaration by the anthropologist Edmund Leach:

> *All* the various non-verbal dimensions of culture, such as styles in cooking, village lay-out, architecture, furniture, food, cooking, music, physical gesture, postural attitudes and so on are organised in patterned sets so as to incorporate coded information in a manner analogous to the sounds and words and sentences of a natural language ... It is just as meaningful to talk about the grammatical rules which govern the wearing of clothes as it is to talk about the grammatical rules which govern speech utterances.
>
> (Leach 1976, 10)

TYPES OF CODES

Semioticians seek to identify codes and the tacit rules and constraints which underlie the production and interpretation of meaning within each code. They have found it convenient to divide codes themselves into groups. Different theorists favour different taxonomies, and while structuralists often follow the 'principle of parsimony' – seeking to find the smallest number of groups deemed necessary – 'necessity' is defined by *purposes*. No taxonomy is innocently neutral and devoid of ideological assumptions. One might start from a fundamental divide between analogue and digital codes, from a division according to sensory channels, from a distinction between verbal and non-verbal, and so on. Many semioticians take human language as their starting point. The primary and most pervasive code in any society is its dominant natural language, within which (as with other codes) there are many 'sub-codes'. A fundamental sub-division of language into spoken and written forms – at least insofar as it relates to whether the text is detached from its maker at the point of reception – is often regarded as representing a broad division into different codes rather than merely sub-codes. One theorist's code is another's sub-code and the value of the distinction needs to be demonstrated. Stylistic and personal codes (or *idiolects*) are often described as subcodes (e.g. Eco 1976, 263, 272). The various kinds of codes overlap, and the semiotic analysis of any text or practice involves considering several codes and the relationships between them. A range of typologies of codes can be found in the literature of semiotics. I refer here only to those which are most widely mentioned in the context of media, communication and cultural studies (this particular tripartite framework is my own).

SOCIAL CODES

- verbal language (phonological, syntactical, lexical, prosodic and paralinguistic subcodes);
- bodily codes (bodily contact, proximity, physical orientation, appearance, facial expression, gaze, head-nods, gestures and posture);
- commodity codes (fashions, clothing, cars);
- behavioural codes (protocols, rituals, role-playing, games).

TEXTUAL CODES

- scientific codes, including mathematics;
- aesthetic codes within the various expressive arts (poetry, drama, painting, sculpture, music, etc.) including classicism, romanticism, realism;
- genre, rhetorical and stylistic codes: exposition, argument, description and narration and so on;
- mass media codes including photographic, televisual, filmic, radio, newspaper and magazine codes, both technical and conventional (including format).

INTERPRETIVE CODES

- perceptual codes: e.g. of visual perception (Hall 1973, 132; Nichols 1981, 11ff.; Eco 1982) (note that this code does not assume intentional communication);
- ideological codes: more broadly, these include codes for 'encoding' and 'decoding' texts – dominant (or 'hegemonic'), negotiated or oppositional (Hall 1980; Morley 1980). More specifically, we may list the '-isms', such as individualism, liberalism, feminism, racism, materialism, capitalism, progressivism, conservatism, socialism, objectivism and populism; (note, however, that *all* codes can be seen as ideological).

These three types of codes correspond broadly to three key kinds of knowledge required by interpreters of a text, namely knowledge of:

1. the world (social knowledge);
2. the medium and the genre (textual knowledge);
3. the relationship between (1) and (2) (modality judgements).

The 'tightness' of semiotic codes themselves varies from the rule-bound closure of logical codes (such as computer codes) to the interpretive looseness of poetic codes. Some theorists question whether some of the looser systems constitute codes at all (e.g. Guiraud 1975, 24, 41, 43–4, 65; Corner 1980).

PERCEPTUAL CODES

Some theorists argue that even our perception of the everyday world around us involves codes. Fredric Jameson declares that 'all perceptual systems are already languages in their own right' (Jameson 1972, 152). As Derrida would put it, perception is always already representation. 'Perception depends on coding the world into iconic signs that can re-present it within our mind. The force of the apparent identity is enormous, however. We think that it is the world itself we see in our "mind's eye", rather than a coded picture of it' (Nichols 1981, 11–12). According to the Gestalt psychologists there are certain universal features in human visual perception which in semiotic terms can be seen as constituting a perceptual code. We owe the concept of 'figure' and 'ground' in perception to this group of psychologists. Confronted by a visual image, we seem to need to separate a dominant shape (a 'figure' with a definite contour) from what our current concerns relegate to 'background' (or 'ground'). An illustration of this is the famous ambiguous figure which initially seems to be either a white vase on a black background or two human faces in silhouette facing each other against a white background. Images such as this are ambiguous concerning figure and ground. In such cases context influences perception, leading us to favour one interpretation over the other ('perceptual set'). When we have identified a figure, the contours seem to belong to it, and it appears to be in front of the ground.

In addition to introducing the terms 'figure' and 'ground', the Gestalt psychologists outlined what seemed to be several fundamental and universal principles (sometimes even called 'laws') of perceptual organization, including:

- *proximity* – features which are close together are associated;
- *similarity* – features which look similar are associated;
- *good continuity* – contours based on smooth continuity are preferred to abrupt changes of direction;
- *closure* – interpretations which produce 'closed' rather than 'open' figures are favoured;
- *smallness* – smaller areas tend to be seen as figures against a larger background;

- *symmetry* – symmetrical areas tend to be seen as figures against asymmetrical backgrounds;
- *surroundedness* – areas which can be seen as surrounded by others tend to be perceived as figures.

All of these principles of perceptual organization serve the over-arching principle of *prägnanz*, which is that the simplest and most stable interpretations are favoured.

What the Gestalt principles of perceptual organization suggest is that we may be predisposed towards interpreting ambiguous images in one way rather than another by universal principles. We may accept such a proposition at the same time as accepting that such predispositions may also be generated by other factors. Similarly, we may accept the Gestalt principles while at the same time regarding other aspects of perception as being *learned* and culturally variable rather than innate. The Gestalt principles can be seen as reinforcing the notion that the world is not simply and objec-tively 'out there' but is constructed in the process of perception. As Bill Nichols comments, 'a useful habit formed by our brains must not be mistaken for an essential attribute of reality. Just as we must learn to read an image, we must learn to read the physical world. Once we have developed this skill (which we do very early in life), it is very easy to mistake it for an automatic or unlearned process, just as we may mistake our particular way of reading, or seeing, for a natural, ahistorical and noncultural given' (Nichols 1981, 12).

We are rarely aware of our own habitual ways of seeing the world. We are routinely anaesthetized to a psychological mechanism called 'perceptual constancy' which stabilizes the relative shifts in the apparent shapes and sizes of people and objects in the world around us as we change our visual viewpoints in relation to them. Without mechanisms such as categorization and perceptual constancy the world would be no more than what William James called a 'great blooming and buzzing confusion' (James 1890, 488). Perceptual constancy ensures that 'the variability of the everyday world becomes translated by reference to less variable codes. The environment becomes a text to be read like any other text' (Nichols 1981, 26).

SOCIAL CODES

Constructionist theorists argue that linguistic codes play a key role in the construction and maintenance of social realities. We learn not the world but the codes into which it has been structured. The Whorfian hypothesis, or Sapir–Whorf theory, is named after the American linguists Edward Sapir and Benjamin Lee Whorf. In its most extreme version the Sapir–Whorf hypothesis can be described as relating two associated principles: *linguistic determinism* and *linguistic relativism*. Applying these two principles, the Whorfian thesis is that people who speak languages with very different phonological, grammatical and semantic distinctions perceive and think about the world quite differently, their worldviews being shaped or determined by their language (Sapir 1958, 69; Whorf 1956, 213–14). The extreme determinist form of the Sapir–Whorf hypothesis is rejected by most contemporary linguists. Critics note that we cannot make inferences about differences in worldview solely on the basis of differences in linguistic structure. While few linguists would accept the Whorfian hypothesis in its 'strong', extreme or deterministic form, many now accept a 'weak', more moderate, or limited Whorfianism, namely that the ways in which we see the world may be *influenced* by the kind of language we use.

Within a culture, social differentiation is overdetermined by a multitude of social codes. We communicate our social identities through the work we do, the way we talk, the clothes we wear, our hairstyles, our eating habits, our domestic environments and possessions, our use of leisure time, our modes of travelling and so on. Language use acts as a key marker of social identity. A controversial distinction regarding British linguistic usage was introduced in the 1960s by the sociologist Basil Bernstein between so-called 'restricted code' and 'elaborated code' (Bernstein 1971). Restricted code was used in informal situations and was characterized by a reliance on situational context, a lack of stylistic variety, an emphasis on the speaker's membership of the group, simple syntax and the frequent use of gestures and tag questions (such as 'Isn't it?'). Elaborated code was used in formal situations and was characterized by less dependence on context, wide stylistic range (including the passive voice), more adjectives, relatively complex syntax and the use of the pronoun 'I'. Bernstein's argument was that middle-class children had access to both of these codes while working-class children had access only to restricted codes. Such clear-cut distinctions and correlations with social class are now widely challenged by linguists (Crystal 1987, 40). However, we still routinely use such linguistic cues as a basis for making inferences about people's social backgrounds.

Social differentiation is observable not only from linguistic codes, but from a host of non-verbal codes. A survey of non-verbal codes is not manageable here, and the interested reader should consult some of the classic texts and specialist guides to the literature (see *Going Further* pp. 238–9, this volume). In the context of the present text a few examples must suffice to illustrate the importance of non-verbal codes. Non-verbal codes which regulate a 'sensory regime' are of particular interest. Within particular cultural contexts there are, for instance, largely inexplicit 'codes of looking' which regulate how people may look at other people (including taboos on certain kinds of looking). Such codes tend to retreat to transparency when the cultural context is one's own. 'Children are instructed to "look at me", not to stare at strangers, and not to look at certain parts of the body . . . People have to look in order to be polite, but not to look at the wrong people or in the wrong place, e.g. at deformed people' (Argyle 1988, 158). In Luo in Kenya one should not look at one's mother-in-law; in Nigeria one should not look at a high-status person; among some South American Indians during conversation one should not look at the other person; in Japan one should look at the neck, not the face; and so on (Argyle 1983, 95).

The duration of the gaze is also culturally variable: in 'contact cultures' such as those of the Arabs, Latin Americans and southern Europeans, people look more than the British or white Americans, while black Americans look less (Argyle 1988, 158). In contact cultures too little gaze is seen as insincere, dishonest or impolite, while in non-contact cultures too much gaze ('staring') is seen as threatening, disrespectful and insulting (Argyle 1983, 95 and 1988, 165). Within the bounds of the cultural conventions, people who avoid one's gaze may be seen as nervous, tense, evasive and lacking in confidence, while people who look a lot may tend to be seen as friendly and self-confident (Argyle 1983, 93). Such codes may sometimes be deliberately violated. In the USA in the 1960s, bigoted white Americans employed a sustained 'hate stare' directed against blacks, which was designed to depersonalize the victims (Goffman 1969a).

Codes of looking are particularly important in relation to gender differentiation. One woman reported to a male friend: 'One of the things I really envy about men is the right to look.' She pointed out that in public places, 'men could look freely at women, but women could only glance back surreptitiously' (Dyer 1992, 103).

We learn to read the world in terms of the codes and conventions which are dominant within the specific socio-cultural contexts and roles within which we are socialized. In the process of adopting a way of seeing, we also adopt an 'identity'. The most important constancy in our understanding of reality is our sense of who we are as an individual. Our sense of self as a constancy is a social construction which is overdetermined by a host of interacting codes within our culture (Berger and Luckmann 1967; Burr 1995). 'Roles, conventions, attitudes, language – to varying degrees these are internalized in order to be repeated, and through the constancies of repetition a consistent locus gradually emerges: the self. Although never fully determined by these internalizations, the self would be entirely undetermined without them' (Nichols 1981, 30). When we first encounter the notion that the self is a social construction we are likely to find it counter-intuitive. We usually take for granted our status as autonomous individuals with unique 'personalities'. We will return later to the notion of our positioning as subjects. For the moment, we will note simply that 'society depends upon the fact that its members grant its founding fictions, myths or codes a taken-for-granted status' (ibid.). Culturally variable perceptual codes are typically inexplicit, and we are not normally conscious of the roles which they play. To users of the dominant, most widespread codes, meanings generated within such codes tend to appear obvious and natural. Stuart Hall comments:

> Certain codes may . . . be so widely distributed in a specific language community or culture, and be learned at so early an

age, that they appear not to be constructed – the effect of an articulation between sign and referent – but to be 'naturally' given. Simple visual signs appear to have achieved a 'near-universality' in this sense: though evidence remains that even apparently 'natural' visual codes are culture-specific. However, this does not mean that no codes have intervened; rather, that the codes have been profoundly *naturalized*.

(Hall 1973, 132)

Learning these codes involves adopting the values, assumptions and worldviews which are built into them without normally being aware of their intervention in the construction of reality. A startling example of this relates to colour codes. When I show my own students a picture of two teddy bears, one clothed in powder blue and the other in pale pink, there is seldom any hesitation in suggesting that this signifies respectively male and female. There follows an almost tangible sense of shock when I confront them with this passage:

Pink or blue? Which is intended for boys and which for girls? This question comes from one of our readers this month, and the discussion may be of interest to others. There has been a great diversity of opinion on this subject, but the generally accepted rule is pink for the boy and blue for the girl. The reason is that pink being a more decided and stronger color, is more suitable for the boy; while blue, which is more delicate and dainty is prettier for the girl.

Widely misattributed to the *Ladies' Home Journal*, this is actually from a Chicago-based trade magazine called *The Infants' Department: A Monthly Magazine of Merchandising Helps for the Infants' Wear Buyer* (vol. 1, no. 10, June 1918, p. 161). Nor is this an isolated source for the same sentiments in the early decades of the twentieth century: for instance, a boy's sailor suit dating from 1908 in the Smithsonian Institution has pink trimmings (object #234865.10 in the National Museum of American History; cf. Paoletti and Kregloh 1989). Only in more recent times has pink acquired such a powerfully marked status as 'feminine' (Taft 1997). The profound sense of amazement or even disbelief generated by encountering such 'counter-intuitive' gendering of colours serves to alert us to a realization that some of the codes which seem most natural may be rather more arbitrary than we had assumed. Reading the justification in the passage for pink being deemed more suitable for boys than for girls may seem initially to be an amusing rationalization, but the realization quickly dawns that our own rationale for the opposite case is hardly immune from the same judgement. Such revelatory moments powerfully suggest the denaturalizing potential of semiotics.

TEXTUAL CODES

Every text is a system of signs organized according to codes and subcodes which reflect certain values, attitudes, beliefs, assumptions and practices. Codes transcend single texts, linking them together in an interpretive framework which is used by their producers and interpreters. In creating texts we select and combine signs in relation to the codes with which we are familiar. Codes help to simplify phenomena in order to make it easier to communicate experiences. In reading texts, we interpret signs with reference to what seem to be appropriate codes. This helps to limit their possible meanings. Usually the appropriate codes are obvious, overdetermined by all sorts of contextual cues. The medium employed clearly influences the choice of codes. In this sense we routinely 'judge a book by its cover'. We can typically identify a text as a poem simply by the way in which it is set out on the page. The use of what is sometimes called 'scholarly apparatus' (such as introductions, acknowledgements, section headings, tables, diagrams, notes, references, bibliographies, appendices and indexes) – is what makes academic texts immediately identifiable as such to readers. Such cueing is part of the *metalingual* function of signs. With familiar codes we are rarely conscious of our acts of interpretation, but occasionally a text requires us to work a little harder – for instance, by pinning down the most appropriate signified for a key signifier (as in jokes based on word play) – before we can identify the relevant codes for making sense of the text as a whole. Textual codes do not *determine* the meanings of texts but dominant codes do tend to *constrain* them. Social conventions ensure that signs cannot mean whatever an individual wants them to mean. The use of codes helps to guide us towards what Stuart Hall calls 'a preferred reading' and away from what Umberto Eco calls 'aberrant decoding', though media texts do vary in the extent to which they are open to interpretation (Hall 1980, 134).

One of the most fundamental kinds of textual code relates to *genre*. Traditional definitions of genres tend to be based on the notion that they constitute particular conventions of content (such as themes or settings) and/or form (including structure and style) which are shared by the texts which are regarded as belonging to them. This mode of defining a genre is deeply problematic. For instance, genres overlap and texts often exhibit the conventions of more than one genre. It is seldom hard to find texts which are exceptions to any given definition of a particular genre. Furthermore, a Saussurean focus on synchronic analysis ignores the way in which genres are involved in a constant process of change.

An overview of genre taxonomies in various media is beyond the scope of the current text, but it is appropriate here to allude to a few key cross-media genre distinctions. The organization of public libraries suggests that one of the most fundamental contemporary genre distinctions is between *fiction* and *non-fiction* – a categorization which highlights the importance of modality judgements. Even such an apparently basic distinction is revealed to be far from straightforward as soon as one tries to apply it to the books on one's own shelves or to an evening's television viewing. Another binary distinction is based on the kinds of language used: *poetry* and *prose* – the 'norm' being the latter, as Molière's Monsieur Jourdain famously discovered: 'Good Heavens! For more than forty years I have been speaking prose without knowing it!' Even here there are grey areas, with literary prose often being regarded as 'poetic'. This is related to the issue of how librarians, critics and academics decide what is 'literature' as opposed to mere 'fiction'. As with the typology of codes in general, no genre taxonomy can be ideologically neutral. Traditional rhetoric distinguishes between four kinds of discourse: *exposition*, *argument*, *description* and *narration* (Brooks and Warren 1972, 44). These four forms, which relate to primary purposes, are often referred to as different genres (e.g. Fairclough 1995a, 88). However, texts frequently involve any combination of these forms and they are perhaps best thought of as 'modes'. More widely described as genres are the four 'modes of emplotment' which Hayden White adopted from Northrop Frye in his study of historiography: *romance*, *tragedy*, *comedy* and *satire* (White 1973). Useful as such interpretive frameworks can be, however, no taxonomy of textual genres adequately represents the diversity of texts.

Despite such theoretical problems, various interpretive communities (at particular periods in time) do operate on the basis of a negotiated (if somewhat loose and fluid) consensus concerning what they regard as the primary genres relevant to their purposes. While there is far more to a genre code than that which may seem to relate to specifically textual features it can still be useful to consider the distinctive properties attributed to a genre by its users. For instance, if we take the case of film, the textual features typically listed by theorists include:

- **narrative** – similar (sometimes formulaic) plots and structures, predictable situations, sequences, episodes, obstacles, conflicts and resolutions;
- **characterization** – similar types of characters (sometimes stereotypes), roles, personal qualities, motivations, goals, behaviour;
- basic **themes**, topics, subject-matter (social, cultural, psychological, professional, political, sexual, moral) and values;
- **setting** – geographical and historical;
- **iconography** (echoing the narrative, characterization, themes and setting) – a familiar stock of images or motifs, the connotations of which have become fixed; primarily but not necessarily visual, including décor, costume and objects, certain 'typecast' performers (some of whom may have become 'icons'), familiar patterns of dialogue, characteristic music and sounds, and appropriate physical topography; and
- **filmic techniques** – stylistic or formal conventions of camerawork, lighting, sound-recording, use of colour, editing, etc. (viewers are often less conscious of such conventions than of those relating to content).

Some film genres tend to be defined primarily by their *subject-matter* (e.g. detective films), some by their *setting* (e.g. the western) and others by their *narrative* form (e.g. the musical). Less easy to place in one of the traditional categories are *mood* and *tone* (which are key features of *film noir*). In addition to *textual* features, different genres (in any medium) also involve different purposes, pleasures, audiences, modes of involvement, styles of interpretation and *text–reader relationships* (an issue to which we will return shortly).

CODES OF REALISM

All representations are systems of signs: they signify rather than represent, and they do so with primary reference to codes rather than to reality. Adopting such a stance need not, of course, entail a denial of the existence of an external reality but it does involve the recognition that textual codes which are 'realistic' are nonetheless (to some degree) conventional. 'Realism is not reality,' as Christian Metz put it (Metz 1968/1974, 21). From the Renaissance until the nineteenth century, Western art was dominated by a mimetic or representational purpose which still prevails in popular culture. Such art denies its status as a signifying system, seeking to represent a world which is assumed to exist before, and independently of, the act of representation. Realism involves an instrumental view of the medium as a neutral means of representing reality. The signified is foregrounded at the expense of the signifier. Realist representational practices tend to mask the processes involved in producing texts, as if they were slices of life 'untouched by human hand'. As Catherine Belsey notes, 'realism is plausible not because it reflects the world, but because it is constructed out of what is (discursively) familiar' (Belsey 1980, 47). Ironically, the 'naturalness' of realist texts comes not from their reflection of reality but from their uses of codes which are derived from other texts. The familiarity of particular semiotic practices renders their mediation invisible. Our recognition of the familiar in realist texts repeatedly confirms the 'objectivity' of our habitual ways of seeing.

However, the codes of the various realisms are not always initially familiar. In the context of painting, Ernst Gombrich has illustrated (for instance, in relation to John Constable) how aesthetic codes which now seem 'almost photographic' to many viewers were regarded at the time of their emergence as strange and radical (Gombrich 1977). Eco adds that early viewers of Impressionist art could not recognize the subjects represented and declared that real life was not like this (Eco 1976, 254; Gombrich 1982, 279). Most people had not previously noticed coloured shadows in nature (Gombrich 1982, 27, 30, 34). Even photography involves a translation from three dimensions into two, and anthropologists have often reported the initial difficulties experienced by people in primal tribes in making sense of photographs and films (Deregowski 1980), while historians note that even in recent times the first instant snapshots confounded Western viewers because they were not accustomed to arrested images of transient movements and needed to go through a process of cultural habituation or training (Gombrich 1982, 100, 273). Photography involved a new 'way of seeing' (to use John Berger's phrase) which had to be learned before it could become transparent. What human beings see does not resemble a sequence of rectangular frames, and camerawork and editing conventions are not direct replications of the way in which we see the everyday world. When we look at things around us in everyday life we gain a sense of depth from our binocular vision, by rotating our head or by moving in relation to what we are looking at. To get a clearer view we can adjust the focus of our eyes. But for making sense of depth when we look at a photograph none of this helps. We have to decode the cues. Semioticians argue that, although exposure over time leads 'visual language' to seem natural, we need to learn how to 'read' even visual and audio-visual texts (though see Messaris 1982 and 1994 for a critique of this stance).

In the cinema, 'the gestural codes and the bodily and facial expressions of actors in silent films belonged to conventions which connoted realism when they were made and watched' (Bignell 1997, 193), whereas now such codes stand out as unrealistic. When the pioneering American film-maker D. W. Griffith initially proposed the use of close-ups, his producers warned him that the audience would be disconcerted since the rest of the actor was missing (Rosenblum and Karen 1979, 37–8). What count as realistic modes of representation are both culturally and historically variable. To most contemporary Western audiences the conventions of American cinema seem more realistic than the conventions of modern Indian cinema, for instance, because the latter are so much less familiar. Even within a culture, over historical time particular codes become increasingly less familiar, and as we look back at texts produced centuries ago we are struck by the strangeness of their codes – their maintenance systems having long since been superseded. In his influential book, *Languages of Art*, the North American philosopher Nelson Goodman (1906–98) insisted that 'realism is relative, determined by the system of representation standard for a given culture or person at a given time' (Goodman 1968, 37).

As noted earlier, Peirce referred to signs in (unedited) photographic media as being *indexical* as well as *iconic* – meaning that the signifiers did not simply resemble their signifieds but were mechanical recordings and reproductions of them (within the limitations of the medium). John Berger also argued that photographs are automatic 'records of things seen' and that 'photography has no language of its own' (Berger 1968, 179, 181). In 'The photographic message' (1961), Roland Barthes famously declared that 'the photographic image . . . is a *message without a code*' (Barthes 1961, 17). Since this phrase is frequently misunderstood, it may be worth clarifying its context with reference to this essay together with another published three years later – 'The rhetoric of the image' (Barthes 1964). Barthes was referring to the 'absolutely analogical, which is to say, *continuous*' character of the medium (Barthes 1961, 20). 'Is it possible', he asks, 'to conceive of an analogical code (as opposed to a digital one)?' (Barthes 1964, 32). The relation between the signifier and the thing signified is not arbitrary as in language (ibid., 35). He grants that photography involves both mechanical *reduction* (flattening, perspective, proportion and colour) and human *intervention* (choice of subject, framing, composition, optical point of view, distance, angle, lighting, focus, speed, exposure, printing and 'trick effects'). However, photography does not involve rule-governed *transformation* as codes can (Barthes 1961, 17, 20–5; Barthes 1964, 36, 43, 44). 'In the photograph – at least at the level of the literal message – the relationship of signifieds to signifiers is not one of "transformation" but of "recording".' Alluding to the indexical nature of the medium, he notes that the image is 'captured mechanically' and that this reinforces the myth of its 'objectivity' (Barthes 1964, 44). Unlike a drawing or a painting, a photograph reproduces 'everything': it 'cannot intervene *within* the object (except by trick effects)' (ibid., 43). 'In order to move from the reality to the photograph it is in no way necessary to divide up this reality into units and to constitute these units as signs, substantially different from the object they communicate; there is no necessity to set up . . . a code, between the object and its image' (Barthes 1961, 17). In consequence, he noted, photographs cannot be reduced to words.

However, 'every sign supposes a code' and at a level higher than the 'literal' level of denotation, a *connotative* code can be identified. Barthes noted that at the 'level of production', 'the press photograph is an object that has been worked on, chosen, composed, constructed, treated according to professional or ideological norms' and, at the 'level of reception', the photograph 'is not only perceived, received, it is *read*, connected by the public that consumes it to a traditional stock of signs' (Barthes 1961, 19). Reading a photograph involved relating it to a 'rhetoric' (ibid., 18, 19). In addition to the photographic techniques already noted, he refers for instance to the signifying functions of: postures, expressions and gestures; the associations evoked by depicted objects and settings; sequences of photographs, e.g. in magazines (which he refers to as 'syntax'); and relationships with accompanying text (ibid., 21–5). He added that 'thanks to the code of connotation the reading of the photograph is . . . always historical; it depends on the reader's "knowledge" just as though it were a matter of a real language, intelligible only if one has learned the signs' (ibid., 28).

Clearly, therefore, it would be a misinterpretation of Barthes' declaration that 'the photographic image . . . is a *message without a code*' to suggest that he meant that no codes are involved in producing or 'reading' photographs. His main point was that it did not (at least yet) seem possible to reduce the photographic image itself to elementary 'signifying units'. Far from suggesting that photographs are purely denotative, he declared that the 'purely "denotative" status of the photograph . . . has every chance of being mythical (these are

the characteristics that commonsense attributes to the photograph)'.
At the level of the analogue image itself, while the connotative code
was implicit and could only be inferred, he was convinced that it was
nonetheless 'active' (Barthes 1961, 19). Citing Bruner and Piaget, he
notes the possibility that 'there is no perception without immediate
categorization' (ibid., 28). Reading a photograph also depends closely
on the reader's culture, knowledge of the world, and ethical and
ideological stances (ibid., 29). Barthes adds that 'the viewer receives
at one and the same time the perceptual message and the cultural
message' (Barthes 1964, 36).

In *Writing Degree Zero*, Roland Barthes sought to demonstrate
that the classical textual codes of French writing (from the mid-
seventeenth century until the mid-nineteenth century) had been used
to suggest that such codes were natural, neutral and transparent
conduits for an innocent and objective reflection of reality (i.e. the
operation of the codes was masked). Barthes argues that while generating the illusion of a 'zero-degree' of style, these codes served the
purpose of fabricating reality in accord with the bourgeois view of
the world and covertly propagating bourgeois values as self-evident
(Barthes 1953; Hawkes 1977, 107–8). In 'The rhetoric of the image'
Barthes developed this line of argument in relation to the medium
of photography, arguing that because it appears to record rather than
to transform or signify, it serves an ideological function. Photography
'seems to found in nature the signs of culture ... masking the
constructed meaning under the appearance of the given meaning'
(Barthes 1964, 45–6).

Most semioticians emphasize that photography involves visual
codes, and that film and television involve both visual and aural
codes. John Tagg argues that 'the camera is never neutral. The representations it produces are highly coded' (Tagg 1988, 63–4; cf. 187).
Cinematic and televisual codes include: genre; camerawork (shot
size, focus, lens movement, camera movement, angle, lens choice,
composition); editing (cuts and fades, cutting rate and rhythm);
manipulation of time (compression, flashbacks, flashforwards, slow
motion); lighting; colour; sound (soundtrack, music); graphics; and
narrative style. Christian Metz added authorial style, and distinguished codes from sub-codes, where a sub-code was a particular

choice from within a code (e.g. western within genre, or naturalistic or expressionist lighting subcodes within the lighting code). The syntagmatic dimension was a relation of combination between different codes and sub-codes; the paradigmatic dimension was that of the film-maker's choice of particular sub-codes within a code. Since, as Metz noted, 'a film is not "cinema" from one end to another' (Metz 1971, 63), film and television involve many codes which are not specific to these media.

While some photographic and filmic codes are relatively arbitrary, many of the codes employed in realistic photographic images or films simulate many of the perceptual cues used in encountering the physical world (Nichols 1981, 35; cf. Messaris 1982 and 1994). This is a key reason for their perceived realism. The depiction of reality even in iconic signs involves variable codes which have to be learned, yet which, with experience, come to be taken for granted as transparent and obvious. Eco argues that it is misleading to regard such signs as less conventional than other kinds of signs (Eco 1976, 190ff.): even photography and film involve conventional codes. Paul Messaris, however, stresses that the formal conventions of representational visual codes (including paintings and drawings) are not arbitrary (Messaris 1994), and Ernst Gombrich offers a critique of what he sees as the 'extreme conventionalism' of Nelson Goodman's stance (Gombrich 1982, 278–97), stressing that 'the so-called conventions of the visual image [vary] according to the relative ease or difficulty with which they can be learned' (Gombrich 1982, 283) – a notion familiar from the Peircean ranking of signifier–signified relationships in terms of relative conventionality.

INVISIBLE EDITING

Semioticians often refer to 'reading' film or television – a notion which may seem strange since the meaning of filmic images appears not to need decoding at all. When we encounter a shot in which someone is looking offscreen we usually interpret the next shot as what he or she is looking at. Consider the following example offered by Ralph Rosenblum, a major professional film editor. In an initial shot, 'a man awakens suddenly in the middle of the night, bolts up in bed, stares ahead intensely, and twitches his nose'. If we then cut to 'a room where two people are desperately fighting a billowing blaze, the viewers realize that through clairvoyance, a warning dream, or the smell of smoke, the man in bed has become aware of danger'. Alternatively, if we cut from the first shot to 'a distraught wife defending her decision to commit her husband to a mental institution, they will understand that the man in bed is her husband and that the dramatic tension will surround the couple'. If it's a Hitchcock movie 'the juxtaposition of the man and the wife will immediately raise questions in the viewers' minds about foul play on the part of the woman'. This form of editing may alert us not only to a link between the two consecutive shots but in some cases to a genre. If we cut to an image of clouds drifting before the full moon, we know that we can expect a 'wolf-man' adventure (Rosenblum and Karen 1979, 2).

Such interpretations are not 'self-evident': they are a feature of a filmic editing code. Having internalized such codes at a very young age we then cease to be conscious of their existence. Once we know the code, decoding it is almost automatic and the code retreats to invisibility. The convention just described is known as an *eyeline match* and it is part of the dominant editing code in film and television narrative which is referred to as 'the continuity system' or as 'invisible editing' (Reisz and Millar 1972; Bordwell et al. 1988, Chapter 16; Bordwell and Thompson 1993, 261ff.). While minor elements within the code have been modified over time, most of the main elements are still much the same now as when they were developed many decades ago. This code was originally developed in Hollywood feature films but most narrative films and television dramas now routinely employ it. Editing supports rather than dominates the narrative: the story and the behaviour of its characters are the centre of attention. While nowadays there may be cuts every few seconds, these are intended to be unobtrusive. The technique gives the impression that the edits are always required and are motivated by the events in the reality that the camera is recording rather than the result of a desire to tell a story in a particular way. The seamlessness convinces us of its realism, but the code consists of an integrated system of technical conventions. These conventions serve to assist viewers in transforming the two-dimensional screen into a plausible three-dimensional world in which they can become absorbed.

A major cinematic convention is the use of the *establishing shot*: soon after a cut to a new scene we are given a long shot of it, allowing us to survey the overall space – followed by closer 'cut-in' shots focusing on details of the scene. Re-establishing shots are used when needed, as in the case of the entry of a new character. Another key convention involved in helping the viewer to make sense of the spatial organization of a scene is the so-called *180° rule*. Successive shots are not shown from both sides of the 'axis of action' since this would produce apparent changes of direction on screen. For instance, a character moving right to left across the screen in one shot is not shown moving left to right in the next shot. This helps to establish where the viewer is in relation to the action. In separate shots of speakers in a dialogue, one speaker always looks left while the other looks right. Even in telephone conversations the characters are oriented as if facing each other.

In *point-of-view (POV) shots*, the camera is placed (usually briefly) in the spatial position of a character to provide a subjective point of view. This is often in the form of alternating shots between two characters – a technique known as *shot/reverse-shot*. Once the 'axis of action' has been established, the alternation of shots with reverse-shots allows the viewer to glance back and forth at the participants in a dialogue (*matched shots* are used in which the shot-size and framing of the subject is similar). In such sequences, some of these shots are *reaction shots*. All of the techniques described so far reflect the goal of ensuring that the same characters are always in the same parts of the screen.

Because this code foregrounds the narrative, it employs what are called *motivated cuts*: changes of view or scene occur only when the action requires it and the viewer expects it. When cuts from one distance and/or angle to another are made, they are normally *matches on action*: cuts are usually made when the subject is *moving*, so that viewers are sufficiently distracted by the action to be unaware of the cut. There is a studious avoidance of *jump-cuts*: the so-called *30° rule* is that a shot of the same subject as the previous shot must differ in camera angle by at least 30° (otherwise it will feel to the viewer like an apparently pointless shift in position).

This cinematic editing code has become so familiar to us that we no longer consciously notice its conventions until they are broken. Indeed, it seems so natural that some will feel that it closely reflects phenomenal reality and thus find it hard to accept it as a code at all. Do we not mentally 'cut' from one image to another all of the time in everyday visual perception? This case seems strongest when all that is involved is a shift corresponding to a turn of our head or a refocusing of our eyes (Reisz and Millar 1972, 213–16). But of course many cuts would require us to change our viewing position. A common response to this – at least if we limit ourselves to moderate changes of angle or distance and ignore changes of scene – is to say that the editing technique represents a reasonable analogy with the normal mental processes involved in everyday perception. A cut to close-up can thus be seen to reflect as well as direct a purposive shift in attention. Of course, when the shot shifts so radically that it would be a physical impossibility to imitate this in everyday life, then the argument by perceptual analogy breaks down. And cuts reflect such shifts more often than not; only fleetingly does film editing closely reflect the perceptual experience of 'being there' in person. But of course a gripping narrative will already have led to our 'suspension of disbelief'. We thus routinely and unconsciously grant the film-maker the same 'dramatic licence' with which we are familiar not only from the majority of films that we watch but also from analogous codes employed in other media – such as theatre, the novel or the comic-strip.

For an argument questioning the interpretive importance of a cinematic editing code and emphasizing real-life analogies, see the lively and interesting book by Paul Messaris entitled *Visual Literacy* (Messaris 1994, 71ff.). However, his main focus of attack is on the stance that the cinematic editing code is *totally arbitrary* – a position which few would defend. Clearly these techniques were designed where possible to be analogous to familiar codes so that they would quickly become invisible to viewers once they were habituated to them. Messaris argues that context is more important than code; it is likely that where the viewer is in doubt about the meaning of a specific cut, interpretation may be aided by applying knowledge either from other textual codes (such as the logic of the narrative) or from relevant social codes (such as behavioural expectations in analogous situations in everyday life). The interpretation of film draws on knowledge of multiple codes. Adopting a semiotic approach to cinematic editing is not simply to acknowledge the importance of conventions and conventionality but to highlight the process of naturalization involved in the 'editing out' of what 'goes without saying'.

The emphasis given to *visual* codes by most theorists is perhaps partly due to their use of printed media for their commentaries – media which are inherently biased towards the visual, and may also derive from a Western tendency to privilege the visual over other channels. We need to remind ourselves that it is not only the visual image which is mediated, constructed and codified in the various media – in film, television and radio, this also applies to *sound*. Film and television are not simply visual media but *audio-visual* media. Even where the mediated character of the visual is acknowledged, there is a tendency for sound to be regarded as largely unmediated. But codes are involved in the choice and positioning of microphones, the use of particular equipment for recording, editing and reproduction, the use of diegetic sound (ostensibly emanating from the action in the story) versus non-diegetic sound, direct versus post-synchronous (dubbed) recording, simulated sounds (such as the highly conventionalized signifier for a punch) and so on (Altman 1992; Stam 2000, 212–23). In the dominant Hollywood tradition, conventional sound codes included features such as:

- *diegesis*: sounds should be relevant to the story;
- *hierarchy*: dialogue should override background sound;
- *seamlessness*: no gaps or abrupt changes in sound;
- *integration*: no sounds without images or vice versa;
- *readability*: all sounds should be identifiable;
- *motivation*: unusual sounds should be what characters are supposed to be hearing.

(Stam 2000, 216–17)

Sound can also assist in making visual editing 'invisible': within the same scene a 'sound-bridge' (carrying the same unbroken sound sequence) is used across a cut from one shot to another, as if there had been no cut at all.

BROADCAST AND NARROWCAST CODES

Some codes are more widespread and accessible than others. Those which are widely distributed and which are learned at an early age may seem natural rather than constructed (Hall 1973, 132). John Fiske distinguishes between *broadcast* codes, which are shared by member of a mass audience, and *narrowcast* codes which are aimed at a more limited audience; pop music is a broadcast code; ballet is a narrowcast code (Fiske 1982, 78ff.). Broadcast codes are learned through experience; narrowcast codes often involve more deliberate learning (Fiske 1989, 315). Following the controversial sociolinguistic theories of Basil Bernstein, what Fiske refers to as broadcast codes are described by some media theorists as 'restricted codes', with Fiske's narrowcast codes being described as 'elaborated codes' (Bernstein 1971). 'Restricted' codes are described as structurally simpler and more repetitive ('overcoded'), having what information theorists call a high degree of *redundancy*. In such codes several elements serve to emphasize and reinforce preferred meanings. Umberto Eco describes as 'closed' those texts (such as many mass media texts) which show a strong tendency to encourage a particular interpretation (Eco 1981). In contrast, literary writing – in particular poetry – has a minimum of redundancy (Lotman 1976a). The distinction between 'restricted' and 'elaborated' codes serves to stress the difference between an élite ('highbrows') and the majority ('lowbrows'). Art for the élite is held to be more 'original' and unpredictable. Fiske suggests that narrowcast (elaborated) codes have the potential to be more subtle; broadcast (restricted) codes can lead to cliché. Terry Eagleton argues that 'literary texts are "code-productive" and "code-transgressive"' rather than merely 'code-confirming' (Eagleton 1983, 125). Insofar as such positions suggest that broadcast codes restrict expressive possibilities this argument has affinities with Whorfianism. The dangers of élitism inherent in such stances make it particularly important that the evidence is closely examined in the context of the particular code under study.

INTERACTION OF TEXTUAL CODES

Any text uses not one code, but many. Theorists vary in their classification of such codes. In his book *S/Z*, Roland Barthes itemized five codes employed in literary texts: *hermeneutic* (narrative turning-points); *proairetic* (basic narrative actions); *cultural* (prior social knowledge); *semic* (medium-related codes) and *symbolic* (themes) (Barthes 1973). Yuri Lotman argued that a poem is a 'system of systems' – lexical, syntactical, metrical, morphological, phonological, and so on – and that the relations between such systems generate powerful literary effects. Each code sets up expectations which other codes violate (Lotman 1976a). The same signifier may play its part in several different codes. The meaning of literary texts may thus be overdetermined by several codes. Just as signs need to be analysed in their relation to other signs, so codes need to be analysed in relation to other codes. Becoming aware of the interplay of such codes requires a potentially recursive process of rereading. Nor can such readings be confined to the internal structure of a text, since the codes utilized within it extend beyond any specific text – an issue of 'intertextuality' to which we will return.

CODIFICATION

The synchronic perspective of Saussurean semioticians tends to give the impression that codes are static. But codes have origins and they do evolve, and studying their evolution is a legitimate semiotic endeavour. Guiraud argues that there is a gradual process of 'codification' whereby systems of implicit interpretation acquire the status of codes (Guiraud 1975, 41). Codes are dynamic systems which change over time and are thus historically as well as socioculturally situated. Codification is a *process* whereby conventions are established. For instance, Metz notes how in Hollywood cinema the white hat became codified as the signifier of a 'good' cowboy; eventually this convention became over-used and was abandoned (Metz 1968).

In the commercial application of semiotics to market research (where consumer trends are of course a key concern) a distinction has been made between three kinds of consumer codes: dominant codes (the prevailing codes of the present day); residual codes (codes in decline) and emergent codes (Alexander 2000). In structuralist accounts, codes tend to be presented as if they evolve autonomously, but socially oriented semioticians emphasize human agency: as Eco puts it, 'in exchanging messages and texts . . . *people* contribute to the changing of codes' (Eco 1976, 152; *my emphasis*). He adds that there is 'a dialectic between codes and messages, whereby the codes control the emission of messages, but new messages can restructure the codes' (ibid., 161). For those in marketing, this comes as no surprise.

In historical perspective, many of the codes of a new medium evolve from those of related existing media (for instance, many televisual techniques owe their origins to their use in film and photography). New conventions are also developed to match the technical potential of the medium and the uses to which it is put. Some codes are unique to (or at least characteristic of) a specific medium or to closely related media (e.g. 'fade to black' in film and television); others are shared by (or similar in) several media (e.g. scene breaks); and some are drawn from cultural practices which are not tied to a medium (e.g. body language) (Monaco 1981, 146ff.). Some are more specific to particular genres within a medium. Some are more broadly linked either to the domain of science ('logical codes', suppressing connotation and diversity of interpretation) or to that of the arts ('aesthetic codes', celebrating connotation and diversity of interpretation), though such differences are differences of degree rather than of kind.

Whatever the nature of any 'embedded' ideology, it has been claimed that as a consequence of their internalization of the codes of the medium, 'those born in the age of radio perceive the world differently from those born into the age of television' (Gumpert and Cathcart 1985). Critics have objected to the degree of technological determinism which is sometimes involved in such stances, but this is not to suggest that our use of such tools and techniques is without influence on our habits of mind. If this is so, the subtle phenomenology of new media is worthy of closer attention than is typically accorded to it. Whatever the medium, learning to notice the operation of codes when representations and meanings seem natural, obvious and transparent is clearly not an easy task. Understanding what semioticians have observed about the operation of codes can help us to denaturalize such codes by making their implicit conventions explicit and amenable to analysis. Semiotics offers us some conceptual crowbars with which to deconstruct the codes at work in particular texts and practices, providing that we can find some gaps or fissures which offer us the chance to exert some leverage.

Codes cannot account for everything in human culture and communication: social behaviour and textual practices cannot simply be reduced to the operation of semiotic codes. They are not autonomous determinants of human action – historical changes in social and textual patterns attest to the importance of human agency and textual 'transgression'. Even in terms of structure and style, few texts (especially those of enduring importance) can be wholly mapped onto existing generic codes. Unless semioticians wish to restrict themselves to trivial codes of limited scope they must take into account the possibility that at least some of the most significant codes in human meaning-making may be quite loosely and transitorily defined. Certainly many social codes have no clearly definable boundaries and the study of human culture requires explorers who are prepared to venture into the shifting sands of border zones as well as beyond them into codically unmapped (and sometimes codically unmappable) territory. However, recognizing the limitations of the concept of *code* does not mean that it has no utility, that there are no recognizable codes, that there is no value in seeking to identify patterns in textual and social practices or even that codes never appear to exhibit some degree of 'relative autonomy'. Nor, as we will see in the next chapter, does endorsement of the concept necessarily require meaning to be related purely to codes – even in structuralist models of human communication.

6

TEXTUAL
INTERACTIONS

In this chapter we will consider semiotic approaches to the interactions between makers, texts and users. First, we will explore the
issue of the encoding and decoding of texts and the ways in which
readers are 'positioned' in this process. Then we will consider *intertextuality* – or the interactions between texts.

MODELS OF COMMUNICATION

In 1972, Pioneer 10, a 'deep-space probe', was launched into inter-
stellar space by NASA; attached to the craft (and to the later Pioneer
11) was a plaque bearing the image shown in Figure 6.1. A press
release noted the possibility that during its long journey the spacecraft might be intercepted by 'intelligent scientifically educated
beings'. One of the designers wrote that the plaque was intended to
'convey, in what is hoped is easily understood scientific language,
some information on the locale, epoch, and nature of the builders
of the spacecraft' (Sagan 1977, 235). Ernst Gombrich wrote an

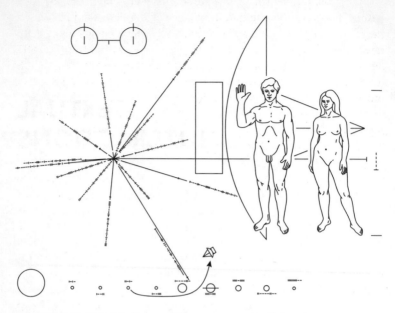

FIGURE 6.1 Pictorial plaque on Pioneer 10 spacecraft (1972)

Source: produced by the Pioneer Project at NASA Ames Research Center and obtained from NASA's National Space Science Data Center

insightful commentary on this endeavour (Gombrich 1972, 55–6). He noted that alien beings 'could not possibly get the message'. The most obvious reason is that on the sensory level they would have to be tuned to the same narrow range of the electromagnetic spectrum as we are, whereas even on Earth other creatures do not share the same sensory apparatus. However, his main point was rather less obvious: 'reading an image, like the reception of any other message, is dependent on prior knowledge of possibilities; we can only recognize what we know'. No one could make sense of this message without access to relevant social and textual codes. 'It is this information alone that enables us to separate the code from the message.'

For us, the human figures are immediately identifiable as such within the overall configuration of lines. We are so familiar with a range of visual conventions used to depict human beings that we are rarely conscious of the intervention of codes – after all, we routinely decode far more schematic images indicating 'male' or 'female' on toilet doors. Our knowledge of representational codes helps us to break the whole picture into separate parts: we know which bits seem to 'belong together' even if we don't know exactly what they all represent. This is not purely due to the apparently global invariance of the gestalt theorists' perceptual code (e.g. *good continuity* and *closure* – which enable us, for instance, to fill in the gaps in the large but backgrounded outline of Pioneer itself), but because we can distinguish several cohesive sets of representational conventions with different degrees of modality (even when they are superimposed). Gombrich notes that in relation to the human figures we recognize which lines are contours and which are conventional modelling. He adds: 'Our "scientifically educated" fellow creatures in space might be forgiven if they saw the figures as wire constructs with loose bits and pieces hovering weightlessly in between. Even if they deciphered this aspect of the code, what would they make of the woman's right arm that tapers off like a flamingo's neck and beak?' (Gombrich 1972). This latter point will give most readers pause for thought because it draws our attention to the familiar – and therefore normally invisible – convention that this represents the occlusion of one shape by another (a convention not adopted, for instance, in ancient Egyptian art).

As for social codes, although the man's raised right hand is presumably intended to signify a greeting this is a nonverbal code which would be alien to those living on large parts of our own planet. It can only be interpreted according to the preferred reading because we have social knowledge of the source of the craft and can infer the likely intentions of its makers: without this knowledge we might assume (from other contexts) that it signified 'stop' (e.g. traffic police); 'go' (as a signal for a train to depart), 'goodbye' or even a dictator acknowledging his followers (Adolf Hitler). Returning to textual codes, relatively few of us have access to the scientific codes which would enable us to interpret the large starburst-like pattern as 'the 14 pulsars of the Milky Way' – it could easily represent an explosion. In case the alien beings would like to track us down to discuss this further, there is a helpful route-map at the bottom of the picture, but since it adopts spatial conventions analogous to those of the London Underground map we probably won't be hearing from them soon, unless that is, they realize that the key to decoding it is the image at the top, which to most of us looks like dumb-bells or eye-glasses, whereas it is apparently intended to represent two hydrogen atoms engaged in 'hyperfine transition'. However, as Gombrich points out, even if they cracked this code, 'The trajectory. . . is endowed with a directional arrowhead; it seems to have escaped the designers that this is a conventional symbol unknown to a race that never had the equivalent of bows and arrows.' The message, one fears, seems likely to be 'lost in translation'.

Gombrich's observations on making sense of the Pioneer plaque capture very well the processes of 'decoding' outlined by semioticians in the structuralist tradition. Paired with the term 'encoding' this sometimes has the unfortunate consequence of making the processes of constructing and interpreting texts (visual, verbal or otherwise) sound too programmatic. The Pioneer plaque example shows that reading (or viewing, or listening) requires reference to relevant codes (*relevance* itself requiring hypothesis-testing). We need 'prior knowledge' of such codes in order 'to separate the code from the message'. Although with practice the process of decoding can become transparent (so that it can seem strange to say that pictures require 'reading'), the process is clearly a cognitively active one. What is 'meant' is invariably more than what is 'said' (Smith 1988; Olson 1994), so *inference* is required to 'go beyond the information given' (in the famous phrase of the American psychologist Jerome Bruner). While psychologists refer to the generation of inferences by invoking familiar social and textual 'scripts', semioticians refer to accessing social and textual codes (and sometimes to the modality judgements needed to compare these codes).

In contrast to the importance accorded to the active process of 'decoding' in this example, everyday references to communication are based on a 'transmission' model in which a sender transmits a message to a receiver – a formula which reduces meaning to explicit 'content' which resides within the text and is delivered like a parcel (Reddy 1979). This model is implicit, for instance, in the Pioneer-plaque designer's reference to the intention to 'convey ... information'. Transmission is also the basis of Claude Shannon and Warren Weaver's well-known model of communication, which makes no allowance for the importance of social codes or contexts – though ironically, to criticize that particular model for this reason would be to ignore the context of telephone engineering for which it was developed (Shannon and Weaver 1949).

Figure 6.2 shows Saussure's model of oral communication. While (for its time) it is innovatingly labelled as a 'speech circuit' and includes directional arrows indicating the involvement of both partici-pants (thus at least implying 'feedback'), it too was nevertheless a linear transmission model (albeit a 'two-track' one). Furthermore, the speaker's role was 'active' and the listener's role was 'passive' (Saussure 1983, 13). In this respect a richer model had appeared in

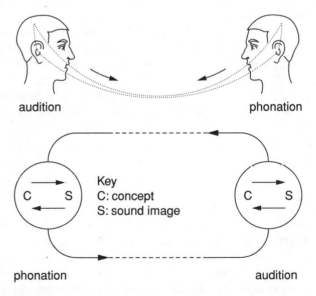

FIGURE 6.2 Saussure's speech circuit

Source: Based on Saussure 1967, 27, 28

print more than three centuries earlier. Michel de Montaigne wrote in 1580: 'Speaking is half his that speaks, and half his that hears; the last of which ought to prepare himself to receive it, according to its motion and rebound. Like tennis players, he that receives the ball, shifts and prepares, according as he sees him move who strikes the stroke, and according to the stroke it self' (*Essays*, trans. Charles Cotton, 1685: 'Of experience' III, 13). The anticipation involved is clearly 'active': you could never return a serve if you simply stood still waiting for the ball. Saussure's 'speech circuit' was based on the notion that comprehension on the part of the listener is a kind of mirror of the speaker's initial process of expressing a thought (ibid., 11–13; Harris 1987, 22–5, 204–18). The shortcomings of this isomorphism would perhaps have been clearer if Saussure had been attempting to account for a broader range of forms of communication than speech alone. A dyslexic student once asked me, 'Why is it so important to read so fast when the writer spent so long writing it?' The answer, of course, is that a significant part of the power of the written word lies in this asymmetry (for the shortcomings of the mirror model for the medium of film, see Larry Gross's critique in Worth 1981, 9–11). Given the prominence of the concept of the code in Saussurean-inspired semiotics, it is also surprising that in Saussure's model there is only the briefest of allusions to the speaker's use of 'the code provided by the language', together with the implicit assumption that a fixed code is shared – a very monolithic conception (Saussure 1983, 14; Harris 1987, 216, 230).

In 1960 another structuralist linguist – Roman Jakobson (drawing on work by Bühler dating from the 1930s) – proposed a model of interpersonal verbal communication which moved beyond the basic transmission model of communication (see Figure 6.3; cf. Eco 1976, 141). Using the somewhat programmatic language mentioned earlier, Jakobson outlines what he regards as the six 'constitutive factors . . . in any act of verbal communication' thus:

> The *addresser* sends a *message* to the *addressee*. To be operative the message requires a *context* referred to ('referent' in another, somewhat ambivalent, nomenclature), seizable by the addressee, and either verbal or capable of being verbalized, a

context

message
addresser -------------- addressee
contact

code

FIGURE 6.3 Jakobson's model of communication

Source: Jakobson 1960, 353

code fully, or at least partially, common to the addresser and
addressee (or in other words, to the encoder and decoder of
the message); and finally, a *contact*, a physical channel and
psychological connection between the addresser and the
addressee, enabling both of them to stay in communication.

(Jakobson 1960, 353)

Jakobson established the principle already noted that we cannot make
sense of signs without relating them to relevant codes. In response
to Bertrand Russell's point that 'no one can understand the word
"cheese" unless he has a nonlinguistic acquaintance with cheese',
Jakobson replied that (likewise) 'the meaning of the word "cheese"
cannot be inferred from a nonlinguistic acquaintance with cheddar
or with camembert without the assistance of the verbal code'
(Jakobson 1958, 261). He noted that 'the efficiency of a speech event
demands the use of a common code by its participants' (Jakobson
1956, 72). However, his model of linguistic codes was not monolithic. He argued that whereas Saussure had posited 'the delusive
fiction' of 'the uniformity of the code', 'as a rule, everyone belongs
simultaneously to several speech communities of different radius and
capacity; any overall code is multiform and comprises a hierarchy
of diverse subcodes freely chosen by the speaker with regard to the
variable functions of the message, to its addressee, and to the relation between the interlocutors' (Jakobson 1971d, 719). It should
already be apparent that although Jakobson was greatly influenced
by Peirce, he did not owe his emphasis on encoding and decoding

to him. In Peirce 'there is no reflection at all, to speak of, on the system to which any individual sign belongs or on the process that produces it . . . His interest is neither in the construction of the message nor in the larger code from which its components are drawn' (Bruss 1978, 93). The Peircean model does not incorporate a code at all. Peirce's influence is nevertheless evident in another key aspect of Jakobson's model of communication.

All codes are social in the sense that their conventions have no existence apart from their application in the social world, but as we have seen Saussure declined his own challenge to study 'the role of signs as part of social life' and proceeded to exclude social life from his monolithic linguistic code. Jakobson's reference to 'speech communities' is one indicator that he did not share Saussure's desire to exclude reference to the social world. However, his model does not account for acts of communication purely in terms of encoding and decoding. Crucially, it highlighted the importance not only of systemic codes but also of the *contexts* involved. Jakobson noted that 'there are two references which serve to interpret the sign – one to the code, and the other to the context' (Jakobson 1956, 75; cf. 1963b, 114), and insisted that 'it is not enough to know the code in order to grasp the message . . . you need to know the context' (Jakobson 1953, 233). We have already seen in Chapter 4 that the identification of irony requires reference to contextual factors in the form of perceived intent and truth status. Like 'meaning', 'context' can be a slippery term and as a linguist Jakobson was initially wary of trespassing too far beyond the notion of *linguistic* contexts into the more *philosophical* territory of referentiality. For instance, he noted that 'truth values . . . as far as they are . . . "extralinguistic entities," obviously exceed the bounds of . . . linguistics in general'. Nevertheless, unlike Saussure, it was clear that he would not seek to exclude from his concerns 'the question of relations between the word and the world' (Jakobson 1960, 351). 'Speech events' take place in the social world, and Jakobson was a linguist who emphasized the social functions of language. He quickly recognized the importance of both 'the place occupied by the given messages within the context of surrounding messages . . . and . . . the relation of the given message to the universe of discourse' (Jakobson 1968, 697).

The philosophical concept of a *universe of discourse* (found also in Peirce) refers to a frame of reference shared by participants in an act of communication. 'Linguistics is likely to explore all possible problems of relation between discourse and the "universe of discourse": what of this universe is verbalized by a given discourse and how it is verbalized' (Jakobson 1960, 351). Later he ventured further, noting that 'the sometimes equivalent term "context" means not only the verbalized context but also the partly or nonverbalized context' (Jakobson 1973, 319). By 1972 he felt able to issue a unequivocal declaration on this issue:

> Fourteen years ago [1958], Quine [the American philosopher] and I agreed diplomatically that the signified (*signatum*) belonged to linguistics and the referent (*designatum*) to logic. Now I think that the referent also belongs to linguistics . . . This does not mean to linguistics only, but it has a linguistic aspect, namely, what we call contextual meaning. The general meaning belongs to semantics; the contextual meaning, given by the whole context, by the universe of discourse, is also a linguistic fact.
>
> (Jakobson 1973, 320)

Elsewhere, he was even more explicit – adding that contextual meaning included *situational* meanings (Jakobson 1972, 44). In definitively including context as well as code, Jakobson's model moves beyond the original Saussurean framework, which 'bracketed' any referential context outside the sign-system itself. It also supports not only the symbolic mode featured in both the Saussurean and the Peircean models but also the referential character of Peirce's iconic and indexical modes. However problematic Jakobson's model of the sign may be regarded as being, his model of communication constitutes a conceptual bridge between the two major semiotic traditions. While the determination of meaning in the Saussurean model depends upon the system of relations within a code and in the Peircean model upon a referential context, only the Jakobsonian model provides for both.

Type	Oriented towards	Function	Example
referential	context	imparting information	It's raining.
expressive	addresser	expressing feelings or attitudes	It's bloody pissing down again!
conative	addressee	influencing behaviour	Wait here till it stops raining!
phatic	contact	establishing or maintaining social relationships	Nasty weather again, isn't it?
metalingual	code	referring to the nature of the interaction (e.g. genre)	This is the weather forecast.
poetic	message	foregrounding textual features	It droppeth as the gentle rain from heaven.

TABLE 6.4 Jakobson's six functions of language

Jakobson, a functionalist as well as a structuralist, proposed that each of the six factors in his model of verbal communication determines a different function of language (ibid.; see Table 6.4; cf. Lévi-Strauss 1969, 29–30 on music and Ashwin 1989 on graphic design). Unlike the basic transmission model, Jakobson's model thus avoids the reduction of language to purely informational communication. Though one of the potential functions is referential (or informational), this function is not always foregrounded. Jakobson argued that in any given situation several functions may operate in a 'hierarchical order', but that a dominant function influences the general character of the 'message'. For instance, the *poetic* function (which is intended to refer to any creative use of language rather than simply to poetry) highlights 'the palpability of signs', undermining any sense of a natural or transparent connection between a signifier and a referent (Jakobson 1960, 356). In Jakobson's model, messages and meanings cannot be isolated from such constitutive factors. He added that 'the question of presence and hierarchy of those basic functions which we observe in language ... must be applied also to the other semiotic systems ... A parallel investigation of verbal, musical, pictorial, choreographic, theatrical, and cinematographic arts belongs to the most imperative and fruitful duties of semiotic science' (Jakobson 1970, 458).

As we have seen, in contrast to the earlier structuralist model, Jakobson allocated a role for a situational context and stressed the importance of *parole* – the contingency of 'speech events'. However, his embedded *functions* are systemic representations of 'frozen' human purposes and he did not address the dynamic, shifting purposes of those involved in particular acts of communication or the social frameworks within which communication occurs. His theoretical frameworks opened up new pathways but he left to sociolinguists and socio-semiotic researchers the task of investigating specific, socially situated acts of communication: this, in practice, was beyond the scope of even the most radical of the original structural linguists.

While these earlier models had focused on *interpersonal communication*, in an essay entitled 'Encoding/decoding' (Hall 1980, originally published as 'Encoding and decoding in television discourse' in 1973), the British sociologist Stuart Hall proposed a model of *mass communication* which highlighted the importance of signifying practices within relevant codes. A televisual text emerged as 'meaningful' discourse from processes of encoding and decoding. Each of these processes involved 'meaning structures' which consisted of 'frameworks of knowledge', 'relations of production' and 'technical infrastructure'. Despite the apparent symmetry, Hall rejected textual determinism, noting that 'decodings do not follow

inevitably from encodings' (Hall 1980, 136). Hall thus gave a significant role to the 'decoder' as well as to the 'encoder' and presented
communication as a socially contingent practice. Mass media codes
offer their readers social identities which some may adopt as their
own. But readers do not necessarily accept such codes. Where those
involved in communicating do not share common codes and social
positions, decodings are likely to be different from the encoder's
intended meaning. Umberto Eco uses the term 'aberrant decoding'
to refer to a text which has been decoded by means of a different
code from that used to encode it (Eco 1965). We will return shortly
to how Hall incorporated into his model a series of alternative
'reading positions' for decoders.

This necessarily brief review of key structuralist models of
communication has shown that while systemic codes (and the
processes of encoding and decoding) are a central feature, post-
Saussurean semiotics also came to recognize the importance of
contexts (including social contexts) in the determination of meanings. Implicit in such models (for instance in the reference of
Jakobson's functions to the roles and modes of relation of the
'addresser' and the 'addressee') there are also implications for the
construction of social identities. In the structuralist tradition, through
the processes of human communication, the structures of language
and texts came to be seen as involved in 'positioning the subject'.

THE POSITIONING OF THE SUBJECT

'A sign ... addresses somebody,' Charles Peirce declared (Peirce
1931–58, 2.228). Signs 'address' us within particular codes. A genre
is a semiotic code within which we are 'positioned' as 'ideal readers'
through the use of particular 'modes of address'. Modes of address
can be defined as the ways in which relations between addresser and
addressee are constructed in a text. In order to communicate, a
producer of any text must make some assumptions about an intended
audience; reflections of such assumptions may be discerned in the
text (advertisements offer particularly clear examples of this).

Rather than a specifically semiotic concept, 'the positioning of
the subject' is a structuralist notion – although it is absent from early

structuralist discourse (Hall 1996, 46); Saussure did not discuss it. It is a concept which has been widely adopted by semioticians and so it needs to be explored in this context. The term 'subject' needs some initial explanation. In 'theories of subjectivity' a distinction is made between 'the subject' and 'the individual'. While the *individual* is an actual person, the *subject* is a set of roles constructed by dominant cultural and ideological values (e.g. in terms of class, age, gender and ethnicity). Ideology turns individuals into subjects. Subjects are not actual people but exist only in relation to interpretive practices and are constructed through the use of signs. The psychoanalytical theorist Jacques Lacan undermined the humanist notion of a unified and consistent subject. The individual can occupy multiple subject positions, some of them contradictory, and 'identity' can be seen as the interaction of subject-positions.

According to theorists of textual positioning, understanding the meaning of a text involves taking on an appropriate ideological identity. In order to make sense of the signs in a text the reader is obliged to adopt a 'subject-position' in relation to it. For instance, to understand an advertisement we would have to adopt the identity of a consumer who desired the advertised product. Some theorists argue that this position already exists within the structure and codes of the text. 'Narratives or images always imply or construct a position or positions from which they are to be read or viewed' (Johnson 1996, 101). What Colin MacCabe famously called the 'classic realist text' is orchestrated to effect closure: contradictions are suppressed and the reader is encouraged to adopt a position from which everything seems 'obvious' (MacCabe 1974). This stance assumes both that a text is homogeneous and that it has only one meaning – that which was intended by its makers – whereas contemporary theorists contend that there may be several alternative (even contradictory) subject-positions from which a text may make sense. While these may sometimes be anticipated by the author, they are not necessarily built into the text itself. Not every reader is the 'ideal reader' envisaged by the producer(s) of the text. The phrase, 'the positioning of the subject' implies a 'necessary "subjection" to the text' (Johnson 1996, 101) and is thus problematic since there is always some freedom of interpretation. We may for instance choose to regard a poorly translated set of instructions for assembling flat-pack furniture as a text constructed purely for our amusement.

The notion that the human subject is 'constituted' (constructed) by pre-given structures (such as texts) is a general feature of structuralism. It constitutes a radical opposition to the liberal humanist (or 'bourgeois') stance which presents society as 'consisting of "free" individuals whose social determination results from their pre-given essences like "talented", "efficient", "lazy", "profligate", etc.' (Coward and Ellis 1977, 2). The French neo-Marxist philosopher Louis Althusser (1918–90) was the first ideological theorist to give prominence to the notion of the subject. For him, ideology was a system of representations of reality offering individuals certain subject positions which they could occupy. He famously declared that 'what is represented in ideology is . . . not the system of real relations which govern the existence of individuals, but the imaginary relation of these individuals to the real relations in which they live' (Althusser 1971, 155). Individuals are transformed into subjects through the ideological mechanism which he called *interpellation* (Althusser 1971, 174).

The Althusserian concept of interpellation is used by Marxist media theorists to explain the political function of mass media texts. According to this view, the subject (viewer, listener, reader) is constituted by the text, and the power of the mass media resides in their ability to position the subject in such a way that their representations are taken to be reflections of everyday reality. Such structuralist framings of positioning reflect a stance of *textual determinism* which has been challenged by contemporary social semioticians who tend to emphasize the 'polysemic' nature of texts (their plurality of meanings) together with the diversity of their use and interpretation by different audiences ('multiaccentuality'). However, a distinction may be appropriate here between *message* and *code*. While resistance at the level of the message is always possible, resistance at the level of the code is generally much more difficult when the code is a dominant one. The familiarity of the codes in realist texts (especially photographic and filmic texts) leads us to routinely 'suspend our disbelief' in the form (even if not necessarily in the manifest content). Recognition of the familiar (in the guise of the natural) repeatedly confirms our conventional ways of seeing and thus reinforces our sense of self while at the same time invisibly contributing to its *construction*. 'When we say "I see (what the image means)" this act simultaneously installs us in a place of knowledge and slips us into place as subject to this meaning . . . All the viewer need do is fall into place as subject' (Nichols 1981, 38). Falling into place in a realist text is a pleasurable experience which few would wish to disrupt with reflective analysis (which would throw the security of our sense of self into question). Thus we freely submit to the ideological processes which construct our sense of ourselves as free-thinking individuals.

A primary textual code involved in the construction of the subject is that of *genre*. Genres are ostensibly neutral, functioning to make *form* (the conventions of the genre) more transparent to those familiar with the genre, foregrounding the distinctive *content* of individual texts. Certainly genre provides an important frame of reference which helps readers to identify, select and interpret texts (as well as helping writers to compose economically within the medium). However, a genre can also be seen as embodying certain values and ideological assumptions and as seeking to establish a particular worldview. Changes in genre conventions may both reflect and help to shape the dominant ideological climate of the time. Some Marxist commentators see genre as an instrument of social control which reproduces the dominant ideology. Within this perspective, the genre is seen as positioning the audience in order to naturalize the reassuringly conservative ideologies which are typically embedded in the text. Certainly, genres are far from being ideologically neutral. Different genres produce different positionings of the subject which are reflected in their modes of address. Tony Thwaites and his colleagues in Australia note that in many television crime dramas in the tradition of *The Saint*, *Hart to Hart*, and *Murder, She Wrote*,

> Genteel or well-to-do private investigators work for the wealthy, solving crimes committed by characters whose social traits and behaviour patterns often type them as members of

a 'criminal class' . . . The villains receive their just rewards not so much because they break the law, but because they are entirely distinct from the law-abiding bourgeoisie. This TV genre thus reproduces a hegemonic ideology about the individual in a class society.

(Thwaites et al. 1994, 158)

Thus, over and above the specific content of the individual text, generic frameworks can be seen as involved in the construction of their readers.

Film and television add a narrative dimension to the positioning of the subject, incorporating dominant narrative devices specific to filmic media. Film theorists refer to the use of 'suture' (surgical stitching) – the 'invisible editing' of shot relationships which seeks to foreground the narrative and mask the ideological processes which shape the subjectivity of viewers. Some Lacanian theorists argue that in the context of conventional narrative (with its possibilities of identification and opposition), the unique character of the cinema (e.g. watching a large bright screen in the dark) offers us the seductive sense of a 'return' to the pre-linguistic 'mirror-phase' of the 'imaginary' in which the self was constructed (Nichols 1981, 300).

MODES OF ADDRESS

The *modes of address* employed by texts are influenced primarily by three interrelated factors:

- **textual context**: the conventions of the genre and of a specific syntagmatic structure;
- **social context** (e.g. the presence or absence of the producer of the text, the scale and social composition of the audience, institutional and economic factors); and
- **technological constraints** (features of the medium employed).

Modes of address differ in their directness, their formality and their narrative point of view. The various narrative points of view in literature are as follows:

- third-person narration
  - *omniscient* narrator
    - *intrusive* (e.g. Dickens)
    - self-effacing (e.g. Flaubert)
  - *selective* point of view of character(s) presented by self-effacing narrator (e.g. Henry James)
- *first-person* narration: narrated directly by a character (e.g. Salinger's *Catcher in the Rye*)

In television and film drama the camera typically offers the viewer a relatively detached perspective on a scene which is independent of any single character in the narrative. This can be seen as resembling the 'third-person' narrative style of an omniscient and self-effacing narrator – which of course does not necessarily entail such a narrator 'revealing all' to the viewer (indeed, in genres such as the 'whodunit' and the thriller the positioning of the subject is most obvious in relation to what information is withheld and when it is released). Camera treatment is called 'subjective' when the camera shows us events as if from a particular participant's visual point of view (encouraging viewers to identify with that person's way of seeing events or even to feel like an eye-witness to the events themselves). This first-person style in filmic media is rarely sustained, however (or we would never see that character). The point of view is *selective* when we are mainly concerned with a single character but the camerawork is not subjective. Voice-overs are sometimes used for first-person narration by a character in a drama; they are also common as a third-person narrative mode in genres such as documentary. Where first-person commentary shifts from person to person within a text, this produces 'polyvocality' (multiple voices) – contrasting strongly with the interpretive omniscience of 'univocal' narrative which offers a single reading of an event. Where the agency of a narrator is backgrounded, events or facts deceptively seem to 'speak for themselves'.

Modes of address also differ in their *directness*. In linguistic codes, this is related to whether 'you' are explicitly addressed, which in literary modes is quite rare. In Laurence Sterne's highly 'unconventional' novel *Tristram Shandy* (1760), one chapter begins thus: 'How could you, Madam, be so inattentive in reading the last chapter?' (vol. 1, ch. 20). Realist fiction avoids such alienatory strategies. In representational visual codes directness is related to whether or not a depicted person appears to look directly at the viewer (in the case of television, film and photography, via the camera lens). A direct gaze simulates interaction with each individual viewer (an impossibility, of course, outside one-to-one communicative media, but a feature of 'cam-to-cam' communication on the internet or in video-conferences). In film and television, directness of address is reflected in linguistic codes as well as camerawork. Films and (especially) television programmes within the documentary genre frequently employ a disembodied voice-over which directly addresses the audience, as do television commercials. On television, directness of address is also a matter of the extent to which participants look directly into the camera lens. In this way too, commercials frequently include direct address. As for programmes, in a book entitled *The Grammar of Television*, an industry professional warned: 'Never let a performer look straight into the lens of a camera unless it is necessary to give the impression that he is speaking directly to the viewer personally' (Davis 1960, 54). In television programmes, a direct mode of address is largely confined to newsreaders, weather forecasters, presenters and interviewers – which is why it seems so strange on the rare occasions when we notice an interviewee glancing at the camera lens. In short, people from outside the television industry are seldom allowed to talk to us directly on television. The head of state or the leader of a political party are among the few outsiders allowed to look directly at the viewer, and then typically only within special genres such as a party political broadcast or an 'address to the nation'. Direct address reflects the power of the addresser and the use of this signifier typically signifies 'authority'. Direct address is rare in the cinema, and when it is used it tends to be for comic effect. *Indirect address* is the principal mode employed in conventional narrative, masking authorial agency in the interests of foregrounding the story. Conventional film and television drama, of course, depends on the illusion that the participants do not know they are being watched.

Additionally, the mode of address varies in its *formality* or *social distance*. Following Edward T. Hall's distinctions, we may distinguish between 'intimate', 'personal', 'social' and 'public' (or 'impersonal') modes of address (Hall 1966; Kress and van Leeuwen 1996, 130–5). In relation to language, formality is quite closely tied to explicitness, so that intimate language tends to be minimally explicit and maximally dependent on non-verbal cues, while public language tends to reverse these features (especially in print). In usage related also to directness of address, social distance can also established through the use of loaded quasi-synonyms to reflect ideological distinctions of 'us' from 'them', as in '*I* am a patriot; *you* are a nationalist; *they* are xenophobes.'

In visual representation, social distance is related in part to *apparent proximity*. In camerawork, degrees of formality are reflected in *shot sizes* – close-ups signifying intimate or personal modes, medium shots a social mode and long shots an impersonal mode (Kress and van Leeuwen 1996, 130–5; cf. Tuchman 1978, 116–20). In visual media, the represented physical distance between the observed and the observer often reflects attempts to encourage feelings of emotional involvement or critical detachment in the viewer. The cultural variability of the degree of formality signified by different zones of proximity was highlighted in relation to face-to-face interaction in Edward T. Hall's influential book – *The Hidden Dimension* (Hall 1966). Proximity is not the only marker of social distance in the visual media: *angles of view* are also significant. High angles (looking down on a depicted person from above) are widely interpreted as making that person look small and insignificant, and low angles (looking up at them from below) are said to make them look powerful and superior (Messaris 1997, 34–5 and 1994, 158; Kress and van Leeuwen 1996, 146).

Note that while the significations such as those listed in relation to photographic and filmic modes of address may represent the currently dominant, conventional or 'default' linkages of signifiers and signifieds, no programmatic decoding based on a 'dictionary' of one-to-one correspondences is possible – in analogue codes in particular there is a sliding relationship between signifiers and signifieds which may be anchored in various ways by the codes of the particular textual systems in which they are employed (Nichols 1981, 108).

Textual codes construct possible reading positions for the addresser and addressee. Building upon Jakobson's model Thwaites *et al.* define 'the functions of address' in terms of the construction of such subjects and of relationships between them.

- *expressive function*: the construction of an addresser (authorial persona);
- *conative function*: the construction of an addressee (ideal reader);
- *phatic function*: the construction of a relationship between these two.

(Thwaites et al. 1994, 14–15)

A textual code can be defined as a set of ways of reading which its producers and readers share. Not everyone has access to the relevant codes for reading (or writing) a text. The phatic function excludes as well as includes certain readers. Those who share the code are members of the same 'interpretive community' (Fish 1980, 167ff., 335–6, 338). Familiarity with particular codes is related to social position, in terms of such factors as class, ethnicity, nationality, education, occupation, political affiliation, age, gender and sexuality.

READING POSITIONS

Stuart Hall stressed the role of social positioning in the interpretation of mass media texts by different social groups. In a model deriving from Frank Parkin's 'meaning systems', Hall suggested three hypothetical interpretive codes or positions for the reader of a text (Parkin 1972; Hall 1973 and 1980, 136–8; Morley 1980, 20–1, 134–7 and 1983, 109–10):

- *dominant (or 'hegemonic') reading*: the reader fully shares the text's code and accepts and reproduces the *preferred reading* (a reading which may not have been the result of any conscious intention on the part of the author(s)) – in such a stance the code seems natural and transparent;

- *negotiated reading*: the reader partly shares the text's code and broadly accepts the preferred reading, but sometimes resists and modifies it in a way which reflects their own position, experiences and interests (local and personal conditions may be seen as exceptions to the general rule) – this position involves contradictions;
- *oppositional ('counter-hegemonic') reading*: the reader, whose social situation places them in a directly oppositional relation to the dominant code, understands the preferred reading but does not share the text's code and rejects this reading, bringing to bear an alternative frame of reference (radical, feminist, etc.) (e.g. when watching a television broadcast produced on behalf of a political party they normally vote *against*).

This framework is based on the assumption that the latent meaning of the text is encoded in the dominant code. This is a stance which tends to reify the medium and to downplay conflicting tendencies within texts. Also, some critics have raised the question of how a 'preferred reading' can be established. Poststructuralist social semioticians would urge us not to seek such a reading within the form and structure of the text. Just as a reductive reading of Hall's model could lead to the reification of a medium or genre, it could also encourage the essentializing of readers (e.g. as 'the resistant reader') whereas reading positions are multiple, dynamic and contradictory. Despite the various criticisms, Hall's model has been very influential, particularly among British theorists.

The British sociologist David Morley employed this model in his studies of how different social groups interpreted a television programme (Morley 1980). Morley demonstrated differential access to the textual codes of a programme in the 'news magazine' genre (Morley 1980). He insisted that he did *not* take a *social determinist* position in which individual 'decodings' of a text are reduced to a direct consequence of social class position. 'It is always a question of how social position, as it is articulated through particular discourses, produces specific kinds of readings or decodings. These readings can then be seen to be patterned by the way in which the structure of access to different discourses is determined by social position' (Morley 1983, 113; cf. Morley 1992, 89–90). Different interpretive communities have access to different textual and interpretive codes (which offer them the potential to understand and sometimes also to produce texts which employ them). Morley added that any individual or group might operate different decoding strategies in relation to different *topics* and different *contexts*. A person might make 'oppositional' readings of the same material in one context and 'dominant' readings in other contexts (Morley 1981, 9 and 1992, 135). He noted that in interpreting viewers' readings of mass media texts attention should be paid not only to the issue of *agreement* (acceptance/rejection) but to *comprehension, relevance* and *enjoyment* (Morley 1981, 10 and 1992, 126–7, 136). There is thus considerable scope for variety in the ways in which individuals engage with such codes.

The interpretation of signs by their users can be seen from a semiotic perspective as having three levels, loosely related to C. W. Morris's framework for branches of semiotics (Morris 1938/1970, 6–7).

1. *syntactic*: recognition of the sign (in relation to other signs);
2. *semantic*: comprehension of the intended meaning of the sign;
3. *pragmatic*: interpretation of the sign in terms of relevance, agreement, etc.

The most basic task of interpretation involves the identification of what a sign represents (denotation) and may require some degree of familiarity with the medium and the representational codes involved. This is particularly obvious in the case of language, but may also apply in the case of visual media such as photographs and films. Some would not grant this low-level process the label of 'interpretation' at all, limiting this term to such processes as the extraction of a 'moral' from a narrative text. However, some theorists take the stance that comprehension and interpretation are inseparable (e.g. Mick and Politi 1989, 85).

Semiotics has not been widely applied to the *practice* of decoding. While social semiotics stakes a claim to the study of situated semiotic practices, research in this area is dominated by ethnographic and phenomenological methodologies and is seldom closely allied to semiotic perspectives (though there is no necessary incompatibility). A notable exception is the research of David Glen Mick in the field of advertising (Mick and Politi 1989, McQuarrie and Mick 1992, Mick and Buhl 1992).

Having explored some of the theoretical issues concerning the interactions between makers, texts and users we turn now to theories of *intertextuality* – which concern interactions between texts.

INTERTEXTUALITY

Although Saussure stressed the importance of the relationship of signs to each other, one of the weaknesses of structuralist textual analysis is the tendency to treat individual texts as discrete, closed-off entities and to focus exclusively on internal structures. Even where texts are studied as a 'corpus' (a unified collection), the overall generic structures tend themselves to be treated as strictly bounded. The structuralist's first analytical task is often described as being to delimit the boundaries of the system (what is to be included and what excluded), which is logistically understandable but ontologically problematic. Even remaining within the structuralist paradigm, we may note that codes transcend structures. The semiotic notion of 'intertextuality' introduced by the literary theorist Julia Kristeva is associated primarily with poststructuralist theorists. Kristeva referred to texts in terms of two axes: a *horizontal axis* connecting the author and reader of a text, and a *vertical axis*, which connects the text to other texts (Kristeva 1980, 69). Uniting these two axes are shared codes: every text and every reading depends on prior codes. Kristeva declared that 'every text is from the outset under the jurisdiction of other discourses which impose a universe on it' (Kristeva 1974, 388–9; translation by Culler 1981, 105). She argued that rather than confining our attention to the structure of a text we should study its 'structuration' (how the structure came into being). This involved siting it 'within the totality of previous or synchronic texts' of which it was a 'transformation' (Kristeva 1970, 67–9; translation by Coward and Ellis 1977, 52).

Intertextuality refers to far more than the 'influences' of writers on each other. For structuralists, language has powers which not only exceed individual control but also determine subjectivity. Structuralists sought to counter what they saw as a deep-rooted bias in literary and aesthetic thought which emphasized the uniqueness of both texts and authors. The ideology of individualism (with its associated concepts of authorial 'originality', 'creativity' and 'expressiveness') is a post-Renaissance legacy which reached its peak in Romanticism but which still dominates popular discourse. 'Authorship' was a historical invention. Concepts such as 'authorship' and 'plagiarism' did not exist in the Middle Ages. Saussure emphasized that language is a system which pre-exists the individual speaker. For structuralists and poststructuralists alike we are (to use the stock Althusserian formulation) 'always already' positioned by semiotic systems – and most clearly by language. Contemporary theorists have referred to the subject as being *spoken by* language. Barthes declares that 'it is language which speaks, not the author; to write is . . . to reach the point where only language acts, "performs", and not "me"' (Barthes 1977a, 143). When writers write they are also *written*. To communicate we must utilize existing concepts and conventions. Consequently, while our intention to communicate and *what* we intend to communicate are both important to us as individuals, meaning cannot be reduced to authorial 'intention'. To define meaning in terms of authorial intention is the so-called 'intentional fallacy' identified by W. K. Wimsatt and M. C. Beardsley of the 'new critical' tendency in literary criticism (Wimsatt and Beardsley 1954). We may, for instance, communicate things without being aware of doing so. As Michel de Montaigne wrote in 1580, 'the work, by its own force and fortune, may second the workman, and sometimes out-strip him, beyond his invention and knowledge' (*Essays*, trans. Charles Cotton, 1685: 'Of the art of conferring' III, 8). Furthermore, in conforming to any of the conventions of our medium, we act as a medium for perpetuating such conventions.

PROBLEMATIZING AUTHORSHIP

Theorists of intertextuality problematize the status of 'authorship', treating the writer of a text as the orchestrator of what Roland Barthes refers to as the 'already-written' rather than as its originator (Barthes 1973, 21). 'A text is . . . a multidimensional space in which a variety of writings, none of them original, blend and clash. The text is a tissue of quotations . . . The writer can only imitate a gesture that is always anterior, never original. His only power is to mix writings, to counter the ones with the others, in such a way as never to rest on any one of them' (Barthes 1977a, 146). In his book *S/Z*, Barthes deconstructed Balzac's short story *Sarrasine*, seeking to 'deoriginate' the text – to demonstrate that it reflects many voices, not just that of Balzac (Barthes 1973). It would be pure idealism to regard Balzac as 'expressing himself' in language since we do not precede language but are *produced* by it. For Barthes, writing did not involve an instrumental process of recording pre-formed thoughts and feelings (working from signified to signifier) but was a matter of working with the signifiers and letting the signifieds take care of themselves (Chandler 1995, 60ff.).

One of the founding texts of semiotics, the *Course in General Linguistics*, itself problematizes the status of authorship. While the text published in French by Payot in Paris bears the name of Ferdinand de Saussure as its author, it was in fact not the work of Saussure at all. Saussure died in 1913 without leaving any detailed outline of his theories on general linguistics or on what he called semiology. The *Course* was first published posthumously in 1916 and was assembled by Charles Bally and Albert Sechehaye ('with the collaboration of Albert Riedlinger') on the basis of the notes which had been taken by at least seven students, together with a few personal notes which had been written by Saussure himself. The students' notes referred to three separate courses on general linguistics which Saussure had taught at the University of Geneva over the period of 1906–11. Saussure thus neither wrote nor read the book which bears his name, although we continually imply that he did by attaching his name to it. It is hardly surprising that various contradictions and inconsistencies and a lack of cohesion in the text have often been noted. Indeed, some commentators have suggested that the *Course* does not always offer 'a faithful reflection' of Saussure's ideas – a hardly unproblematic notion (Saussure 1983, xii). On top of all this, English readers have two competing translations of the

Course (Saussure 1974; Saussure 1983). Each translation is, of course, a re-authoring. No neutral translation is possible, since languages involve different value systems – as is noted in the *Course* itself. Nor can specialist translators be expected to be entirely disinterested. Furthermore, anyone who treats the *Course* as a founding text in semiotics does so by effectively 'rewriting' it, since its treatment of semiology is fragmentary. Finally, we are hardly short of commentaries to bring both this foundational text and us as readers into line with the interpreter's own theories (e.g. Harris 1987; Thibault 1997).

READING AS REWRITING

This rather extreme but important example thus serves to highlight that every reading is always a rewriting. It is by no means an isolated example. The first critique of the ideas outlined in the *Course* was in a book entitled *Marxism and the Philosophy of Language* which was published in Russian in 1929 under the name Valentin Voloshinov, but it has subsequently been claimed that this book had in fact been written by Mikhail Bakhtin, and the authorship of this text is still contested (Morris 1994, 1). Readers, in any case, construct authors. They perform a kind of amateur archaeology, reconstructing them from textual shards while at the same time feeling able to say about anyone whose writings they have read, 'I *know* her (or him).' The reader's 'Roland Barthes' (for example) never existed. If one had total access to everything he had ever written throughout his life it would be marked by contradiction. The best we can do to reduce such contradictions is to construct yet more authors, such as 'the early Barthes' and 'the later Barthes'. Barthes died in 1981, but every invocation of his name creates another Barthes.

In 1968 Barthes announced 'the death of the author' and 'the birth of the reader', declaring that 'a text's unity lies not in its origin but in its destination' (Barthes 1977a, 148). The framing of texts by other texts has implications not only for their *writers* but also for their *readers*. Fredric Jameson argued that 'texts come before us as the always-already-read; we apprehend them through the sedimented layers of previous interpretations, or – if the text is brand-new –

through the sedimented reading habits and categories developed by those inherited interpretive traditions' (cited in Rodowick 1994, 286, where it was, with delicious irony in this context, cited from Tony Bennett). A famous text has a history of readings. 'All literary works . . . are "rewritten", if only unconsciously, by the societies which read them' (Eagleton 1983, 12). No one today – even for the first time – can read a famous novel or poem, look at a famous painting, drawing or sculpture, listen to a famous piece of music or watch a famous play or film without being conscious of the contexts in which the text had been reproduced, drawn upon, alluded to, parodied and so on. Such contexts constitute a primary frame which the reader cannot avoid drawing upon in interpreting the text.

NO TEXT IS AN ISLAND

The concept of intertextuality reminds us that each text exists in relation to others. In fact, texts owe more to other texts than to their own makers. Michel Foucault declared that:

> The frontiers of a book are never clear-cut: beyond the title, the first lines and the last full stop, beyond its internal configuration and its autonomous form, it is caught up in a system of references to other books, other texts, other sentences: it is a node within a network . . . The book is not simply the object that one holds in one's hands . . . Its unity is variable and relative.
>
> (Foucault 1974, 23)

Texts are framed by others in many ways. Most obvious are formal frames: a television programme, for instance, may be part of a series and part of a genre (such as *soap* or *sitcom)*. Our understanding of any individual text relates to such framings. Texts provide contexts within which other texts may be created and interpreted. The art historian Ernst Gombrich goes further, arguing that all art, however naturalistic, is 'a manipulation of vocabulary' rather than a reflection of the world (Gombrich 1982, 70, 78, 100). Texts draw upon multiple codes from wider contexts – both textual and social. The assignment of a text to a genre provides the interpreter of the text with a key intertextual framework. Genre theory is an important field in its own right, and genre theorists do not necessarily embrace semiotics. Within semiotics genres can be seen as sign-systems or codes – conventionalized but dynamic structures. Each example of a genre utilizes conventions which link it to other members of that genre. Such conventions are at their most obvious in 'spoof' versions of the genre. But intertextuality is also reflected in the fluidity of genre boundaries and in the blurring of genres and their functions which is reflected in such recent coinages as 'advertorials', 'infomercials', 'edutainment', 'docudrama' and 'faction' (a blend of 'fact' and 'fiction').

The debts of a text to other texts are seldom acknowledged (other than in the scholarly apparatus of academic writing). This serves to further the mythology of authorial 'originality'. However, some texts allude directly to each other – as in 'remakes' of films, extra-diegetic references to the media in the animated cartoon *The Simpsons*, and many amusing contemporary TV ads. This is a particularly self-conscious form of intertextuality: it credits its audience with the necessary experience to make sense of such allusions and offers them the pleasure of recognition. By alluding to other texts and other media this practice reminds us that we are in a mediated reality, so it can also be seen as an alienatory mode which runs counter to the dominant realist tradition which focuses on persuading the audience to believe in the ongoing reality of the narrative. It appeals to the pleasures of critical detachment rather than of emotional involvement.

In order to make sense of many contemporary advertisements one needs to be familiar with others in the same series. Expectations are established by reference to one's previous experience in looking at related advertisements. Modern visual advertisements make extensive use of intertextuality in this way. Sometimes there is no direct reference to the product at all. Instant identification of the appropriate interpretive code serves to identify the interpreter of the advertisement as a member of an exclusive club, with each act of interpretation serving to renew one's membership.

Links also cross the boundaries of formal frames, for instance, in sharing topics with treatments within other genres (the theme of war is found in a range of genres such as action-adventure film, documentary, news, current affairs). Some genres are shared by several media: the genres of *soap*, *game show* and *phone-in* are found on both television and radio; the genre of the *news report* is found on TV, radio and in newspapers; the *advertisement* appears in all mass media forms. Texts in the genre of the *trailer* are directly tied to specific texts within or outside the same medium. The genre of the *programme listing* exists within the medium of print (listings magazines, newspapers) to support the media of TV, radio and film. TV soaps generate substantial coverage in popular newspapers, magazines and books; the 'magazine' format was adopted by TV and radio. And so on.

The notion of intertextuality problematizes the idea of a text having boundaries and questions the dichotomy of 'inside' and 'outside': where does a text 'begin' and 'end'? What is 'text' and what is 'context'? The medium of television highlights this issue: it is productive to think of television in terms of a concept which Raymond Williams called 'flow' rather than as a series of discrete texts (Williams 1974, 86, 93). Much the same applies to the World Wide Web, where hypertext links on a page can link it directly to many others. However, texts in any medium can be thought of in similar terms. The boundaries of texts are permeable. Each text exists within a vast 'society of texts' in various genres and media: no text is an island entire of itself. A useful semiotic technique is comparison and contrast between differing treatments of similar themes (or similar treatments of different themes), *within* or *between* different genres or media.

INTRATEXTUALITY

While the term intertextuality would normally be used to refer to allusions to other texts, a related kind of allusion is what might be called 'intratextuality' – involving internal relations within the text. Within a single code (e.g. a photographic code) these would be simply syntagmatic relationships (e.g. the relationship of the image of one person to another within the same photograph). However, a text may involve several codes: a newspaper photograph, for instance, may have a caption (indeed, such an example serves to remind us that what we may choose to regard as a discrete 'text' for analysis lacks clear-cut boundaries: the notion of intertextuality emphasizes that texts have contexts).

Roland Barthes introduced the concept of *anchorage* (Barthes 1964, 38ff.). Linguistic elements can serve to 'anchor' (or constrain) the preferred readings of an image: 'to *fix* the floating chain of signi-fieds' (ibid., 39). Barthes employed this concept primarily in relation to advertisements, but it applies of course to other genres such as cap-tioned photographs, maps, narrated television and film documentaries, and cartoons and comics ('comic books' to North Americans) with their speech and thought 'balloons'. Barthes argued that the principal function of anchorage was ideological (ibid., 40). This is perhaps most obvious when photographs are used in contexts such as newspapers. Photograph captions typically present themselves as neutral labels for what self-evidently exists in the depicted world while actually serv-ing to define the terms of reference and point of view from which it is to be seen. For instance, 'It is a very common practice for the cap-tions to news photographs to tell us, in words, exactly how the sub-ject's expression *ought to be read*' (Hall 1981, 229). You may check your daily newspaper to verify this claim. Such textual anchorages can have a more subversive function, however. For instance, in the 1970s, the photographer Victor Burgin exhibited posters in the form of images appropriated from print advertisements together with his own printed text which ran counter to the intended meaning of the original ads.

Barthes used the term *relay* to describe text–image relation-ships which were 'complementary', instancing cartoons, comic strips and narrative film (Barthes 1964, 41). He did not coin a term for 'the paradoxical case where the image is constructed according to the text' (ibid., 40). Even if it were true in the 1950s and early 1960s that the verbal text was primary in the relation between texts and images, in contemporary society visual images have acquired far more importance in contexts such as advertising, so that what he called 'relay' is far more common. There are also many instances where the 'illustrative use' of an image provides anchorage for ambiguous text – as in assembly instructions for flat-pack furni-ture (note that when we talk about 'illustrating' and 'captioning' we logocentrically imply the primacy of verbal text over images). Awareness of the importance of intertextuality should lead us to examine the functions of those images and written or spoken text used in close association within a text, not only in terms of their respective codes, but also in terms of their overall rhetorical orchestration.

In media such as film, television and the World Wide Web, multiple codes are involved. As the film theorist Christian Metz put it, codes 'are not . . . added to one another, or juxtaposed in just any manner; they are organized, articulated in terms of one another in accordance with a certain order, they contract unilateral hierarchies . . . Thus a veritable *system of intercodical relations* is generated which is itself, in some sort, another code' (Metz 1971, 242). The interaction of film and soundtrack in chart music videos offers a good example of the dynamic nature of their modes of relationship and patterns of relative dominance. The codes involved in such textual systems clearly cannot be considered in isolation: the dynamic patterns of dominance between them contribute to the generation of meaning. Nor need they be assumed to be always in complete accord with each other – indeed, the interplay of codes may be particularly revealing of incoherences, ambiguities, contradictions and omissions which may offer the interpreter scope for deconstructing the text.

BRICOLAGE

Claude Lévi-Strauss's notion of the *bricoleur* who creates improvized structures by appropriating pre-existing materials which are ready to hand is now fairly well known within cultural studies (Lévi-Strauss 1962, 16–33, 35–6, 150n.; cf. Lévi-Strauss 1964). Lévi-Strauss saw 'mythical thought' as 'a kind of bricolage' (Lévi-Strauss 1962/1974, 17): 'it builds ideological castles out of the debris of what was once a social discourse' (ibid., 21n.). The *bricoleur* works with signs, constructing new arrangements by adopting existing signifieds as signifiers and 'speaking' 'through the medium of things' – by the choices made from 'limited possibilities' (ibid., 20, 21). 'The first aspect of bricolage is . . . to construct a system of paradigms with the fragments of syntagmatic chains', leading in turn to new syntagms (ibid., 150n.). 'Authorship' could be seen in similar terms.

Lévi-Strauss certainly saw artistic creation as in part a dialogue with the materials (ibid., 18, 27, 29). Logically (following Quintilian), the practice of *bricolage* can be seen as operating through several key transformations: addition, deletion, substitution and transposition. Elsewhere, I have explored *bricolage* in relation to the construction of personal home pages on the web (Chandler 2006).

TYPES AND DEGREES OF INTERTEXTUALITY

Gérard Genette proposed the term 'transtextuality' as a more inclusive term than 'intertextuality' (Genette 1997). He listed five subtypes:

1. *intertextuality*: quotation, plagiarism, allusion;
2. *paratextuality*: the relation between a text and its 'paratext' – that which surrounds the main body of the text – such as titles, headings, prefaces, epigraphs, dedications, acknowledgements, footnotes, illustrations, dustjackets, etc.;
3. *architextuality*: designation of a text as part of a genre or genres (Genette refers to designation by the text itself, but this could also be applied to its framing by readers);
4. *metatextuality*: explicit or implicit critical commentary of one text on another text (metatextuality can be hard to distinguish from the following category);
5. *hypotextuality* (Genette's term was *hypertextuality*): the relation between a text and a preceding 'hypotext' – a text or genre on which it is based but which it transforms, modifies, elaborates or extends (including parody, spoof, sequel, translation).

To such a list, computer-based *hypertextuality* should be added: text which can take the reader directly to other texts (regardless of authorship or location). This kind of intertextuality disrupts the conventional 'linearity' of texts. Reading such texts is seldom a question of following standard sequences predetermined by their authors.

It may be useful to consider the issue of 'degrees of intertextuality'. Would the 'most intertextual' text be an indistinguishable copy of another text, or would that have gone beyond what it means to be intertextual? Would the 'most intratextual' text be one which approached the impossible goal of referring only to itself? Even if no specific text is referred to, texts are written within genres and use language in ways which their authors have seldom invented. Intertextuality does not seem to be simply a continuum on a single dimension and there does not seem to be a consensus about what dimensions we should be looking for. Intertextuality is not a feature of the text alone but of the 'contract' which reading it forges between its author(s) and reader(s). Since the dominant mode of producing texts seems to involve masking their debts, *reflexivity* seems to be an important issue – we need to consider how *marked* the intertextuality is. Some defining features of intertextuality might include the following:

- *reflexivity*: how reflexive (or self-conscious) the use of intertextuality seems to be (if reflexivity is important to what it means to be intertextual, then presumably an indistinguishable copy goes beyond being intertextual);
- *alteration*: the alteration of sources (more *noticeable* alteration presumably making it more reflexively intertextual);
- *explicitness*: the specificity and explicitness of reference(s) to other text(s) (e.g. direct quotation, attributed quotation) (is *assuming* recognition more reflexively intertextual?);
- *criticality to comprehension*: how important it would be for the reader to *recognize* the intertextuality involved;
- *scale of adoption*: the overall scale of allusion/incorporation within the text; and
- *structural unboundedness*: to what extent the text is presented (or understood) as part of or tied to a larger structure (e.g. as part of a genre, of a series, of a serial, of a magazine, of an exhibition, etc.) – factors which are often not under the control of the author of the text.

Useful as the concept can be, it is important to remember that intertextuality is not purely a relation between texts. Nor does Kristeva's horizontal axis – that connecting the author and reader of a text – adequately represent the frequently neglected dimension of intertextuality. As the Peircean model suggests, the meaning of a sign is in its interpretation. Long before Barthes announced the death of the author, Plato (in the *Phaedrus*) had foreseen (with regret) that once the text left the author, the *reader* was in control. Socrates observed:

> The fact is, Phaedrus, that writing involves a similar disadvantage to painting. The productions of painting look like living beings, but if you ask them a question they maintain a solemn silence. The same holds true of written words; you might suppose that they understand what they are saying, but if you ask them what they mean by anything they simply return the same answer over and over again. Besides, once a thing is committed to writing it circulates equally among those who understand the subject and those who have no business with it; a writing cannot distinguish between suitable and unsuitable readers.
>
> (Plato 1973, 97)

Ultimately readers, not authors, are the determinants of the meaning of texts and the relations between them – textual interactions do not even exist without readers ('suitable' or otherwise). This is not to suggest that texts may mean whatever their readers want them to mean or relate to whatever readers decide they relate to. Nor is it only textual support that the reader must seek for a sustainable reading. Meanings and meaningful textual relations are socially negotiated; readings don't last without interpretive communities. Similarly, the intergeneric blending and blurring that characterizes the evolution of genres depends not on texts but on shifting expectations within interpretive communities. Genre codes are a key intertextual framework, but we noted in the previous chapter the frequent absence of text–reader relations in the classification of generic features. Intertextuality is not about purely textual features. Although assumptions about 'model' readers may be discerned in textual cues, text–reader relations cannot be determined by them. Readers do not necessarily adopt the anticipated 'reading positions', even if they have access to the relevant codes. Nor should we neglect the *pleasures* of recognition (alluded to earlier) that have made intelligent television programmes such as *The Simpsons* so popular and amusing.

Confounding the realist agenda that 'art imitates life,' inter-textuality suggests that art imitates art. Oscar Wilde (typically) took this notion further, declaring provocatively that 'life imitates art'. Texts are instrumental not only in the construction of other texts but in the construction of experiences. Our behaviour is not determined by texts, but much of what we know about the world is derived from what we have read in books, newspapers and magazines, from what we have seen in the cinema and on television and from what we have heard on the radio. Life is thus lived through texts and framed by texts to a greater extent than we are normally aware of. As the sociologist Scott Lash observes, 'We are living in a society in which our *perception* is directed almost as often to representations as it is to "reality"' (Lash 1990, 24). Intertextuality blurs the boundaries not only between texts but between texts and the world of lived experience. Those who radically privilege code over context may argue that we know no pre-textual experience; the world as we know it is merely its current representation. On the other hand, members of an interpretive community whose everyday behaviour is guided by such a relativistic stance might have difficulty in communicating with each other, still less with 'unsuitable readers' such as visitors from other planets.

7

PROSPECT AND RETROSPECT

The definition, scope and methodologies of semiotics vary from theorist to theorist, so it is important for newcomers to be clear about whose version of semiotics they are dealing with. There are many semioticians whose work has not been discussed in this brief introduction to the subject, and other theorists – notably Derrida and Foucault – have been included because they address semiotic issues even though they are not semioticians. The Appendix lists some 'key figures and schools' but this little book cannot perform the functions of the encyclopedias of semiotics (Sebeok 1994b, Bouissac 1998) or of Nöth's magisterial handbook (Nöth 1990). Even in these three great reference works, the only dedicated entries appearing in all of them are for Barthes, Hjelmslev, Jakobson, Peirce and Saussure. Those included in both Bouissac's one-volume encyclopedia and Nöth's handbook who are noticeable by their absence from Sebeok's three-volume work are: Algirdas Greimas, Julia Kristeva and Umberto Eco (though Eco was a contributor). My own account of semiotics is partial in both senses; the biases of which I am conscious were outlined in the Preface – the critical reader will no doubt discern others. Regarding semiotics as unavoidably ideological alienates those semioticians who see it as a purely objective science, but the history of its exposition reveals that semiotics is clearly a 'site of struggle'.

STRUCTURALIST SEMIOTICS

Semiotics has become closely identified with structuralist approaches but it is not tied to any particular theory or methodology. The current review has focused primarily on the European tradition deriving from Saussure (although we have also taken account of the impact of the Peircean approach within this tradition). As we have seen, even the European tradition has been far from monolithic: there have been various inflections of both structuralist and poststructuralist semiotics. Whatever the limitations of some of its manifestations, the legacy of structuralism is a toolkit of analytical methods and concepts which have not all outlived their usefulness. Particular tools have subsequently been applied, adapted, replaced or discarded. Some have even been used 'to dismantle the master's house.' Saussure's framework was thus dismantled not only by deconstructionists such as Jacques Derrida but also by the structuralist linguist Roman Jakobson. Yet even from the ruins of the crumbling creation which bears Saussure's name, valuable concepts have still been salvaged. Jakobson commented: 'Saussure's *Course* is the work of a genius, and even its errors and contradictions are suggestive' (Jakobson 1984b, 85).

Saussure's provocative stance on the radical arbitrariness of signs has long been demonstrated to be unsustainable. It was another structuralist linguist and semiotician who argued that the radical arbitrariness of the sign advocated by Saussure (in contrast to the variability of arbitrariness in the Peircean model) was an 'illusory' 'dogma' (Jakobson 1963a, 19; 1966, 419). Even language incorporates iconic and indexical modes (Jakobson 1966, 420). As we have seen, Saussure did in fact allude to 'relative arbitrariness'. However, this potentiality was little more than a footnote in his exposition of the 'first principle' of the sign, and as we have seen it was through the influence of Peirce that this concept gained widespread acceptance. Nevertheless, the enduring value of Saussure's emphasis on arbitrariness lies in alerting us to the conventional character of many signs which we experience as natural. All signs, texts and codes need to be read. When we interpret television or photography as 'a window on the world' we treat the signified as unmediated or transparent. Saussurean-inspired semiotics demonstrates that the transparency of the medium is illusory.

Saussure's emphasis on arbitrariness was based on his adoption of language as his model for semiotic systems – even Jakobson acknowledged 'the predominantly symbolic character of language' (Jakobson 1966, 420). Subsequent structuralists sought to apply verbal language as a model to media which are non-verbal or not solely or primarily verbal. Such attempts at a unifying approach were seen by critics as failing to allow for the diversity of media, though Jakobson rejected this criticism: 'I have looked forward to the development of semiotics, which helps to delineate the specificity of language among all the various systems of signs, as well as the invariants binding language to related sign systems' (Jakobson 1981, 65; cf. 1960, 351 and 1970, 455). Despite the Jakobsonian stance, a key example of the problem identified by critics is that analogical images (such as in traditional painting and photography) cannot be unproblematically reduced to discrete and meaningfully recombinable units in the way that verbal language can. Yet some semioticians have insisted that a 'grammar' can nevertheless be discerned at some level of analysis in visual and audio-visual media. While we may acknowledge the role of conventions in painting, in the case of an indexical medium such as photography, common sense suggests that we are dealing with 'a message without a code'. Thus, semiotic references to 'reading' photographs, films and television lead some to dispute that we need to learn the formal codes of such media, and to argue that the resemblance of their images to observable reality is not merely a matter of cultural convention: 'to a substantial degree the formal conventions encountered in still or motion pictures should make a good deal of sense even to a first-time viewer' (Messaris 1994, 7). Semioticians in the Saussurean tradition insist that such stances underestimate the intervention of codes (even if their familiarity renders them transparent): relative arbitrariness should not be equated with an absence of conventions. The indexical character of the medium of film does not mean that a documentary film lacks formal codes or guarantee its 'reflection of reality' (Nichols 1991).

While the concept of codes that need to be read can shed light on familiar phenomena, critics have objected to the way in which some semioticians have treated almost anything as a code, while leaving the details of some of these codes inexplicit. It has been argued that we draw on both social and textual codes in making sense even of representational pictures, as indeed we do, but we also draw more broadly on both social and textual *knowledge*. Not all of such knowledge is reducible to codes. In 'bracketing the referent' Saussure excluded social context. We cannot identify which codes to invoke in making sense of any act of communication without knowing the context (or alternatively, being there). The single word 'coffee', spoken with the rising inflection we associate with a question, can be interpreted in a host of ways depending largely on the context in which it is spoken (just try stopping yourself thinking of some!). It is indeed only in social contexts that codes can be learned and applied. However, as we have seen, excluding context is not necessarily a defining feature of structuralist approaches. Roman Jakobson showed that the context counts at least as much as the code in interpreting signs. Such a stance challenges the reductive transmission model of communication.

There are no ideologically neutral sign-systems: signs function to persuade as well as to refer. Valentin Voloshinov declared that 'whenever a sign is present, ideology is present too' (Voloshinov 1973, 10). Sign-systems help to naturalize and reinforce particular framings of 'the way things are', although the operation of ideology in signifying practices is typically masked. Consequently, on these principles semiotic analysis always involves ideological analysis. Victor Shklovsky of the Moscow school argued in 1916 that the key function of art was estrangement, defamiliarization or 'making strange' (*ostranenie*) (Hawkes 1977, 62–7). Many cultural semioticians have seen their primary task as denaturalizing dominant codes; denaturalization was at the heart of Roland Barthes' analytical approach. Semiotic denaturalization has the potential to show ideology at work and to demonstrate that 'reality' can be challenged. In this respect, although Saussure excluded the social and therefore the political, his concept of arbitrariness can be seen as having inspired Barthes and his more socially oriented followers.

As we have seen, the Saussurean legacy was a focus on synchronic rather than diachronic analysis. Synchronic analysis studies a phenomenon as if it were frozen at one moment in time; diachronic analysis focuses on change over time. The synchronic approach underplays the dynamic nature of sign systems (for instance, television conventions change fairly rapidly compared to conventions for written English). It can also underplay dynamic changes in the cultural myths which signification both alludes to and helps to shape. Structuralist semiotics in a purely Saussurean mode ignores process and historicity – unlike historical theories like Marxism. However, once again we should beware of reducing even structuralist semiotics to its Saussurean form. As we have already noted, even other structuralists such as Jakobson rejected the Saussurean splitting of synchronic from diachronic analysis while Lévi-Strauss's approach did at least allow for structural transformation.

Semiotics is invaluable if we wish to look beyond the manifest content of texts. Structuralist semioticians seek to look behind or beneath the surface of the observed in order to discover underlying organizational relations. The more obvious the structural organization of a text or code may seem to be, the more difficult it may be to see beyond such surface features, but searching for what is hidden beneath the obvious can lead to fruitful insights. The quest for underlying structures has, however, led some critics to argue that the focus on underlying structures which characterizes the structural formalism of theorists such as Propp, Greimas and Lévi-Strauss tends to over-emphasize the similarities between texts and to deny their distinctive features (e.g. Coward and Ellis 1977, 5). This is particularly vexatious for literary critics, for whom issues of stylistic difference are a central concern. Some semiotic analysis has been criticized as nothing more than an abstract and 'arid formalism'. In Saussurean semiotics the focus was on *langue* rather than *parole*, on formal systems rather than on social practices. Lévi-Strauss is explicit about his lack of interest in specific *content* – for him, structure *is* the content (e.g. Lévi-Strauss 1962, 75–6; cf. Caws 1968, 203). Jakobson's challenge to Saussure's emphasis on *parole* demonstrates that structuralism should not be equated with the Saussurean model in this respect. Nevertheless, structuralist studies have tended to be purely textual analyses (including Jakobson and Lévi-Strauss 1970), and critics complain that the social dimension (such as how people interpret texts) tends to be dismissed as (or reduced to) 'just another text'. Semiotics can appear to suggest that meaning is purely explicable in terms of determining textual structures. Such a stance is subject to the same criticisms as linguistic determinism. In giving priority to the determining power of the system it can be seen as fundamentally conservative.

However, as an antidote to dominant myths of individualism, it is instructive to be reminded that individuals are not unconstrained in their construction of meanings. Common sense suggests that 'I' am a unique individual with a stable, unified identity and ideas of my own. Semiotics can help us to realize that such notions are created and maintained by our engagement with sign-systems: our sense of identity is established through signs. We derive a sense of self from drawing upon conventional, pre-existing repertoires of signs and codes which we did not ourselves create. As the sociologist Stuart Hall puts it, our 'systems of signs . . . *speak us* as much as we speak in and through them' (Hall 1977, 328). We are thus the subjects of our sign-systems rather than being simply instrumental 'users' who are fully in control of them. While we are not determined by semiotic processes we are shaped by them far more than we realize.

In this context it is perhaps hardly surprising that structuralist semiotic analysis downplays the *affective* domain. Connotation was a primary concern of Barthes, but even he did not undertake research into the diversity of connotative meanings – though the study of connotations ought to include the sensitive exploration of highly variable and subjective emotional nuances. Socially oriented semiotics should alert us to how the same text may generate different meanings for different readers. However, although admirable studies do exist which have investigated the personal meanings of signs (e.g. Csikszentmihalyi and Rochberg-Halton 1981, Chalfen 1987 – both of which include some explicit references to semiotics), research into this aspect of signification has not characterized 'mainstream' semiotic studies.

Purely structuralist approaches have not addressed processes of textual production or audience interpretation. They have downplayed or even ignored the contingencies of particular practices, institutional frameworks and cultural, social, economic and political contexts. Even Roland Barthes, who argued that texts are codified to encourage a reading which favours the interests of the dominant class, did not investigate the social context of interpretation (though his ideological analysis will be discussed in relation to poststructuralist semiotics). It cannot be assumed that preferred readings will go unchallenged (Hall 1980; Morley 1980). The failure of structuralist semiotics to relate texts to social relations has been attributed to its functionalism (Slater 1983, 259). Sociologists insist that we must consider not only *how* signs signify (structurally) but also *why* (socially): structures are not causes. The creation and interpretation of texts must be related to social factors outside the structures of texts.

POSTSTRUCTURALIST SEMIOTICS

Many contemporary theorists have rejected a purely structuralist semiotics, though as we have seen, structuralism has taken a variety of forms, and not all of them are subject to the same catalogue of criticisms. However, even those who choose to reject structuralist priorities need not abandon every tool employed by structuralists, and whether they do or not, they need not reject semiotics whole sale. Influential as it has been, structuralist analysis is but one approach to semiotics. Many of the criticisms of semiotics are directed at a form of semiotics to which few contemporary semioticians adhere. It is only fair to note that much of the criticism of semiotics has taken the form of self-criticism by those within the field. The theoretical literature of semiotics reflects a constant attempt by many semioticians to grapple with the implications of new theories for their framing of the semiotic enterprise. Poststructuralism evolved from the structuralist tradition in the late 1960s, problematizing many of its assumptions. Seeking to account for the role of social change and the role of the subject, poststructuralist semiotics has sometimes adopted Marxist and/or psychoanalytical inflections. Another inflection derives from Foucault – emphasizing power relations in discursive practices. Such shifts of direction are not an abandonment of semiotics but of the limitations of purely structuralist semiotics.

Theorists such as Roland Barthes used semiotics for the 'revelatory' political purpose of 'demystifying' society. However, the semiotic 'decoding' and denaturalization of textual and social codes tends to suggest that there is a literal truth or pre-given objective reality underlying the coded version, which can be revealed by the skilled analyst's banishing of 'distortions' (Watney 1982, 173–4). This strategy is itself ideological. Poststructuralist theorists have argued that the structuralist enterprise is impossible – we cannot stand outside our sign-systems. While we may be able to bypass one set of conventions we may never escape the framing of experience by convention. The notion of 'codes within codes' spells doom for a structuralist quest for a fundamental and universal underlying structure but it does not represent the demise of the semiotic enterprise conceived more broadly. More socially oriented semioticians accept that there can be no 'exhaustive' semiotic analyses because every analysis is located in its own particular social and historical circumstances. In his widely cited essays on the history of photographic practices, John Tagg comments that he is 'not concerned with exposing the manipulation of a pristine "truth", or with unmasking some conspiracy, but rather with the analysis of the specific "political economy" within which the "mode of production" of "truth" is operative' (Tagg 1988, 174–5).

Whereas both common sense and positivist realism involve an insistence that reality is independent of the signs that refer to it, socially oriented semioticians tend to adopt constructionist stances, emphasizing the role of sign-systems in the construction of reality. They usually refer only to 'social reality' (rather than physical reality) as constructed. Some argue that there is nothing natural about our values: they are social constructions which are peculiar to our location in space and time. Assertions which seem to us to be obvious, natural, universal, given, permanent and incontrovertible may be generated by the ways in which sign-systems operate in our discourse communities. Although Saussure's principle of arbitrariness can be seen as an influence on this perspective, the social constructionist stance is not an idealist denial of external physical reality but rather an insistence that although things may exist independently of signs we know them only through the mediation of signs and see only what our socially generated sign-systems allow us to see. Social semioticians have also emphasized the materiality of signs – a dimension ignored by Saussure.

As noted in Chapter two, the emphasis on the mediation of reality (and on representational convention in the form of codes) is criticized by realists as relativism (or conventionalism). Such philosophical critics often fear an extreme relativism in which every representation of reality is regarded as being as good as any other. There are understandable objections to any apparent sidelining of referential concerns such as truth, facts, accuracy, objectivity, bias and distortion. This is a legitimate basis for concern in relation to Saussurean semiotics because of its bracketing of reality. However, socially oriented semioticians are very much aware that representations are far from equal. If signs do not merely reflect (social) reality but are involved in its construction then those who control the sign-systems control the construction of reality. Dominant social groups seek to limit the meanings of signs to those which suit their interests and to naturalize such meanings. For Roland Barthes, various codes contributed to reproducing bourgeois ideology, making it seem natural, proper and inevitable. One need not be a Marxist to appreciate that it can be liberating to become aware of whose view of reality is being privileged in the process. What we are led to accept as 'common sense' involves incoherences, ambiguities, inconsistencies, contradictions, omissions, gaps and silences which offer leverage points for potential social change. The role of ideology is to suppress these in the interests of dominant groups. Consequently, reality construction occurs on 'sites of struggle'.

Since the second half of the 1980s 'social semiotics' has been adopted as a label by members and associates of the Sydney semiotics circle, much-influenced by Michael Halliday's *Language as Social Semiotic* (1978). Halliday (b. 1925) is a British linguist who retired from a chair in Sydney in 1987 and whose functionalist approach to language stresses the contextual importance of social roles. Members of the original Sydney group include Gunther Kress, Theo van Leeuwen, Paul J. Thibault, Terry Threadgold and Anne Cranny-Francis; other associates include Robert Hodge, Jay Lemke and Ron and Suzie Scollon. Members of the group established the journal *Social Semiotics* in 1991. The Sydney school version of 'social semiotics' is not a 'branch' of semiotics in the same sense as 'visual semiotics': it is a 'brand' of semiotics positioned in opposition to 'traditional semiotics'. While the terminology of this school is often distinctive, many of its concepts derive from structuralism (and others from Peirce). There is, of course, nothing new about semiotics having a social dimension (albeit widely neglected): the roots of social semiotics can be traced to the early theorists. It is true that neither Saussure nor Peirce studied the social use of signs. However, Saussure did have a vision of semiotics as 'a science *which studies the role of signs as part of social life*' (even if he did not pursue it himself). As for Peirce, he emphasized that signs do not exist without interpreters (even if he did not allow for the social dimension of codes). Furthermore, as we have seen, it was the structuralist Jakobson (stressing both code and context) who had already upturned the Saussurean priorities along some of the lines outlined by Hodge and Kress (1988). The Sydney school has adopted and adapted some of its analytical concepts partly from (primarily Jakobsonian) structuralism (with a Hallidayan twist) while (like Jakobson) defining itself largely in opposition to Saussure's analytical priorities. The key difference in this respect is that this Australian school has set itself the task of investigating actual meaning-making practices (theoretically prioritized but not pursued by Jakobson). A key concern of socially oriented semioticians is with what they call 'specific signifying practices' or 'situated social semiosis' (Jensen 1995, 57).

Published research into such practices has been rare until recently outside of specialized academic journals, though studies by Hodge and Tripp (1986) and by the Scollons (2003) are commendable examples of book-length treatments explicitly within this school of thought. The influence of socially oriented semioticians such as those associated with the Sydney circle will hopefully stimulate many more. Not the least of the values of such stances is the potential to attract back to semiotics some of those who were alienated by structuralist excesses and who had reductively defined semiotics according to these. The Sydney school has nailed its colours to the mast in reprioritizing the social (Hodge and Kress 1988, van Leeuwen 2005). The extent to which socially oriented semiotics has so far met the concerns of sociologists is debatable. However, 'social semiotics' is still under construction and the Australian strategy is not the only game in town – socio-semiotics is not limited to those adopting it. Semiotics transcends its various schools.

METHODOLOGIES

Certainly there is room for challenging 'traditional semiotics'. Semiotics has not become widely institutionalized as a formal academic discipline and it has not (yet) achieved the status of (social) 'science' which Saussure anticipated. There is little sense of a unified enterprise building on cumulative research findings. Sometimes semioticians present their analyses as if they were purely objective accounts rather than subjective interpretations. Few semioticians seem to feel much need to provide empirical evidence for particular interpretations, and much semiotic analysis is loosely impressionistic and highly unsystematic (or alternatively, generates elaborate taxonomies with little evident practical application). Some seem to choose examples which illustrate the points they wish to make rather than applying semiotic analysis to an extensive random sample. Semiotic analysis requires a highly skilled analyst if it is not to leave readers feeling that it merely buries the obvious in obscurity. In some cases, it seems little more than an excuse for interpreters to display the appearance of mastery through the use of jargon which excludes most people from participation. In practice, semiotic analysis invariably consists of individual readings. We are seldom presented with the commentaries of several analysts on the same text, to say nothing of evidence of any kind of consensus among different semioticians. Few semioticians make their analytical strategy sufficiently explicit for others to apply it either to the examples used or to others. Many make no allowance for alternative readings, assuming either that their own interpretations reflect a general consensus or a meaning which resides within the text. Semioticians who reject the investigation of other people's interpretations privilege what has been called the 'élite interpreter' – though socially oriented semioticians would insist that the exploration of people's interpretive practices is fundamental to semiotics.

Semioticians do not always make explicit the limitations of their techniques, and semiotics is sometimes uncritically presented as a general-purpose tool. A semiotic approach suits some purposes better than others and makes certain kinds of questions easier to ask than others. Signs in various media are not alike – different types may need to be studied in different ways. The empirical testing of semiotic claims requires a variety of methods. Structuralist semiotic analysis is just one of many techniques which may be used to explore sign practices. In relation to textual analysis, other approaches include critical discourse analysis (e.g. Fairclough 1995b) and content analysis. Whereas semiotics is now closely associated with cultural studies, content analysis is well established within the mainstream tradition of social science research. Content analysis involves a quantitative approach to the analysis of the manifest content of texts, while semiotics seeks to analyse texts as structured wholes and investigates latent, connotative meanings. Semioticians have often rejected quantitative approaches: just because an item occurs frequently in a text or cultural practice does not make it significant. The structuralist semiotician is more concerned with the relation of elements to each other while a social semiotician would also emphasize the importance of the significance which readers attach to the signs within a text. Whereas content analysis focuses on explicit content and tends to suggest that this represents a single, fixed meaning, semiotic studies focus on the system of rules governing the discourse involved in texts and practices, stressing the role of semiotic context in shaping meaning. However, some researchers have combined semiotic analysis and content analysis (e.g. Glasgow University Media Group 1980; Leiss et al. 1990; McQuarrie and Mick 1992). Semiotics is not incompatible with quantitative methods – for instance, a highly enlightening study of the signification of domestic objects for their owners made effective use of both qualitative and quantitative data (Csikszentmihalyi and Rochberg-Halton 1981).

Rejecting content analysis, Bob Hodge and David Tripp's classic empirical study of *Children and Television* (1986) linked semiotics with both psychology and social and political theory, employing structural analysis, interviews and a developmental perspective. Semiotic investigations need to range beyond textual analysis, which does not shed light on how people in particular social contexts actually interpret signs – an issue which may require ethnographic and phenomenological approaches (McQuarrie and Mick 1992).

AN ECOLOGICAL AND MULTIMODAL APPROACH

The primary value of semiotics is its central concern for the investigation of meaning-making and representation which conventional academic disciplines have tended to treat as peripheral. Specific semiotic modalities are addressed by such specialists as linguists, art historians, musicologists and anthropologists, but we must turn to semioticians if our investigations are to span a range of modalities. Semiotic analysis has been applied to a vast range of modes and media – including gesture, posture, dress, writing, speech, photography, the mass media and the internet. Since this involves 'invading' the territory of different academic disciplines, it is understandable that semiotics has often been criticized as imperialistic. Aldous Huxley once wryly noted, 'our universities possess no chair of synthesis' (Huxley 1941, 276). Semiotics has an important synthesizing function, seeking to study meaning-making and representation in cultural artifacts and practices of whatever kind on the basis of unified principles, at its best counteracting cultural chauvinism and bringing some coherence to communication theory and cultural studies. While semiotic analysis has been widely applied to the literary, artistic and musical canon, it has also been applied to a wide variety of popular cultural phenomena. It has thus helped to stimulate the serious study of popular culture.

While all verbal language is communication, most communication is non-verbal. In an increasingly visual age, an important contribution of semiotics from Roland Barthes onwards has been a concern with imagistic as well as linguistic signs, particularly in the context of advertising, photography and audio-visual media. Semiotics may encourage us not to dismiss a particular medium as of less worth than another: literary and film critics often regard television as of less worth than 'literary' fiction or 'artistic' film. To élitist critics, of course, this would be a weakness of semiotics. Potentially, semiotics could help us to avoid the routine privileging of one semiotic mode over another, such as the spoken over the written or the verbal over the non-verbal. We need to realize the affordances and constraints of different semiotic modes – visual, verbal, gestural and so on. We live within an ecology of signs that both reflects and gives shape to our experience (Csikszentmihalyi and Rochberg-Halton 1981, 16–17). We must identify and recognize the importance of new 'literacies' in this ever-changing semiotic ecology. Thinking in 'ecological' terms about the interaction of different semiotic structures and languages led the Tartu school cultural semiotician Yuri Lotman to coin the term 'semiosphere' to refer to 'the whole semiotic space of the culture in question' (Lotman 1990, 124–5). This conception of a semiosphere may once again connote semiotic imperialism, but it also offers a more unified and dynamic vision of semiosis than the study of a specific medium as if each existed in a vacuum.

Human experience is inherently multisensory, and every representation of experience is subject to the constraints and affordances of the medium involved. Every medium is constrained by the channels that it utilizes. For instance, even in the very flexible medium of language 'words fail us' in attempting to represent some experiences, and we have no way at all of representing smell or touch with conventional media. Different media and genres provide different frameworks for representing experience, facilitating some forms of expression and inhibiting others. The differences between media led Émile Benveniste to argue that the 'first principle' of semiotic systems is that they are not 'synonymous': 'we are not able to say "the same thing"' in systems based on different units (Benveniste 1969, 235). There is a growing theoretical interest in 'multimodality' (e.g. Kress and van Leeuwen 2001 and Finnegan 2002). This is 'the combination of different semiotic modes – for example, language and music – in a communicative artefact or event' (van Leeuwen 2005, 281). It was foreshadowed in structuralist studies of what Metz called 'intercodical relations' (Metz 1971, 242), including Barthes' exploration of relations such as anchorage between images and words.

In the educational framing of such relations, images are still the marked category, as also are makers as opposed to users. At present, 'with regard to images, most people in most societies are mostly confined to the role of spectator of other people's productions' (Messaris 1994, 121). Most people feel unable to draw, paint or use graphics software, and even among those who own cameras and camcorders not everyone knows how to make effective use of them. This is a legacy of an educational system which still focuses almost exclusively on the acquisition of one kind of symbolic literacy (that of verbal language) at the expense of other semiotic modes. This institutional bias disempowers people not only by excluding many from engaging in those representational practices which are not purely linguistic but by handicapping them as critical readers of the majority of texts to which they are routinely exposed throughout their lives. A working understanding of key concepts in semiotics – including their practical application – can be seen as essential for everyone who wants to understand the complex and dynamic communication ecologies within which we live. As Peirce put it, 'the universe . . . is perfused with signs, if it is not composed exclusively of signs' (Peirce 1931–58, 5.449n.). There is no escape from signs. Those who cannot understand them and the systems of which they are a part are in the greatest danger of being manipulated by those who can. In short, semiotics cannot be left to semioticians.

APPENDIX
KEY FIGURES
AND SCHOOL

Note Those who are *not* generally regarded as semioticians are marked with asterisk.

Barthes, Roland (1915–80) French semiotician and cultural theorist famous for his ideologically inflected analysis of images, literary texts and the 'myths' of popular culture. **Hjelmslev** influenced his ideas on connotation; **Lévi-Strauss** influenced his conception of *myth*. Barthes evolved from a structuralist to a poststructuralist – in *S/Z* (1970) he abandoned his former structural narratology and focused on intertextuality, eventually treating himself as 'an effect of language' (Barthes 1977b, 79).

Bateson, Gregory* (1904–80) American anthropologist and philosopher (born in England), whose ideas on 'the ecology of mind', metacommunication and codes have implications for semiotics and communication theory.

Bogatyrev, Petr *See* **Moscow school**.

Brøndal, Viggo *See* **Copenhagen school**.

Burke, Kenneth* (1897–1993) American rhetorician who identified metaphor, metonymy, synecdoche and irony as the four
'master tropes'.

Cassirer, Ernst* (1874–1945) German philosopher who moved to
the USA in 1941. He is best known for *The Philosophy of
Symbolic Forms* (4 vols), which explores the symbolic forms
underlying human thought, language and culture. He saw
symbolism as distinctively human. His ideas were a key influence on the emergence of semiotics as a subject of study.

Copenhagen school Structuralist and formalist group of linguists
founded by Danish linguists **Hjelmslev** and Viggo Brøndal
(1887–1953). **Jakobson** was associated with this group from
1939–49. Influenced by **Saussure**, its most distinctive contribution was a concern with 'glossematics'. It is a formalist
approach in that it considers semiotic systems without regard
for their social context.

Derrida, Jacques* (b. 1930) French poststructuralist literary
philosopher and linguist who established the critical technique
of deconstruction (applying it, for instance, to **Saussure**'s
Course), emphasizing the instability of the relationship
between the signifier and the signified and the way in which
the dominant ideology seeks to promote the illusion of a transcendental signified.

Eco, Umberto (b. 1932) Italian semiotician and novelist. In his
Theory of Semiotics (1976) he sought 'to combine the structuralist perspective of **Hjelmslev** with the cognitive–
interpretative semiotics of **Peirce**' (Eco 1999, 251). He introduced terms such as: 'unlimited semiosis' (the Peircean notion
of successive interpretants), 'closed texts' and 'aberrant
decoding'. Hjelmslev's influence is evident in relation to deno-
tation/connotation and expression/content.

Eikhenbaum, Boris *See* **Moscow school**.

Foucault, Michel* (1926–84) French historian of ideas and poststructuralist theorist who emphasized power relations and
sought to identify the dominant discourses of specific historical

and socio-cultural contexts – the *episteme* of the age which determines what can be known.

Gombrich, Ernst* (1909–2001) Viennese-born art historian who emigrated to Britain. Intrigued by the psychology of pictorial representation, he initially rejected the idea of a natural likeness and emphasized the role of codes and conventions in art. However, he later criticized the theoretical stance of 'extreme conventionalism' (e.g. **Goodman**).

Goodman, Nelson* (1906–98) An explicitly nominalist American philosopher who rejected the principle of similarity in pictorial representation and argued that '[pictorial] realism is relative'.

Greimas, Algirdas (1917–92) Lithuanian-born semiotician who (in the early 1960s) established the Paris school of semiotics to which Barthes initially belonged. This school, influenced by Edmund Husserl (1859–1938) and Maurice Merleau-Ponty (1908–61), defined semiotics as a 'theory of signification'. Greimas focused on textual analysis and his narratology was influenced by the work of **Vladimir Propp** (1895–1970) and **Lévi-Strauss** (notably in relation to binary oppositions and structural transformation). His contributions to semiotic methodology include the semiotic square and the *seme* as the basic unit of meaning.

Havránek, Bohuslav *See* **Prague school**.

Hjelmslev, Louis (1899–1966) Hjelmslev was a structuralist and formalist linguist who established the **Copenhagen school**. While Hjelmslev did accord a privileged status to language, his 'glossematics' included both linguistics and 'non-linguistic languages'. He adopted **Saussure**'s dyadic model of the sign, though he renamed the signifier as 'expression' and the signified as 'content' and stratified the sign into intersecting planes: content-form, expression-form, content-substance and expression-substance. Hjelmslev was a major influence on the structuralism of **Greimas** and on **Eco**. To a lesser extent he was also an influence on **Barthes** (notably in relation to connotation and metalanguage) and on **Metz**.

Jakobson, Roman (1896–1982) Russian stucturalist and function-alist linguist. Jakobson was involved in the establishment of both the **Moscow school** (in 1915) and the **Prague school** (in 1926) and he was also associated with the **Copenhagen school** from 1939–49. He coined the term 'structuralism'. His version of structuralism was partly a reaction against **Saussure**'s ana-lytical priorities but from the early 1950s onward he was also much influenced by **Peirce**an concepts. His key contributions included: binary oppositions; markedness; the axes of selec-tion–combination, metaphor–metonymy, and similarity–conti-guity; the code–message distinction; and semiotic functions. Jakobson influenced the structuralism of **Lévi-Strauss** and the early **Lacan**.

Karcevski, Sergei *See* **Prague school**.

Korzybski, Alfred* (1879–1950) The founder of 'general seman-tics', who declared that 'the map is not the territory' and that 'the word is not the thing'.

Kristeva, Julia (b. 1941) Feminist poststructuralist linguist, psycho-analyst and cultural theorist whose *semanalysis* combines semi-otics (both **Saussure**an and **Peirce**an) and psychoanalysis (Freud, **Lacan** and Melanie Klein). Signification for her con-sists of a dialectic between 'the symbolic' (the 'translinguistic' or 'nonlinguistic' structure or grammar enabling signification) and 'the semiotic' (*le sémiotique*, not to be confused with *la sémiotique* or semiotics) – the organization of bodily drives which motivates communication. She also introduced the con-cept of intertextuality.

Lacan, Jacques* (1901–81) French psychoanalytical theorist who sought to undermine the concept of a unified human subject. He reworked **Saussure**an concepts in Freudian terms. He adopted Saussure's principle of arbitrariness, his differential relational system and his non-referential view of language. However, he gave primacy to the signifier rather than the sig-nified, referring to 'the incessant sliding of the signified under the signifier'. His early structuralism evolved into a poststruc-turalist stance. Other influences on his work were **Lévi-Strauss** and **Jakobson** (metaphor and metonymy). He is best known for 'the mirror stage' and the realms of the Imaginary, the Symbolic and the Real.

Lévi-Strauss, Claude (b. 1908) French anthropologist, widely regarded as the principal structuralist theorist. He was strongly influenced by **Jakobson** (particularly in relation to binary oppositions) and the functionalist **Prague school**. He draws upon **Saussure**an concepts such as signifier and signified, langue and parole, and syntagmatic and paradigmatic axes as well as Jakobson's metaphoric and metonymic modes. His analytical concepts included the alignment of homologous oppositions, structural transformation, bricolage, 'mythemes', and the idea of myth as a kind of language performing the function of naturalization (a concept taken up by **Barthes**).

Lotman, Yuri (1922–93) was a semiotician who worked in Tartu University, Estonia and founded the **Tartu school**. Lotman worked within the tradition of formalist structuralist semiotics but broadened his semiotic enterprise by establishing 'cultural semiotics', his goal being to develop a unified semiotic theory of culture.

Mathesius, Vilem *See* **Prague school**.

Metz, Christian (1931–93) was a French linguist and structuralist semiotician influenced in particular by **Hjelmslev** and **Lacan**. Metz focused on film semiotics, in particular in relation to cinematic codes. The concepts he is associated with include the *grande syntagmatique*, 'the imaginary signifier', intercodical relations and spectator positioning.

Morris, Charles William (1901–79) Morris, an American semiotician who worked within the Peircean model, defined semiotics as 'the science of signs' (Morris 1938, 1–2). Unlike **Peirce**, he included within semiotics the study of communication by animals and other organisms. He was a behaviourist who sought to develop a biological approach. His contributions include the division of semiotics into syntactics (later called syntax), semantics and pragmatics and the term 'sign vehicle' (for the signifier or representamen).

Moscow school The Moscow linguistics circle was co-founded in 1915 by the Russian linguists **Jakobson** and Petr Bogatyrev

(1893–1971). Together with the Petrograd Society for the Study of Poetic Language – which included Victor Shklovsky (1893–1984), Yuri Tynyanov (1894–1943) and Boris Eikhenbaum (1886–1959) – the Moscow school was the origin of Russian formalism. The primary focus of the formalists was on form, structure, technique or medium rather than on content. Formalism evolved into structuralism in the late 1920s and 1930s.

Moscow–Tartu school *See* **Tartu school**.

Mukarovsky, Jan *See* **Prague school**.

Paris school School of structuralist semiotic thinking established in the early 1960s by **Greimas**. **Barthes** was involved until 1970. Strongly influenced by **Hjelmslev**, it seeks to identify basic structures of signification. Greimas focused primarily on the semantic analysis of textual structures but the Paris school has expanded its rigorous (critics say arid) structural analysis to cultural phenomena such as gestural language, legal discourse and social science. It is formalist in treating semiotic systems as autonomous rather than exploring the importance of social context.

Peirce, Charles Sanders (pronounced 'purse') (1839–1914) American philosopher whose 'semeiotic' (or 'semiotic') was the 'formal doctrine of signs' (closely related to logic). Founder of the American semiotic tradition.

poststructuralism While poststructuralism is often interpreted simply as 'anti-structuralism', the label refers to a school of thought which developed *after*, out of, and in relation to structuralism. Poststructuralism built on and adapted structuralist notions in addition to problematizing many of them. Both schools of thought are built on the assumption that we are the subjects of language rather than being simply instrumental users of it, and poststructuralist thinkers have developed further the notion of 'the constitution of the subject'. Poststructuralist semiotics involves a rejection of structuralist hopes for semiotics as a systematic science which could reveal some fundamental 'deep structures' underlying forms in an external world. Poststructuralist theorists include **Derrida**, **Foucault**, the later **Lacan**, **Kristeva** and the later **Barthes**.

Prague school This influential structuralist and functionalist group of linguists/semioticians was established in 1926 in Prague by Czech and Russian linguists. Principal members of this group included: Vilem Mathesius (1882–1946), Bohuslav Havránek (1893–1978), Sergei Karcevski (1884–1955), Jan Mukarovsky (1891–1975), **Nikolai Trubetzkoy** (1890–1938) and **Jakobson**. It was functionalist in analysing semiotic systems in relation to social functions such as communication rather than treating them purely as autonomous forms (in contrast to **Saussure** and **Hjelmslev**). While they are known for their identification of the 'distinctive features' of language, these theorists also explored culture and aesthetics.

Propp, Vladimir* (1895–1970) Russian narrative theorist best known for his influential book, *The Morphology of the Folktale* (1928).

Saussure, Ferdinand de (1857–1913) Swiss-born founder of modern linguistics. Founder of the structuralist tradition of semiology who envisaged it as 'a science which studies the role of signs as part of social life'.

Sebeok, Thomas (1920–2001) was an American linguist, anthropologist and semiotician who worked within the **Peirce**an semiotic tradition of 'the doctrine of signs', rejecting the linguistic tradition of Saussure as 'the minor tradition'. He was initially influenced by **Jakobson** and **Morris**. He had a particular interest in animal communication, for which he introduced the term *zoosemiotics*.

Shklovsky,Victor *See* **Moscow school**.

structuralism The primary concern of the structuralists is with relational systems or structures which are seen as 'languages'. Structuralists search for 'deep structures' underlying the surface features of phenomena (such as language, society, thought and behaviour). Their analysis of texts and cultural practices seeks to delineate underlying codes and rules by comparing those perceived as belonging to the same system (e.g. a genre) and identifying invariant constituent units. The structuralists include:

Saussure, **Lévi-Strauss**, **Hjelmslev** and the **Copenhagen school**, **Jakobson** and the **Prague** and **Moscow schools**, **Greimas** and the **Paris school**, **Metz**, **Lotman**, the early **Barthes** and the early **Lacan**.

Tartu school What is sometimes called the Moscow–Tartu school was founded in the 1960s by **Lotman**.

Trubetzkoy, Nikolai *See* **Prague school**.

Tynyanov, Yuri *See* **Moscow school**.

Voloshinov, Valentin N.* (1884/5–1936) Russian linguist who probably wrote *Marxism and the Philosophy of Language* (published in 1929) – which included a strident materialist critique of Saussure's exclusion of the social, the historical and the ideological. Authorship is contested: it may actually have been written by (or at least heavily influenced by) Mikhail Bakhtin (1895–1975).

Whorf, Benjamin Lee* (1897–1941) American linguist who, with the linguist Edward Sapir (1884–1939), developed the 'Sapir–Whorf hypothesis' of linguistic relativity and linguistic determinism.

GOING FURTHER

There are several useful works of general reference on semiotics: Nöth 1990, Colapietro 1993, Sebeok 1994b, Bouissac 1998, Danesi 2000, Martin and Ringham 2000 and Cobley 2001. Any serious student should consult the work of the foundational theorists, Saussure and Peirce, since they are frequently misrepresented in popular texts. There are two English translations of Saussure – that by Wade Baskin dating from 1959 (Saussure 1974) and a later British translation by Roy Harris (Saussure 1983). Watch out for Harris's quirky substitution of 'signal' and 'signification' for what are still invariably known as the signifier and the signified. Peirce's writings are voluminous and the references to semiotics are scattered. There is an eight-volume edition (Peirce 1931–58) which may be available in libraries, the most useful volume perhaps being volume two. A searchable but expensive CD-ROM version is available from InteLex. A chronological edition has reached its sixth volume so far (Peirce 1982–93). Useful selections are also available (e.g. Peirce 1966, 1998).

The main works of the leading semioticians are listed here in the references. Two collections of essays by Barthes offer a fairly gentle introduction to his version of cultural semiotics – *Mythologies* (1957/1987) and *Image–Music–Text* (1977). The work of Jakobson (e.g. 1990) and Lévi-Strauss (e.g. 1972) is an essential foundation for structuralist theory. Greimas's *On Meaning* (1987) is not for beginners. Eco's *Theory of Semiotics* (Eco 1976) is widely cited but difficult – it should be read in conjunction with his more recent *Kant and the Platypus* (Eco 1999). The writings of the key poststructuralists, Derrida (1976, 1978), Foucault (1970, 1974) and Lacan (1977), are initially daunting, and a beginner's guide may be helpful (e.g. Sarup 1993). Readers offering affordable selections are available for some of the major theorists (e.g. Barthes 1983, Foucault 1991, Kristeva 1997, Derrida 1998).

In the few years since the first edition of this book was published there has been something of a publishing revival in books on semiotic topics and in public interest in the field. This has encouraged me to provide a list of suggested texts in English on selected topics. It includes material already referenced in the text but I have also responded to readers' requests for further reading on subject areas not necessarily featured in the book. The topic list was thus generated reactively and it is far from comprehensive. For instance, I have resisted the temptation to include general dictionaries of 'symbolism'. However, I hope that within its areas of coverage this list is a useful resource for readers. To keep it within manageable proportions I have restricted it to material available in book form and in English. In some topic areas I have also included a number of authors who are not explicitly semiotic and even a few posing as 'anti-semiotic'. Reading the texts suggested for a topic should at least introduce the reader to some of the issues and debates in the field and will hopefully inspire further exploration.

ADVERTISING, MARKETING AND CONSUMER CULTURE

Leymore 1975, Williamson 1978, Goffman 1979, Dyer 1982, Vestergaard and Schrøder 1985, Jhally 1987, Umiker-Sebeok 1987, Leiss et al. 1990, McCracken 1990, Cook 1992, Goldman 1992,

Holbrook and Hirschman 1993, McKracken 1993, Nadin and Zakia 1994, Forceville 1996, Goldman and Papson 1996, Messaris 1997, Mollerup 1997, Nava et al. 1997, Goldman and Papson 1998, Stern 1998, Budd et al. 1999, Beasley et al. 2000, Floch 2000, Richards et al. 2000, Scanlon 2000, Floch 2001, Beasley and Danesi 2002, Schroeder 2002, McFall 2004

ARCHITECTURE AND THE BUILT ENVIRONMENT

Agrest and Gandelsonas 1977, Krampen 1979, Preziosi 1979a, Preziosi 1979b, Broadbent et al. 1980, Cable 1981, Colquhoun 1981, Rapoport 1983, Minai 1985, Gottdiener and Lagopoulos 1986, Carlson 1993, Lukken and Searle 1993, Jencks 2002

CINEMA AND FILM

Metz 1968, Wollen 1969, Kitses 1970, Metz 1971, Reisz and Millar 1972, Lotman 1976b, Metz 1977, Carroll 1980, Eaton 1981, Monaco 1981, Nichols 1981, Peters 1981, Worth 1981, Branigan 1984, de Lauretis 1984, Bordwell et al. 1988, Lapsley and Westlake 1988, Whittock 1990, Nichols 1991, Stam 1992, Bordwell and Thompson 1993, Rodowick 1994, Buckland 1995, Lapsley and Westlake 1988, Dyer 1992, Iampolski 1998, Altman 1999, Buckland 2000, Mitry 2000, Stam 2000, Tamburri 2002, Ehrat 2004

COMMUNICATION AND MEDIA

McLuhan 1962, Cherry 1966, McLuhan 1967, Hall 1973, Eakins and Eakins 1978, Tuchman 1978, Galtung and Ruge 1981, Fiske 1982, Hartley 1982, Davis and Walton 1983, Wilden 1987, Leeds-Hurwitz 1993, Jensen 1995, Bignell 1997, Nöth 1998, Danesi 2002, Finnegan 2002, Katz and Aakhus 2002

COMPUTERS, INFORMATION SCIENCE AND THE INTERNET

Bolter 1991, Warner 1994, Aarseth 1997, Andersen 1997, Yazdani and Barker 2000, Manovich 2001, Myers 2003, Perron et al. 2003, Boardman 2004, Burnett 2005, de Souza 2005

LANGUAGE, WRITING AND PRINT

Saussure 1916, Ogden and Richards 1923, Richards 1932, Bloomfield 1939, Jakobson and Halle 1956, Sebeok 1960, Hjelmslev 1961, McLuhan 1962, Gelb 1963, Whorf 1967, Lanham 1969, Jameson 1972, Voloshinov 1973, Derrida 1976, Coward and Ellis 1977, Lyons 1977, Derrida 1978, Reddy 1979, Lakoff and Johnson 1980, Silverman and Torode 1980, Shapiro 1983, Eco 1984, Pharies 1985, Jakobson 1990, Meggs 1992, Harris 1995, Eco 1997, Keller 1998, Cobley 2001, Harris 2001, Kress 2001, Scollon and Scollon 2003

LAW

Jackson 1985, Benson 1989, Jackson 1995, Kevelson 1988a, Kevelson 1988b, Kevelson 1990, Kevelson 1991, Liu 2000, Wagner et al. 2005

LITERATURE

Propp 1928, Barthes 1953, Jakobson and Lévi-Strauss 1970, Abrams 1971, Barthes 1974, Culler 1975, Lotman 1976, Hawkes 1977, Lodge 1977, Belsey 1980, Kristeva 1980, Culler 1981, Eco 1981, Eagleton 1983, Scholes 1983, Silverman 1983, Halle et al. 1984, Genette 1997, Petrilli and Ponzio 2004

MUSIC AND SOUND

Lévi-Strauss 1969, Ostwald 1973, Barthes 1977a, Nattiez 1977, Tarasti 1979, Steiner 1981b, Middleton 1990, Agawu 1991, Barthes 1991, Shepherd 1991, Altman 1992, Monelle 1992, Nattiez 1992, Hatten 1994, Tarasti 1994, Tarasti 1995, van Baest 1995, Elicker 1997, Lidov 1999, van Leeuwen 1999, Monelle 2000, Cumming 2001, Tamburri 2002, Tarasti 2002, Nattiez 2004, van Baest 2004

NONVERBAL COMMUNICATION

Hall 1959, Hall 1966, Argyle 1969, Goffman 1969b, Birdwhistell 1971, Benthall and Polhemus 1975, Hinde 1975, Henley 1977,

Eakins and Eakins 1978, LaFrance and Mayo 1978, Polhemus 1978, Kendon 1981, Mayo and Henley 1981, Argyle 1983, Argyle 1988, Burgoon et al. 1989, Malandro et al. 1989, Guerrero et al. 1990, Hall 1990, McNeill 1995, Remland 2000, Knapp and Hall 2002, Beattie 2003, Collett 2003

ORGANIZATIONS

Holmqvist et al. 1996, Jablin and Putnam 2000, Liu et al. 2000, Liu et al. 2002, Gazendam 2003, Liu 2004, Desouza and Hensgen 2005

PEIRCE

Gallie 1952, Zeman 1977, Shapiro 1983, Pharies 1985, Fisch 1986, Kevelson 1991, Merrell 1991, Shapiro 1993, Sebeok 1994a, Merrell 1995a, Merrell 1995b, Muller 1995, van Baest 1995, Liszka 1996, Merrell 1997, Sonesson 1998, Kevelson 1999, Deledalle 2000, Muller and Brent 2000, Merrell 2001, Shapiro 2003, Ehrat 2004, Freadman 2004

PHOTOGRAPHY

Barthes 1961, Barthes 1964, Berger 1968, Sontag 1979, Hirsch 1981, Burgin 1982, Chalfen 1987, Tagg 1988, Ziller 1990, Spence and Holland 1991, Barthes 1993, Bertelsen et al. 1999, Scott 1999, Alvarado et al. 2001

SAUSSURE AND STRUCTURALISM

Hjelmslev 1961, Lévi-Strauss 1964, Douglas 1966, Barthes 1967a, Barthes 1967b, Metz 1968, Lévi-Strauss 1968, Lévi-Strauss 1969, Lane 1970, Hayes and Hayes 1970, Leach 1970, Metz 1971, Jameson 1972, Lévi-Strauss 1972, Macksey and Donato 1972, Douglas 1973, Needham 1973, Culler 1975, Douglas 1975, Leach 1976, Barthes 1977, Hawkes 1977, Sturrock 1979, Greimas and Courtés 1982, Leach 1982, Culler 1985, Sturrock 1986, Harland 1987, Harris 1987, Jakobson 1990, Holdcroft 1991, Seiter 1992, Stam 1992,

Thibault 1997, Dosse 1998, Harris 2001, Harris 2003, Sanders 2004, Barthes 2006

TELEVISION

Williams 1974, Fiske and Hartley 1978, Morley 1980, Hodge and Tripp 1987, Fiske 1987, Threadgold and Gillard 1990, Lewis 1991, Morley 1992, Seiter 1992, Bignell 1997, Budd et al. 1999, Page 2000, Gray 2005

THEATRE AND PERFORMANCE

Elam 1980, Esslin 1988, Alter 1990, Yell 1990, Aston and Savona 1991, Fischer-Lichte 1992, Carlson 1993, de Marinis 1993, Donahue 1993, Pavis 1993, Melrose 1994, de Toro and Hubbard 1995, Quinn 1995, Counsell 1996, Ubersfeld 1999

VISUAL ART, VISUAL REPRESENTATION, AND VISUAL RHETORIC

Goodman 1968, Panofsky 1970, Berger 1972, Kennedy 1974, Gombrich 1977, Goodman 1978, Mitchell 1980, Steiner 1981a, Worth 1981, Gombrich 1982, Bertin 1983, Bryson 1983, Foucault 1983, Mitchell 1987, Ashwin 1989, Sonesson 1989, Saint-Martin 1990, Barthes 1991, Bryson et al. 1991, Miller 1992, Messaris 1994, Mitchell 1994, O'Toole 1994, Block 1996, Forceville 1996, Kress and van Leeuwen 1996, Schapiro 1996, Tomaselli 1996, Dyer 1997, Walker and Chaplin 1997, Andrews 1998, Elkins 1998, Stephens 1998, Evans and Hall 1999, Ewen 1999, Thomas 2000, Carson and Pajaczkowska 2001, van Leeuwen and Jewitt 2001, Bogdan 2002, Schroeder 2002, Crow 2003, Fuery and Fuery 2003, Howells 2003, Jones 2003, Kostelnick and Hassett 2003, Handa 2004, Hill and Helmers 2004, Schirato and Webb 2004, Barnard 2005

Semiotics is served by a range of journals addressing more specialized academic interests. These include (with title, ISSN and date established): *Sign Systems Studies* (1406–4243, 1964), *Transactions of the Charles S. Peirce Society* (0009–1774, 1965), *Semiotica* (0037–1998, 1969), *Kodikas/Code: An International Journal of*

Semiotics (0171–0834, 1977), *Zeitschrift für Semiotik* (0170–6241, 1979), *American Journal of Semiotics* (0277–7126, 1982), *International Journal for the Semiotics of Law* (0952–8059, 1988), *European Journal for Semiotic Studies* (1015–0102, 1989), *Semiotic Review of Books* (0847–1622, 1990), *Social Semiotics* (1035–0330, 1991), *Cybernetics and Human Knowing* (0907–0877, 1993), *Elementa: Journal of Slavic Studies and Comparative Cultural Semiotics* (1064–6663, 1993), *Interdisciplinary Journal for Germanic Linguistics and Semiotic Analysis* (1087–5557, 1996), *Visio: Revue internationale de sémiotique visuelle/International Journal for Visual Semiotics* (1026–8340, 1996), *Applied Semiotics/Sémiotique appliquée* (1715–7374, 1996) and *International Journal of Applied Semiotics* (1488–0733, 1999). Articles written from a semiotic perspective can, of course, be found in many other academic journals.

The scholarly societies and associations for semiotics at an international level include the International Association for Semiotic Studies, the International Association for Visual Semiotics and the International Association for the Semiotics of Law. There are also regional and national bodies. Current contact details are best obtained via a search engine. Some useful resources on the Web at the time of writing included:

- International Association for Semiotic Studies
  http://www.arthist.lu.se/kultsem/AIS/IASS/
- International Semiotics Institute
  http://www.isisemiotics.fi/
- Martin Ryder's Semiotics links page
  http://carbon.cudenver.edu/~mryder/itc_data/semiotics.html
- Open Semiotics Resource Center
  http://www.semioticon.com/
- Text Semiotics
  http://www.text-semiotics.org/
- Wikipedia entry for Semiotics
  http://en.wikipedia.org/wiki/Semiotics

The online version of the text of this present volume includes gateways to additional resources. This is currently at: http://www.aber.ac.uk/media/Documents/S4B/

GLOSSARY

aberrant decoding Eco's term referring to decoding a text by means of a different code from that used to encode it. *See also* **codes, decoding**.

absent signifiers Signifiers which are absent from a text but which (by contrast) nevertheless influence the meaning of a signifier actually used (which is drawn from the same paradigm set). *See also* **deconstruction, paradigm, paradigmatic analysis, signifier**.

addresser and addressee Jakobson used these terms to refer to what, in transmission models of communication, are called the 'sender' and the 'receiver' of a message. Other commentators have used them to refer more specifically to constructions of these two roles within the text, so that *addresser* refers to an authorial persona, while *addressee* refers to an 'ideal reader'. *See also* **codes, functions of signs**.

analogue oppositions (antonyms) Pairs of oppositional signifiers in a paradigm set representing categories with comparative grading on the same implicit dimension, e.g. good–bad where 'not good' is not necessarily 'bad' and vice versa. *See also* **binary oppositions**.

analogue signs Analogue signs are signs in a form in which they are perceived as involving graded relationships on a continuum rather than as discrete units (in contrast to digital signs). Note, however, that digital technology can transform analogue signs into digital reproductions which may be perceptually indistinguishable from the 'originals'. *See also* **digital signs**.

anchorage Roland Barthes introduced the concept of *anchorage*. Linguistic elements in a text (such as a caption) can serve to 'anchor' (or constrain) the preferred readings of an image (conversely the illustrative use of an image can anchor an ambiguous verbal text). *See also* **preferred reading**.

arbitrariness Saussure emphasized that the relationship between the linguistic signifier and signified is *arbitrary*: the link between them is not necessary, intrinsic or natural. Many subsequent theorists apply this also to the relation between the signifier and any real-world referent. Peirce noted that the relationship between signifiers and their signifieds varies in arbitrariness. Other semioticians argue that *all* signs are to some extent arbitrary and conventional. *See also* **conventionality**, **motivation and constraint**, **primacy of the signifier**, **relative autonomy**.

articulation of codes *Articulation* refers to structural levels within semiotic codes. Semiotic codes have either single articulation, double articulation or no articulation. *See also* **double articulation**, **relative autonomy**, **single articulation**, **unarticulated codes**.

associative relations This was Saussure's term for what later came to be called paradigmatic relations. The 'formulaic' associations of linguistic signs include synonyms, antonyms, similar-sounding words and words of similar grammatical function. *See also* **paradigm**.

binarism The ontological division of a domain into two discrete categories (dichotomies) or polarities. *Binarism* is a loaded term which critics have applied to what they regard as the obsessive dualism of structuralists such as Lévi-Strauss and

Jakobson. Hjelmslev argued against binarism. Derridean deconstruction demonstrates the inescapability of binary logic. *See also* **binary oppositions, deconstruction**.

binary oppositions (or digital oppositions) Pairs of mutually exclusive signifiers in a paradigm set representing categories which are logically opposed, e.g. alive–not-alive. *See also* **analogue oppositions (antonyms), markedness**.

bricolage Lévi-Strauss's term for the appropriation of pre-existing materials which are ready to hand is widely used to refer to the intertextual authorial practice of adopting and adapting signs from other texts. *See also* **intertextuality**.

broadcast codes Fiske's term for codes which are shared by members of a mass audience and which are learned informally through experience rather than deliberately or institutionally. In contrast to narrowcast codes, broadcast codes are structurally simpler, employing standard conventions and 'formulas'. They are more repetitive and predictable – 'overcoded' – having a high degree of redundancy. *See also* **codes, intertextuality, narrowcast codes**.

channel A sensory mode utilized by a medium (e.g. visual, auditory, tactile). Available channel(s) are dictated by the technical features of the medium in which a text appears. The sensory bias of the channel limits the codes for which it is suitable. *See also* **medium**.

codes Semiotic codes are procedural systems of related conventions for correlating signifiers and signifieds in certain domains. Codes provide a framework within which signs make sense: they are interpretive devices which are used by interpretive communities. *See also* **articulation of codes, broadcast codes, codification, dominant (or 'hegemonic') code and reading, interpretive community, narrowcast codes, negotiated code and reading, oppositional code and reading, unarticulated codes**.

code-switching Term usually used by sociolinguists referring to interlingual switching by bilingual speakers or sometimes to intralingual switching between discourse types; more generally switching between sub-codes in any sign-system.

codification A historical social process whereby the conventions of a particular code (e.g. for a genre) become widely established (Guiraud).

combination, axis of A structuralist term for the 'horizontal' axis in the analysis of a textual structure: the plane of the syntagm (Jakobson). *See also* **selection, axis of**.

commutation test A structuralist analytical technique used in the paradigmatic analysis of a text to determine whether a change on the level of the signifier leads to a change on the level of the signified. *See also* **markedness**, **paradigmatic analysis**, **transformation, rules of**.

complex sign Saussure's term for a sign which contains other signs. A text is usually a complex sign. *See also* **simple sign**, **text**.

conative function *See* **functions of signs**.

connotation The socio-cultural and personal associations produced as a reader decodes a text. For Barthes, connotation was a second 'order of signification' which uses the denotative sign (signifier and signified) as its signifier and attaches to it an additional signified. In this framework, connotation is a sign which derives from the signifier of a denotative sign (so denotation leads to a chain of connotations). *See also* **denotation**, **orders of signification**.

constitution of the subject *See* **interpellation**, **subject**.

constraint *See* **motivation and constraint**.

contiguity In ordinary use, this term refers to something which touches or adjoins something else; semioticians (e.g. Jakobson) use it to refer to something which is in some sense part of (or part of the same domain as) something else. Contiguity may be causal, cultural, spatial, temporal, physical, conceptual, formal or structural. *See also* **metonymy**.

conventionalism This term is used by realists to describe a position which they associate with epistemological relativism and the denial of the existence of any knowable reality outside representational conventions. They associate it with the 'severing' of signs from real world referents and with the notion that reality is a construction of language or a product of theories. They regard 'conventionalists' (or constructivists) as reducing reality to nothing more than signifying practices. They criticize as 'extreme conventionalism' the stance that theories (and the worlds which they construct) are incommensurable.

conventionality A term often used in conjunction with the term *arbitrary* to refer to the relationship between the signifier and the signified. In the case of a symbolic system such as verbal language this relationship is purely conventional – dependent on social and cultural conventions (rather than in any sense natural). The conventional nature of codes means that they have to be *learned* (not necessarily formally). *See also* **arbitrariness, primacy of the signifier, relative autonomy**.

decoding The comprehension and interpretation of texts by decoders with reference to relevant codes. Most commentators assume that the reader actively constructs meaning rather than simply 'extracting' it from the text. *See also* **codes, encoding**.

deconstruction This is a poststructuralist strategy for textual analysis, which was developed by Jacques Derrida. Practitioners seek to dismantle the rhetorical structures within a text to demonstrate how key concepts within it depend on their unstated oppositional relation to absent signifiers. Deconstructionists have also exposed culturally embedded conceptual oppositions in which the initial term is privileged, leaving 'Term B' negatively 'marked'. Radical deconstruction is not simply a *reversal* of the valorization in an opposition but a demonstration of the instability of such oppositions. *See also* **denaturalization, markedness, analogue oppositions, binary oppositions, paradigmatic analysis**.

denaturalization The denaturalization of signs and codes is a Barthesian strategy seeking to reveal the socially coded basis of phenomena which are taken for granted as natural. The goal is to make more explicit the underlying rules for encoding and decoding them, and often also to reveal the usually invisible operation of ideological forces. *See also* **deconstruction, naturalization**.

denotatum Latin term for a referent. In relation to language, the denonatum is extralinguistic as distinct from the *signatum* (Morris, Jakobson). *See also* **designatum, object, referent**.

denotation The term refers to the relationship between the signifier and its **signified** (*or* **referent**). In the pairing *denotation/designation* it signifies the relation of *reference* (Sebeok). In the pairing *denotation/connotation*, denotation is routinely treated as the definitional, literal, obvious or common-sense meaning of a sign, but semioticians tend to treat it as a signified about which there is a relatively broad *consensus*. *See also* **connotation, designation, orders of signification**.

designation refers to the relation of **sense** or meaning as opposed to **denotation** (Sebeok). *See also* **meaning, sense**.

designatum Latin term sometimes used for a **referent** (Morris, Jakobson). *See also* **denotatum*, object, referent**.

diachronic analysis Diachronic analysis studies change in a phenomenon (such as a code) over time (in contrast to synchronic analysis). Saussure saw the development of language in terms of a series of synchronic states. *See also* **langue and parole, synchronic analysis**.

différance Derrida coined this term to allude simultaneously to 'difference' and 'deferral'. He deliberately ensured that (in French) the distinction from the word for 'difference' was apparent only in writing. Adding to Saussure's notion of meaning being differential (based on differences between signs), the term is intended to remind us that signs also defer the presence of what they signify through endless substitutions of signifiers. *See also* **deconstruction, transcendent(al) signified, unlimited semiosis**.

digital signs Digital signs involve discrete units such as words and numerals, in contrast to analogue signs. *See also* **tokens and types**.

directness of address Modes of address differ in their directness. This is reflected in the use of language ('you' may be directly addressed), and in the case of television and photography, in whether or not someone looks directly into the camera lens. *See also* **modes of address**.

discourse Many contemporary theorists influenced by Michel Foucault treat language as structured into different discourses such as those of science, law, government, medicine, journalism and morality. A discourse is a system of representation consisting of a set of representational codes (including a distinctive interpretive repertoire of concepts, tropes and myths) for constructing and maintaining particular forms of reality within the ontological domain (or topic) defined as relevant to its concerns. Representational codes thus reflect relational principles underlying the symbolic order of the 'discursive field'. *See also* **interpretive community, representation, signifying practices**.

discourse community *See* **interpretive community**.

dominant (or 'hegemonic') code and reading Within Stuart Hall's framework, this is an ideological code in which the decoder fully shares the text's code and accepts and reproduces the preferred reading (a reading which may not have been the result of any conscious intention on the part of the author(s)). *See also* **negotiated code and reading, oppositional code and reading, preferred reading**.

double articulation A semiotic code which has double articulation (as in the case of verbal language) can be analysed into two abstract structural levels. At the *level of first articulation* the system consists of the smallest meaningful units available (e.g. morphemes or words in a language). These meaningful units are complete signs, each consisting of a signifier and a signified. At the *level of second articulation*, a semiotic code is divisible into minimal functional units which lack meaning in themselves (e.g. phonemes in speech or graphemes in writing). They are not signs in themselves (the code must have a first level of articulation for these lower units to be combined into meaningful signs). *See also* **articulation of codes, single articulation**.

elaborated codes *See* **narrowcast codes**.

élite interpreter Semioticians who reject the investigation of other people's interpretations privilege what has been called the 'élite interpreter' whereas socially oriented semioticians would insist that the exploration of people's interpretive practices is fundamental to semiotics.

empty signifier An 'empty' or 'floating' signifier is variously defined as a signifier with a vague, highly variable, unspecifiable or non-existent signified. Such signifiers mean different things to different people: they may stand for many or even *any* signifieds; they may mean whatever their interpreters want them to mean. *See also* **signifier**, **transcendent(al) signified**.

encoding The production of texts by encoders with reference to relevant codes. Encoding involves foregrounding some meanings and backgrounding others. *See also* **codes**, **decoding**.

expressive function *See* **functions of signs**.

foregrounding, stylistic This term was used by the Prague school linguists to refer to a stylistic feature in which signifiers in a text attract attention to themselves rather than simulating transparency in representing their signifieds. This primarily serves a 'poetic' function (being used 'for its own sake') rather than a 'referential' function. *See also* **denaturalization**, **reflexivity**.

functions of signs In Jakobson's model of linguistic communication, the dominance of any one of six factors within an utterance reflects a different linguistic function: *referential*, oriented towards the *context*; *expressive*, oriented towards the *addresser*; *conative*, oriented towards the *addressee*; *phatic*, oriented towards the *contact*; *metalingual*, oriented towards the *code*; *poetic*, oriented towards the *message*.

hegemonic code *See* **dominant (or 'hegemonic') code and reading**.

homology *See* **isomorphism**.

iconic A mode in which the signifier is perceived as resembling or imitating the signified (recognizably looking, sounding, feeling, tasting or smelling like it) – being similar in possessing some of its qualities. *See also* **indexical**, **isomorphism**, **symbolic**.

ideal readers This is a term often used to refer to the roles in which readers of a text are 'positioned' as subjects through the use of particular modes of address. For Eco this term is not intended to suggest a 'perfect' reader who entirely echoes any authorial intention but a 'model reader' whose reading could be justified in terms of the text. *See also* **addresser and addressee, modes of address, preferred reading, subject**.

imaginary signifier This term was used by Christian Metz to refer to the cinematic signifier. The term is used in more than one sense. The cinematic signifier is 'imaginary' by virtue of an apparent perceptual transparency which suggests the unmediated presence of its absent signified – a feature widely regarded as the key to the power of cinema. The term is also related to Lacan's term, 'the Imaginary' – the cinematic signifier is theorized as inducing identifications similar to those of 'the mirror stage'.

indexical A mode in which the signifier is *not* purely arbitrary but is directly connected in some way (physically or causally) to the signified – this link can be observed or inferred (e.g. fingerprint). *See also* **iconic, symbolic**.

interpellation Interpellation is Althusser's term to describe a mechanism whereby the human subject is 'constituted' (constructed) by pre-given structures or texts (a structuralist stance). *See also* **subject**.

interpretant In Peirce's model of the sign, the *interpretant* is *not* an interpreter but rather the sense made of the sign. *See also* **unlimited semiosis**.

interpretive community Those who share the same codes are members of the same 'interpretive community'. Linguists tend to use the logocentric term, 'discourse community'. Individuals belong simultaneously to several interpretive communities. *See also* **code, signifying practices**.

intertextuality Intertextuality refers to the various links in form and content which bind a text to other texts. *See also* **bricolage, intratextuality**.

intratextuality While the term intertextuality would normally be used to refer to links to other texts, a related kind of link is what might be called 'intratextuality' – involving internal relations *within* the text. *See also* **anchorage, intertextuality**.

irony Irony is a rhetorical trope. It is a kind of double-coded sign in which the 'literal sign' combines with another sign to signify the opposite meaning (although understatement and overstatement can also be ironic). *See also* **metaphor, metonymy, synecdoche, trope**.

isomorphism The term is used to refer to correspondences, parallels, or similarities in the properties, patterns or relations of (a) two different structures; (b) structural elements in two different structures and (c) structural elements at different levels within the same structure. Some theorists use the term *homology* in much the same way. *See also* **iconic, transformation, rules of**.

langue and parole These are Saussure's terms. *Langue* refers to the abstract system of rules and conventions of a signifying system – it is independent of, and pre-exists, individual users. *Parole* refers to concrete instances of its use. *See also* **diachronic analysis, synchronic analysis**.

literalism The fallacy that the meaning of a text is contained within it and is completely determined by it so that all the reader must do is to 'extract' this meaning from the signs within it. This stance ignores the importance of 'going beyond the information given' and limits comprehension to the decoding (in the narrowest sense) of textual properties (without even reference to codes). *See also* **decoding, meaning**.

logocentrism Derrida used this term to refer to the 'metaphysics of presence' in Western culture – in particular its phonocentrism, and its foundation on a mythical 'transcendent signified'. Logocentrism can also refer to a typically unconscious interpretive bias which privileges linguistic communication over the revealingly named 'non-verbal' forms of communication and expression. *See also* **channel, phonocentrism**.

markedness The concept of markedness introduced by Jakobson can be applied to the poles of a paradigmatic opposition. Paired signifiers (such as male–female) consist of an unmarked form and a 'marked' form distinguished by some special semiotic feature. A marked or unmarked status applies not only to signifiers but also to their signifieds. The marked form (typically the second term) is presented as 'different' and is (implicitly) negative. The unmarked form is typically dominant (e.g. statistically within a text or corpus) and therefore seems to be neutral, normal and natural. *See also* **analogue oppositions, binary oppositions, deconstruction, paradigm, transcendent(al) signified**.

meaning Osgood and Richards (1923) listed 23 meanings of the term 'meaning'. The key distinction in relation to models of the sign is between: (a) *sense* – referred to by various theorists simply as 'meaning', or as conceptual meaning (e.g. linguistic meaning), content, **designation**, *signatum*, *significatum*, **signified, signification, interpretant**, idea or thought; and (b) *reference* to something beyond the sign-system (e.g. extralinguistic) – what is 'represented', variously termed **denotation**, *denotatum*, *designatum*, **object, reference, referent**, or simply 'thing'.

medium The term 'medium' is used in a variety of ways by different theorists, and may include such broad categories as speech and writing, or print and broadcasting or relate to specific technical forms within the media of mass communication or the media of interpersonal communication. Signs and codes are always anchored in the material form of a medium – each of which has its own constraints and affordances. A medium is typically treated instrumentally as a transparent vehicle of representation by readers of texts composed within it, but the medium used may itself contribute to meaning. *See also* **channel, sign vehicle**.

message This term variously refers either to a text or to the meaning of a text – referents which literalists tend to conflate. *See also* **text**.

metalingual function *See* **functions of signs**.

metaphor Metaphor expresses the unfamiliar (known in literary jargon as the 'tenor') in terms of the familiar (the 'vehicle'). In semiotic terms, a metaphor involves one signified acting as a signifier referring to a rather different signified. Since metaphors apparently disregard literal or denotative resemblance they can be seen as symbolic as well as iconic. *See also* **irony, metonymy, synecdoche, trope**.

metonymy A metonym is a figure of speech that involves using one signified to stand for another signified which is directly related to it or closely associated with it in some way, notably the substitution of effect for cause. It is sometimes considered to include the functions ascribed by some to synecdoche. Metonymy simulates an indexical mode. *See also* **irony**, **metaphor**, **synecdoche**, **trope**.

modality Modality refers to the reality status accorded to or claimed by a sign, text or genre.

modelling systems, primary and secondary Secondary modelling systems are described, following Lotman, as semiotic super-structures built upon primary modelling systems. Saussure treated spoken language as primary and saw the written word as secondary. Since this stance grants primacy to the spoken form, it has been criticized as phonocentric. Other theorists have extended this notion to texts in other media, seeing them as secondary modelling systems built out of a primary 'language'. *See also* **phonocentrism**.

modes of address Implicit and explicit ways in which aspects of the style, structure and/or content of a text function to position readers as subjects ('ideal readers') (e.g. in relation to class, age, gender and ethnicity). *See also* **functions of signs**.

motivation and constraint The term 'motivation' (used by Saussure) is sometimes contrasted with 'constraint' in describing the extent to which the signified determines the signifier. The more a signifier is constrained by the signified, the more 'motivated' the sign is: iconic signs are highly moti-vated; symbolic signs are unmotivated. The less motivated the sign, the more learning of an agreed code is required. *See also* **arbitrariness**.

multiaccentuality of the sign Voloshinov's term is used to refer to the diversity of the use and interpretation of texts by different audiences.

myth For Lévi-Strauss, myths were systems of binary alignments mediating between nature and culture. For Barthes, myths were the dominant discourses of contemporary culture. He argued that myths were a metalanguage operating through codes and serving the ideological function of naturalization.

narrowcast codes In contrast to broadcast codes, narrowcast codes are aimed at a limited audience, structurally more complex, less repetitive and tend to be more subtle, original and unpredictable. *See also* **broadcast codes**, **codes**.

natural signs (a) (in classical theory) representational visual images as opposed to 'conventional signs' (words); (b) signs not intentionally created but nevetheless interpreted as signifying, such as smoke signifying fire (St Augustine); (c) signs (apparently) produced without the intervention of a code (as in Barthes' initial characterization of photographs); (d) (allegedly in popular perception) metonyms (in contrast to metaphors). *See also* **iconic**, **indexical**.

naturalization Codes which have been naturalized are those which are so widely distributed in a culture and which are learned at such an early age that they appear not to be constructed but to be naturally given. Myths serve the ideological function of naturalization. *See also* **denaturalization**.

negotiated code and reading Within Stuart Hall's framework, this is an ideological code in which the reader partly shares the text's code and broadly accepts the preferred reading, but sometimes resists and modifies it in a way which reflects their own social position, experiences and interests (local and personal conditions may be seen as exceptions to the general rule). *See also* **dominant (or 'hegemonic') code and reading**, **oppositional code and reading**.

object Term used in Peirce's triadic model of the sign to describe the **referent** of the sign – what the sign 'stands for'.

open and closed texts Eco describes as 'closed' those texts which show a strong tendency to encourage a particular interpretation – in contrast to more 'open' texts. *See also* **broadcast codes**.

oppositional code and reading Within Stuart Hall's framework, this is an ideological code in which the reader, whose social situation places them in a directly oppositional relation to the dominant code, understands the preferred reading but does not share the text's code and rejects this reading, bringing to bear an alternative ideological code. *See also* **dominant (or 'hegemonic') code and reading**, **negotiated code and reading**.

oppositions, semantic *See* **analogue oppositions, binary oppositions**.

orders of signification Barthes adopted from Hjelmslev the notion that there are different orders of signification (levels of meaning) in semiotic systems. The first order of signification is that of denotation: at this level there is a sign consisting of a signifier and a signified. Connotation is a second order of signification which uses the denotative sign (signifier and signified) as its signifier and attaches to it an additional signified. Barthes argued that myth is also a higher order of signification built upon language. *See also* **connotation, denotation, myth**.

overcoding 'Overcoding' refers to structurally simple, conventional and repetitive texts having what information theorists call a high degree of redundancy. These are alleged to be features of broadcast codes. Under-coding is a feature of texts using less conventional narrowcast codes. *See also* **broadcast codes, preferred reading**.

pansemiotic features Jakobson's term for properties shared by all systems of signs (not just verbal language).

paradigm A paradigm is a set of associated signifiers which are all members of some defining category, but in which each signifier is significantly different. In natural language there are grammatical paradigms such as verbs or nouns. In a given context, one member of the paradigm set is structurally replaceable with another. *See also* **paradigmatic analysis, syntagm**.

paradigmatic analysis Paradigmatic analysis is a structuralist technique which seeks to identify the various paradigms which underlie the 'surface structure' of a text. This aspect of structural analysis involves a consideration of the positive or negative connotations of each signifier (revealed through the use of one signifier rather than another), and the existence of 'underlying' thematic paradigms (e.g. binary oppositions). *See also* **analogue oppositions, binary oppositions, commutation test, markedness, paradigm, syntagmatic analysis**.

parole *See* **langue**.

phatic function *See* **functions of signs**.

phonocentrism Phonocentrism is a typically unconscious interpretive bias which privileges speech over writing (and consequently the oral–aural over the visual). *See also* **channel**, **logocentrism**.

poetic function *See* **functions of signs**.

positioning of the subject *See* **subject**.

poststructuralism *See* Appendix.

preferred reading (Stuart Hall). Readers of a text are guided towards a preferred reading and away from 'aberrant decoding' through the use of codes. A preferred reading is not necessarily the result of any conscious intention on the part of the producer(s) of a text. The term is often used as if it refers to a meaning which is in some way built into the form and/or content of the text – a notion which is in uneasy accord with a textual determinism which Hall rejected. *See also* **dominant (or hegemonic) code and reading**.

primacy of the signifier The argument that reality or the world is at least partly created by the language (and other media) we use insists on *the primacy of the signifier* – suggesting that the signified is shaped by the signifier rather than *vice versa*. Some theorists stress the *materiality* of the signifier. Poststructuralist theorists such as Lacan, Barthes, Derrida, Foucault have developed the notion of the primacy of the signifier, but its roots can be found in structuralism. *See also* **arbitrariness**, **conventionality**, **relative autonomy**.

reading, dominant, negotiated and oppositional *See* **dominant code and reading**, **negotiated code and reading**, **oppositional code and reading**.

reference The **meaning** of a sign in relation to something beyond the sign-system. Sometimes a synonym for **referent**.

referent Term used by some theorists (e.g. Ogden and Richards) for what the sign 'stands for'. In Peirce's triadic model of the sign this is called the **object**. In Saussure's dyadic model of the sign a referent in the world is not explicitly featured – this is sometimes referred to as 'bracketing the referent'. Note that referents can include ideas, events and material objects. *See also* **representation**.

referential function *See* **functions of signs**.

reflexivity Some 'reflexive' aesthetic practices foreground their textuality – the signs of their production (the materials and techniques used) – thus reducing the transparency of their style. Texts in which the poetic function is dominant foreground the act and form of expression and undermine any sense of a natural or transparent connection between a signifier and a referent. Postmodernism often involves a highly reflexive intertextuality. *See also* **denaturalization, foregrounding, materiality of the sign, poetic function**.

relative autonomy Saussure's model of the sign assumes the relative autonomy of language in relation to reality (it does not directly feature a 'real world' referent); there is no essential bond between words and things. In a semiotic system with double articulation the levels of the signifier and of the signified are relatively autonomous. The signifier and the signified in a sign are autonomous to the extent that their relationship is arbitrary. *See also* **arbitrariness, articulation of codes, conventionality, primacy of the signifier**.

representamen The *representamen* is one of the three elements of Peirce's model of the sign and it refers to the form which the sign takes (not necessarily material). *See also* **signifier**.

representation Standard dictionaries note that a representation is something which stands for or in place of something else – which is of course what semioticians call a sign. Semiotics foregrounds and problematizes the process of representation. Representation always involves the construction of reality. All texts, however realistic they may seem to be, are constructed representations rather than simply transparent reflections, recordings, transcriptions or reproductions of a pre-existing reality. Both structuralist and poststructuralist theories lead to reality and truth being regarded as the products of particular systems of representation. *See also* **referent**.

restricted codes *See* **broadcast codes**.

selection, axis of A structuralist term for the 'vertical' axis in the analysis of a textual structure: the plane of the paradigm (Jakobson). *See also* **combination, axis of**.

semeiosis This term (also spelled *semiosis*) was used by Peirce to refer to the *process* of meaning-making – specifically to the interaction between the representamen, the object and the interpretant. *See also* **signification, signifying practices, unlimited semiosis**.

semeiotic This was Peirce's term (also spelled *semiotic*) for the 'formal doctrine of signs', which was closely related to logic.

scmiology Saussure's term *sémiologie* dates from a manuscript of 1894. 'Semiology' is sometimes used to refer to the study of signs by those within the Saussurean tradition (e.g. Barthes, Lévi-Strauss, Kristeva and Baudrillard), while 'semiotics' sometimes refers to those working within the Peircean tradition (e.g. Morris, Richards, Ogden and Sebeok). Sometimes 'semiology' refers to work concerned primarily with textual analysis while 'semiotics' refers to more philosophically oriented work. *See also* **semiotics**.

semiosphere The Russian cultural semiotician Yuri Lotman coined this term to refer to 'the whole semiotic space of the culture in question' – it can be thought of as a semiotic ecology in which different languages and media interact.

semiotic square Greimas introduced the semiotic square as a means of mapping the key semantic oppositions in a text or practice. If we begin by drawing a horizontal line linking two familiarly paired terms such as 'beautiful' and 'ugly', we turn this into a semiotic square by making this the upper line of a square in which the two other logical possibilities – 'not ugly' and 'not beautiful' occupy the lower corners. The semiotic square reminds us that this is not simply a binary opposition because something which is not beautiful is not necessarily ugly and that something which is not ugly is not necessarily beautiful.

semiotic triangle Peirce's triadic model of the sign is a semiotic triangle. *See also* **referent, sense, sign vehicle**.

semiotics, definition of Semiotics is 'the study of signs'. It is not purely a method of textual analysis, but involves both the theory and analysis of signs, codes and signifying practices. *See also* **semiology, sign**.

sense In some semiotic triangles, this refers to the sense made of the sign (what Peirce called the *interpretant*). *See also*: **interpretant, meaning, semiotic triangle**.

shifters Term adopted by Jakobson from Otto Jespersen for 'indexical symbols' in language – grammatical units with an **indexical** (deictic) character (such as personal pronouns) – which can be decoded only by reference to the specific context of particular messages.

sign A sign is a meaningful unit which is interpreted as 'standing for' something other than itself. Signs are found in the physical form of words, images, sounds, acts or objects (this physical form is sometimes known as the sign vehicle). Signs have no *intrinsic* meaning and become signs only when sign-users invest them with meaning with reference to a recognized code. *See also* **analogue signs, digital signs, functions of signs, signification**.

sign vehicle A term sometimes used to refer to the physical or material form of the sign (e.g. words, images, sounds, acts or objects). For some commentators this means the same as the *signifier* (which for Saussure himself did *not* refer to *material* form). The Peircean equivalent is the *representamen*: the form which the sign takes, but even for Peirce this was not necessarily a material form. *See also* **medium, representamen, signifier, tokens and types**.

signans Latin term favoured by Jakobson for the signifier or perceptible form of the sign (*signum*) – its 'sound form' in the case of words. *See also signatum*, **signifier**, *signum*.

signatum In Jakobson's dyadic model the *signatum* is the signified or conceptual meaning of the sign; in language it refers to linguistic meaning as distinct from the ***denotatum***. *See also signans*, **signified**, *signum*.

signification In Saussurean semiotics, the term *signification* refers to the relationship between the signifier and the signified. It is also variously used to refer to: the defining function of signs (i.e. that they signify, or 'stand for', something other than themselves); the *process* of signifying (semiosis); signs as part of an overall semiotic *system*; *what* is signified; the reference of language to reality; a representation. *See also* **semiosis**, **value**.

significatum Morris's term for the sense of the sign (as distinct from *denotatum*).

signified (*signifié*) For Saussure, the signified was one of the two parts of the sign. Saussure's *signified* is the mental *concept* represented by the signifier (and is *not* a material thing). This does not exclude the reference of signs to physical objects in the world as well as to abstract concepts and fictional entities, but the signified is not itself a referent in the world. *See also* **referent**, **signifier**, **transcendent(al) signified**.

signifier (signifiant) In the Saussurean tradition, the signifier is the *form* which a sign takes. For Saussure himself, in relation to linguistic signs, this meant a non-material form of the spoken word. Subsequent semioticians have treated it as the material (or physical) form of the sign – something which can be seen, heard, felt, smelt or tasted (also called the sign vehicle). *See also* **empty signifier**, **primacy of the signifier**, **representamen**, **sign vehicle**, **signified**.

signifying practices These are the meaning-making behaviours in which people engage (including the production and reading of texts) following particular conventions or rules of construction and interpretation. *See also* **interpretive community**.

signum Jakobson's favoured Latin term for a sign, uniting a *signans* and *signatum* in his dyadic model.

simple sign A sign which does not contain any other signs, in contrast to a complex sign. *See also* **complex sign**, **sign**.

simulacrum This was Baudrillard's term (borrowed from Plato); 'simulacra' are 'copies without originals' – the main form in which we encounter texts in postmodern culture. More broadly, he used the term to refer to a representation which bears no relation to any reality. See also **digital signs**, **empty signifier**, **tokens and types**.

single articulation, codes with Codes with single articulation have either first articulation or second articulation only. Codes with *first articulation only* (e.g. traffic signs) consist of signs – meaningful elements which are systematically related to each other – but there is no second articulation to structure these signs into minimal, non-meaningful elements. Other semiotic codes lacking double articulation have *second articulation only*. These consist of signs which have specific meanings which are not derived from their elements (e.g. binary code). They are divisible only into *figurae* (minimal functional units). *See also* **articulation of codes**, **double articulation**, **unarticulated codes**.

structuralism *See* Appendix.

subject In theories of subjectivity a distinction is made between 'the subject' and 'the individual'. While the individual is an actual person, the *subject* is a set of *roles* constructed by dominant cultural and ideological values. Poststructuralist theorists critique the concept of the unified subject. *See also* **addresser and addressee**, **interpellation**, **preferred reading**.

symbol (a) for some theorists (e.g. Goodman), and in popular usage, simply a **sign**; (b) a **symbolic** (i.e. conventional) sign, as distinct from an **iconic** or an **indexical** sign.

symbolic A mode in which the signifier does *not* resemble the signified but which is arbitrary or purely conventional – so that the relationship must be learnt (e.g. the word 'stop', a red traffic light, a national flag, a number). *See also* **arbitrariness**, **iconic**, **indexical**.

synchronic analysis Synchronic analysis studies a phenomenon (such as a code) as if it were frozen at one moment in time. Saussurean structuralism focused on synchronic rather than diachronic analysis and was criticized for ignoring historicity. *See also* **langue and parole**.

synecdoche A figure of speech involving the substitution of part for whole, genus for species or vice versa. Some theorists do not distinguish it from metonymy. *See also* **irony**, **metaphor**, **metonymy**, **trope**.

syntagm A syntagm is an orderly combination of interacting signifiers which forms a meaningful whole. *Syntagmatic relations* are the various ways in which constituent units within the same text may be structurally related to each other. These can be either *sequential* (e.g. in film and television narrative sequences), or *spatial* (e.g. in paintings or photographs). *See also* **paradigmatic analysis, syntagmatic analysis**.

syntagmatic analysis Syntagmatic analysis is a structuralist technique which seeks to establish the 'surface structure' of a text and the relationships between its parts. *See also* **paradigmatic analysis, syntagm**.

text Most broadly, this term is used to refer to anything which can be 'read' for meaning; to some theorists, the world is 'social text'. Although the term appears to privilege written texts (it seems *graphocentric* and *logocentric*), to most semioticians a text is a system of signs (in the form of words, images, sounds and/or gestures). The term is often used to refer to *recorded* (e.g. written) texts which are independent of their users (used in this sense the term excludes unrecorded speech). *See also* **representation**.

tokens and types Peirce made a distinction between *tokens* and *types*. In relation to words in a text, a count of the tokens would be a count of the total number of words used (regardless of type), while a count of the types would be a count of the *different* words used (ignoring any repetition). The medium used may determine whether a text is a type which is its own sole token (unique original) or simply one token among many of its type ('a copy without an original'). *See also* **digital signs**.

transcendent(al) signified Derrida argued that dominant ideological discourse relies on the metaphysical illusion of a transcendental signified – an ultimate referent at the heart of a signifying system which is portrayed as 'absolute and irreducible', stable, timeless and transparent – as if it were *independent of* and *prior to* that system. All other signifieds within that signifying system are subordinate to this dominant central signified which is the final meaning to which they point. Without such a foundational term to provide closure for meaning, every signified functions as a signifier in an endless play of signification. *See also* **deconstruction, empty signifier, markedness**.

transformation, rules of Lévi-Strauss argued that new structural patterns within a culture are generated from existing ones through formal rules of transformation based on systematic similarities, equivalences, parallels, or symmetrical inversions. The patterns on different levels of a structure (e.g. within a myth) or in different structures (e.g. in different myths) are seen as logical transformations of each other. Rules of transformation enable the analyst to reduce a complex structure to some more basic constituent units. *See also* **commutation test**, **isomorphism**.

transmission model of communication Everyday references to communication are based on a 'transmission' model in which a 'sender' 'transmits' a message to a 'receiver' – a formula which reduces meaning to content (delivered like a parcel) and which tends to support the intentional fallacy. Such models make no allowance for the importance of either codes or social contexts.

trope Tropes are rhetorical 'figures of speech' such as **metaphor**, **metonymy**, **synecdoche** and **irony**.

types and tokens *See* **tokens and types**.

unarticulated codes Codes without articulation consist of a series of signs bearing no direct relation to each other. These signs are not divisible into recurrent compositional elements (e.g. the folkloristic 'language of flowers'). *See also* **articulation of codes**.

unlimited semiosis Umberto Eco coined the term 'unlimited semiosis' to refer to the way in which, for Peirce (via the 'interpretant'), for Barthes (via connotation), for Derrida (via 'freeplay') and for Lacan (via 'the sliding signified'), the signified is endlessly commutable – functioning in its turn as a signifier for a further signified. *See also* **interpretant**, **transcendent(al) signified**.

value Saussure distinguished the value of a sign from its signification or referential meaning. A sign does not have an absolute value in itself – its value is dependent on its relations with other signs within the signifying system as a whole. Words in different languages can have equivalent referential meanings but different values since they belong to different networks of associations. *See also* **signification**.

Note: A more extensive glossary is available in the online version of this text, currently at: http://www.aber.ac.uk/media/Documents/S4B/

BIBLIOGRAPHY

Aarseth, Espen J. (1997) *Cybertext: Perspectives on Ergodic Literature*.
    Baltimore, MD: Johns Hopkins University Press.
Abrams, Meyer H. (1971) *The Mirror and the Lamp: Romantic Theory
    and the Critical Tradition*. London: Oxford University Press.
Agawu, V. Kofi (1991) *Playing with Signs: A Semiotic Interpretation of
    Classic Music*. Princeton, NJ: Princeton University Press.
Agrest, Diana and Mario Gandelsonas (1977) 'Semiotics and the Limits
    of Architecture', in Sebeok (ed.) (1977), pp. 90 120.
Alcoff, Linda and Elizabeth Potter (eds) (1993) *Feminist Epistemologies*.
    London: Routledge.
Alexander, Monty (1995) 'Big Talk, Small Talk: BT's Strategic Use of
    Semiotics in Planning its Current Advertising' [WWW document]
    http://www.semioticsolutions.com/ref.aspx?id=72.
—— (2000) 'Codes and Contexts: Practical Semiotics for the Qualita-
    tive Researcher' [WWW document] http://www.semioticsolutions.
    com/ref.aspx?id=78.
Allen, Graham (2000) *Intertextuality*. London: Routledge.
Allen, Robert C. (ed.) (1992) *Channels of Discourse, Reassembled*.
    London: Routledge.

Allport, Gordon W. and Leo J. Postman (1945) 'The basic psychology of rumour', *Transactions of the New York Academy of Sciences*, Series II, 8: 61–81. Reprinted in Eleanor E. Maccoby, Theodore M. Newcomb and Eugene L. Hartley (eds) (1959) *Readings in Social Psychology* (3rd edn). London: Methuen, pp. 54–65.

Alter, Jean (1990) *A Sociosemiotic Theory of Theatre*. Philadelphia, PA: University of Pennsylvania Press.

Althusser, Louis (1971) *Lenin and Philosophy* (trans. Ben Brewster). London: New Left Books.

Altman, Rick (1992) 'The material heterogeneity of recorded sound', in Rick Altman (ed.) (1992) *Sound Theory, Sound Practice*. New York: Routledge, pp. 15–31.

—— (1999) *Film/Genre*. London: BFI.

Alvarado, Manuel, Edward Buscombe and Richard Collins (eds) (2001) *Representation and Photography: A Screen Education Reader*. Basingstoke: Palgrave.

Andersen, Peter Bøgh (1997) *A Theory of Computer Semiotics*. Cambridge: Cambridge University Press.

Andrews, Lew (1998) *Story and Space in Renaissance Art: The Rebirth of Continuous Narrative*. Cambridge: Cambridge University Press.

Ang, Ien (1985) *Watching 'Dallas': Soap Opera and the Melodramatic Imagination*. London: Methuen.

Argyle, Michael (1969) *Social Interaction*. London: Tavistock/Methuen.

—— (1983) *The Psychology of Interpersonal Behaviour* (4th edn). Harmondsworth: Penguin.

—— (1988) *Bodily Communication* (2nd edn). London: Methuen.

Aristotle (2004) *On Interpretation* (trans. E. M. Edghill). Whitefish, MT: Kessinger.

Ashwin, Clive (1989) 'Drawing, design and semiotics', in Victor Margolis (ed.) (1989) *Design Discourse: History, Theory, Criticism*. Chicago: University of Chicago Press, pp. 199–212.

Aston, Elaine and George Savona (1991) *Theatre as Sign-system: A Semiotics of Text and Performance*. London: Routledge.

Baggaley, Jon and Steve Duck (1976) *Dynamics of Television*. Farnborough: Saxon House.

Bakhtin, Mikhail (1981) *The Dialogic Imagination: Four Essays* (trans. C. Emerson and M. Holquist). Austin, TX: University of Texas Press.

Barnard, Malcolm (2005) *Graphic Design as Communication*. London: Routledge.

Barthes, Roland (1953/1967) *Writing Degree Zero* (trans. Annette Lavers and Colin Smith). London: Jonathan Cape.

——— (1957/1987) *Mythologies*. New York: Hill & Wang.
——— (1961) 'The photographic message', in Barthes (1977a), pp. 15–31; also in Barthes (1991), pp. 3–20.
——— (1964) 'The rhetoric of the image', in Barthes (1977a), pp. 32–51; also in Barthes (1991), pp. 21–40.
——— (1967a) *Elements of Semiology* (trans. Annette Lavers and Colin Smith). London: Jonathan Cape.
——— (1967b/1985) *The Fashion System* (trans. Matthew Ward and Richard Howard). London: Jonathan Cape.
——— (1973/1974) *S/Z*. London: Jonathan Cape.
——— (1977a) *Image–Music–Text*. London: Fontana.
——— (1977b) *Roland Barthes* (trans. Richard Howard). Berkeley, CA: University of California Press.
——— (1982) *Empire of Signs* (trans. Richard Howard). New York: Hill & Wang.
——— (1983) *A Barthes Reader* (ed. Susan Sontag). New York: Hill & Wang.
——— (1991) *The Responsibility of Forms: Critical Essays on Music, Art, and Representation* (trans. Richard Howard). Berkeley, CA: University of California Press.
——— (1993) *Camera Lucida* (trans. Richard Howard). London: Vintage.
——— (2006) *The Language of Fashion* (trans. Andy Stafford). Oxford: Berg.
Baudrillard, Jean (1984) 'The precession of simulacra', in Brian Wallis (ed.)
——— (1984) *Art After Modernism: Rethinking Representations*, vol. 1. New York: Museum of Contemporary Art (reprinted from *Art and Text* 11 (September 1983): 3–47.
——— (1988) *Selected Writings* (ed. Mark Poster). Cambridge: Polity Press.
——— (1995) *The Gulf War Did Not Take Place* (trans. Paul Patton). Bloomington, IN: Indiana University Press.
Bazin, André (1974) *Jean Renoir*. London: W. H. Allen.
Beasley, Ron and Marcel Danesi (2002) *Persuasive Signs: The Semiotics of Advertising*. Berlin: Mouton de Gruyter.
Beasley, Ron, Marcel Danesi and Paul Perron (2000) *Signs for Sale: An Outline of Semiotic Analysis for Advertisers and Marketers*. New York: Legas.
Beattie, Geoffrey (2003) *Visible Thought: The New Psychology of Body Language*. London: Routledge.
Belsey, Catherine (1980) *Critical Practice*. London: Methuen.
Benjamin, Walter (1992) *Illuminations* (ed. Hannah Arendt, trans. Harry Zohn). London: Fontana.
Benson, Robert W. (1989) *Semiotics, Modernism and the Law*. Berlin: Mouton.

Benthall, Jonathan and Ted Polhemus (1975) *The Body as a Medium of Expression*. Harmondsworth: Penguin.

Benveniste, Émile (1969/1986) 'The Semiology of Language', in Innis (ed.) (1986), pp. 228–46.

Berger, John (1968) 'Understanding a Photograph', in John Berger (1972) *Selected Essays and Articles*. Harmondsworth: Penguin, pp. 178–82.

—— (1972) *Ways of Seeing*. London: BBC/Penguin.

Berger, Peter and Thomas Luckmann (1967) *The Social Construction of Reality*. New York: Anchor/Doubleday.

Bernard, Michael, Melissa Mills, Michelle Peterson and Kelsey Storrer (2001) 'A Comparison of Popular Online Fonts: Which is Best and When?' *Usability News* 3.2 http://psychology.wichita.edu/surl/usability news/3S/font.htm

Bernstein, Basil (1971) *Class, Codes and Control*, vol. 1. London: Routledge & Kegan Paul.

Bertelsen, Lars Kiel, Rune Gade and Mette Sandbye (1999) *Symbolic Imprints: Essays on Photography and Visual Culture*. Aarhus: Aarhus University Press.

Bertin, Jacques (1983) *Semiology of Graphics* (trans. William J. Berg). Madison, WI: University of Wisconsin Press.

Bignell, Jonathan (1997) *Media Semiotics: An Introduction*. Manchester: Manchester University Press.

Birdwhistell, Ray L. (1971) *Kinesics and Context: Essays on Body–Motion Communication*. London: Allen Lane.

Block (ed.) (1996) *The Block Reader in Visual Culture*. London: Routledge.

Bloomfield, Leonard (1939) *Linguistic Aspects of Science*. Chicago, IL: University of Chicago Press.

Boardman, Mark (2004) *The Language of Websites*. London: Routledge.

Bogdan, Catalina (2002) *The Semiotics of Visual Languages*. New York: Columbia University Press.

Bolter, Jay David (1991) *Writing Space: The Computer, Hypertext and the History of Writing*. Hillsdale, NJ: Lawrence Erlbaum.

Boorstin, Daniel J. (1961) *The Image, or What Happened to the American Dream*. London: Weidenfeld & Nicolson.

Bordwell, David, Janet Staiger and Kristin Thompson (1988) *The Classical Hollywood Cinema: Film Style and Mode of Production to 1960*. London: Routledge.

Bordwell, David and Kristin Thompson (1993) *Film Art: An Introduction* (4th edn). New York: McGraw-Hill.

Bouissac, Paul (ed.) (1998) *Encyclopedia of Semiotics*. Oxford: Oxford University Press.

Branigan, Edward (1984) *Point of View in the Cinema*. Berlin: Mouton de Gruyter.

Broadbent, Geoffrey, Richard Bunt and Charles Jencks (1980) *Signs, Symbols and Architecture*. New York: Wiley.

Brooks, Cleanth and Robert Penn Warren (1972) *Modern Rhetoric* (shorter 3rd edn). New York: Harcourt Brace Jovanovich.

Bruner, Jerome S. (1966) 'Culture and cognitive growth', in J. S. Bruner, R. R. Olver and P. M. Greenfield (eds) (1966) *Studies in Cognitive Growth*. New York. Wiley.

—— (1990) *Acts of Meaning*. Cambridge, MA: Harvard University Press.

Bruner, Jerome S., Jacqueline S. Goodnow and George A. Austin ([1956] 1962) *A Study of Thinking*. New York: Wiley.

Bruss, Elizabeth W. (1978) 'Peirce and Jakobson on the Nature of the Sign', in Richard W. Bailey, Ladislav Matejka and Peter Steiner (eds) (1978) *The Sign: Semiotics Around the World*. Ann Arbor, MI: University of Michigan Press, pp. 81–98.

Bryson, Norman (1983) *Vision and Painting: The Logic of the Gaze*. New Haven, CT: Yale University Press.

Bryson, Norman, Michael Ann Holly and Keith Moxey (eds) (1991) *Visual Theory: Painting and Interpretation*. Oxford: Polity.

Buckland, Warren (ed.) (1995) *The Film Spectator: From Sign to Mind*. Amsterdam: Amsterdam University Press.

—— (2000) *The Cognitive Semiotics of Film*. Cambridge: Cambridge University Press.

Budd, Mike, Steve Craig and Clay Steinman (1999) *Consuming Environments: Television and Consumer Culture*. New Brunswick, NJ: Rutgers University Press.

Burgin, Victor (ed.) (1982a) *Thinking Photography*. London: Macmillan.

—— (1982b) 'Photographic practice and art theory', in Burgin (ed.) (1982a), pp. 39–83.

Burgoon, Judee K., David B. Buller and W. Gill Woodall (1989) *Nonverbal Communication: The Unspoken Dialogue*. New York: Harper & Row.

Burke, Kenneth (1969) *A Grammar of Motives*. Berkeley, CA: University of California Press.

Burnett, Ron (2005) *How Images Think*. Cambridge, MA: MIT Press.

Burr, Vivien (1995) *An Introduction to Social Constructionism*. London: Routledge.

Butler, Judith (1999) *Gender Trouble: Feminism and the Subversion of Identity*. London: Routledge.

Cable, Carole (1981) *Semiotics and Architecture*. Monticello, IL: Vance Bibliographies.

Carlson, Marvin A. (1993) *Places of Performance: Semiotics of Theatre Architecture*. Ithaca, NY: Cornell University Press.

Carroll, John M. (1980) *Toward a Structural Psychology of Cinema*. The Hague: Mouton.

Carson, Fiona and Claire Pajaczkowska (eds) (2001) *Feminist Visual Culture*. New York: Routledge.

Caws, Peter (1968) 'What is Structuralism?', in Hayes and Hayes (eds) (1970), pp. 197–214.

Chalfen, Richard (1987) *Snapshot Versions of Life*. Bowling Green, OH: Bowling Green State University Popular Press.

Chandler, Daniel (1995) *The Act of Writing: A Media Theory Approach*. Aberystwyth: University of Wales, Aberystwyth.

—— (1998) *Semiótica para Principiantes* (trans. Vanessa Hogan Vega and Iván Rodrigo Mendizábal). Quito, Ecuador: Ediciones Abya-Yala/ Escuela de Comunicación Social de la Universidad Politécnica Salesiana.

—— (2002) *Semiotics: The Basics* (1st edn). London: Routledge.

—— (2006) 'Identities Under Construction', in Janet Maybin and Joan Swann (eds) (2006) *The Art of English: Everyday Creativity*. Basingstoke: Palgrave Macmillan, pp. 303–11.

Chandler, Daniel and Merris Griffiths (2000) 'Gender-Differentiated Production Features in Toy Commercials', *Journal of Broadcasting and Electronic Media* 44(3): 503–20.

Chase, Stuart (1938) *The Tyranny of Words*. New York: Harcourt, Brace & World.

Cherry, Colin (1966) *On Human Communication* (2nd edn). Cambridge, MA: MIT Press.

Clark, Herbert H. and Eve V. Clark (1977) *Psychology and Language: An Introduction to Psycholinguistics*. New York: Harcourt Brace Jovanovich.

Cobley, Paul (ed.) (2001) *The Routledge Companion to Semiotics and Linguistics*. London: Routledge.

Cockburn, Cynthia and Susan Ormrod (1993) *Gender and Technology in the Making*. London: Sage.

Cohen, Stanley and Jock Young (eds) (1981) *The Manufacture of News: Social Problems, Deviance and the Mass Media*. London: Constable.

Colapietro, Vincent Michael (1993) *Glossary of Semiotics*. New York: Paragon House.

Collett, Peter (2003) *The Book of Tells: How to Read People's Minds From their Actions*. London: Doubleday.

Colquhoun, Alan (1981) *Essays in Architectural Criticism. Modern Architecture and Historical Change*. Cambridge, MA: MIT Press.

Cook, Guy (1992) *The Discourse of Advertising*. London: Routledge.

Corner, John (1980) 'Codes and Cultural Analysis', *Media, Culture and Society* 2: 73–86.

Corner, John and Jeremy Hawthorne (eds) (1980) *Communication Studies: An Introductory Reader*. London: Edward Arnold.

Counihan, Carole and Penny van Esterik (eds) (1997) *Food and Culture: A Reader*. London: Routledge.

Counsell, Colin (1996) *Signs of Performance: Introduction to Twentieth Century Theatre*. London: Routledge.

Coward, Rosalind and John Ellis (1977) *Language and Materialism: Developments in Semiology and the Theory of the Subject*. London: Routledge & Kegan Paul.

Crow, David (2003) *Visible Signs: An Introduction to Semiotics*. Crans-près-Céligny: AVA.

Crystal, David (1987) *The Cambridge Encyclopedia of Language*. Cambridge: Cambridge University Press.

Csikszentmihalyi, Mihaly and Eugene Rochberg-Halton (1981) *The Meaning of Things: Domestic Symbols and the Self*. Cambridge: Cambridge University Press.

Culler, Jonathan (1975) *Structuralist Poetics: Structuralism, Linguistics and the Study of Literature*. London: Routledge & Kegan Paul.

—— (1981) *The Pursuit of Signs: Semiotics, Literature, Deconstruction*. London: Routledge & Kegan Paul.

—— (1985) *Saussure*. London: Fontana.

Cumming, Naomi (2001) *The Sonic Self: Musical Subjectivity and Signification*. Bloomington, IN: Indiana University Press.

Danesi, Marcel (2000) *Encyclopedic Dictionary of Semiotics, Media, and Communication*. Toronto: University of Toronto Press.

—— (2002) *Understanding Media Semiotics*. London: Arnold.

Davis, Desmond (1960) *The Grammar of Television Production* (revised by John Elliot). London: Barrie & Rockliff.

Davis, Howard and Paul Walton (eds) (1983a) *Language, Image, Media*. Oxford: Basil Blackwell.

—— (1983b) 'Death of a premier: consensus and closure in international news', in Davis and Walton (eds), (1983a), pp. 8–49.

de Lauretis, Teresa (1984) *Alice Doesn't: Feminism, Semiotics, Cinema*. London: Macmillan.

de Marinis, Marco (1993) *The Semiotics of Performance*. Bloomington, IN: Indiana University Press.

de Souza, Clarisse Sieckenius (2005) *The Semiotic Engineering of Human-Computer Interaction*. Cambridge, MA: MIT Press.

de Toro, Fernando and Carole Hubbard (1995) *Theatre Semiotics: Text and Staging in Modern Theatre*. Toronto: University of Toronto Press.

Deledalle, Gérard (2000) *Charles S. Peirce's Philosophy of Signs: Essays in Comparative Semiotics*. Bloomington, IN: Indiana University Press.

Deregowski, Jan B. (1980) *Illusions, Patterns and Pictures: A Cross-Cultural Perspective*. New York: Academic Press.

Derrida, Jacques (1967a/1976) *Of Grammatology* (trans. Gayatri Chakravorty Spivak). Baltimore, MD: Johns Hopkins University Press.

—— (1967b/1978) *Writing and Difference* (trans. Alan Bass). London: Routledge & Kegan Paul.

—— (1974) 'White Mythology: Metaphor in the Text of Philosophy', *New Literary History* 6(1): 5–74.

—— (1981) *Positions* (trans. Alan Bass). London: Athlone Press.

—— (1998) *A Derrida Reader* (ed. Peggy Kamuf). New York: Columbia University Press.

Desouza, Kevin C. and Tobin Hensgen (2005) *Managing Information in Complex Organizations: Semiotics and Signals, Complexity and Chaos*. New York: Sharpe.

Donahue, Thomas John (1993) *Structures of Meaning: A Semiotic Approach to the Play Text*. Madison, NJ: Fairleigh Dickinson University Press.

Dosse, François (1998) *History of Structuralism: The Rising Sign, 1945–66*, vol. 1 (trans. Deborah N. Glassman). Minneapolis, MN: University of Minnesota Press.

Douglas, Mary (1966) *Purity and Danger: An Analysis of the Concepts of Pollution and Taboo*. London: Routledge & Kegan Paul.

—— (ed.) (1973) *Rules and Meanings: The Anthropology of Everyday Knowledge*. Harmondsworth: Penguin.

—— (1975) 'Deciphering a Meal', in Counihan and van Esterik (eds) (1997), pp. 36–54.

Dyer, Gillian (1982) *Advertising as Communication*. New York: Methuen.

Dyer, Richard (1992) *Only Entertainment*. London: Routledge.

—— (1997) *White*. London: Routledge.

Eagleton, Terry (1983) *Literary Theory: An Introduction*. Oxford: Basil Blackwell.

Eakins, Barbara Westbrook and R. Gene Eakins (1978) *Sex Differences in Human Communication*. Boston, MA: Houghton Mifflin.

Easthope, Antony (1988) *British Post-structuralism Since 1968.* London: Routledge

—— (1990) *What a Man's Gotta Do.* Boston, MA: Unwin Hyman.

Eaton, Mick (ed.) (1981) *Cinema and Semiotics* (*Screen* Reader 2). London: Society for Education in Film and Television.

Eco, Umberto (1965) 'Towards a semiotic enquiry into the television message', in Corner and Hawthorn (eds) (1980), pp. 131–50.

—— (1976) *A Theory of Semiotics.* Bloomington, IN: Indiana University Press/London: Macmillan.

—— (1981) *The Role of the Reader: Explorations in the Semiotics of Texts.* London: Hutchinson.

—— (1982) 'Critique of the image', in Burgin (ed.) (1982a), pp. 32–8.

—— (1984) *Semiotics and the Philosophy of Language.* Bloomington, IN: Indiana University Press.

—— (1997) *The Search for the Perfect Language.* London: Fontana.

—— (1999) *Kant and the Platypus: Essays on Language and Cognition.* London: Secker and Warburg.

Ehrat, Johannes (2004) *Cinema and Semiotic: Peirce and Film Aesthetics, Narration, and Representation.* Toronto: University of Toronto Press.

Elicker, Martina (1997) *Semiotics of Popular Music: The Theme of Loneliness in Mainstream Pop and Rock Songs.* Tubingen: Narr.

Elkins, James (1998) *On Pictures and the Words that Fail Them.* Cambridge: Cambridge University Press.

Esslin, Martin (1988) *The Field of Drama: How the Signs of Drama Create Meaning on Stage and Screen.* London: Methuen.

Evans, Jessica and Stuart Hall (eds) (1999) *Visual Culture: The Reader.* Thousand Oaks, CA: Sage.

Ewen, Stuart (1999) *All Consuming Images: The Politics of Style in Contemporary Culture.* New York: Basic Books.

Fairclough, Norman (1995a) *Media Discourse.* London: Edward Arnold.

—— (1995b) *Critical Discourse Analysis.* Harlow: Longman.

Finnegan, Ruth (2002) *Communicating: The Multiple Modes of Human Interconnection.* London: Routledge.

Fisch, Max H. (1986) *Peirce, Semiotic and Pragmatism* (ed. Kenneth Laine Ketner and Christian J. W. Kloesel). Bloomington, IN: Indiana University Press.

Fischer-Lichte, Erika (1992) *The Semiotics of Theatre* (trans. Jeremy Gaines and Doris L Jones). Bloomington, IN: Indiana University Press.

Fish, Stanley (1980) *Is There A Text In This Class? The Authority Of Interpretive Communities.* Cambridge, MA: Harvard University Press.

Fiske, John (1982) *Introduction to Communication Studies*. London: Routledge.

—— (1987) *Television Culture*. London: Routledge.

—— (1989) 'Codes', in Tobia L. Worth (ed.) *International Encyclopedia of Communications*, vol. 1. New York: Oxford University Press, pp. 312–16.

Fiske, John and John Hartley (1978) *Reading Television*. London: Methuen.

Fleming, Dan (1996) *Powerplay: Toys as Popular Culture*. Manchester: Manchester University Press.

Floch, Jean-Marie (2000) *Visual Identities* (trans. Pierre Van Osselaer and Alec McHoul). London: Continuum.

—— (2001) *Semiotics, Marketing and Communication* (trans. Robin Orr Bodkin). London: Palgrave Macmillan.

Forceville, Charles (1996) *Pictorial Metaphor in Advertising*. London: Routledge.

Foucault, Michel (1970) *The Order of Things*. London: Tavistock.

—— (1974) *The Archaeology of Knowledge*. London: Tavistock.

—— (1983) *This is Not a Pipe*. Berkeley: University of California Press.

—— (1991) *The Foucault Reader* (ed. Paul Rabinow). Harmondsworth: Penguin.

Freadman, Anne (2004) *The Machinery of Talk: Charles Peirce and the Sign Hypothesis*. Stanford, CT: Stanford University Press.

Freud, Sigmund (1938) *The Basic Writings of Sigmund Freud*. New York: Modern Library.

Fuery, Patrick and Kelli Fuery (2003) *Visual Cultures and Critical Theory*. London: Arnold.

Fuss, Diane (ed.) (1991) *Inside/Out: Lesbian Theories, Gay Theories*. London: Routledge.

Gallie, W. B. (1952) *Peirce and Pragmatism*. Harmondsworth: Penguin.

Galtung, Johan and Eric Ruge (1981) 'Structuring and selecting news', in Cohen and Young (eds) (1981), pp. 52–63.

Gardiner, Michael (1992) *The Dialogics of Critique: M. M. Bakhtin and the Theory of Ideology*. London: Routledge.

Gazendam, H.W. (2003) *Dynamics and Change in Organizations: Studies in Organizational Semiotics*. Berlin: Springer.

Gelb, I. J. (1963) *A Study of Writing*. Chicago: University of Chicago Press.

Genette, Gérard (1997) *Palimpsests* (trans. Channa Newman and Claude Doubinsky). Lincoln, NB: University of Nebraska Press.

Glasgow University Media Group (1980) *More Bad News*. London: Routledge & Kegan Paul.

Goffman, Erving (1969a) *Behaviour in Public Places*. Harmondsworth: Penguin.
—— (1969b) *The Presentation of Self in Everyday Life*. Harmondsworth: Penguin.
—— (1979) *Gender Advertisements*. New York: Harper & Row/London: Macmillan.
Goldman, Robert (1992) *Reading Ads Socially*. London: Routledge.
Goldman, Robert and Stephen Papson (1996) *Sign Wars: The Cluttered Landscape of Advertising*. New York: Guilford Press.
—— (1998) *Nike Culture*. London: Sage.
Gombrich, Ernst H. (1972) 'The Visual Image', in *Scientific American* (eds) *Communication*. San Francisco, CA: Freeman, pp. 46–60; originally in a special issue of *Scientific American*, September 1972; republished in Gombrich (1982), pp. 137–61.
—— (1977) *Art and Illusion: A Study in the Psychology of Pictorial Representation*. London: Phaidon.
—— (1982) *The Image and the Eye: Further Studies in the Psychology of Pictorial Representation*. London: Phaidon.
Goodman, Nelson (1968) *Languages of Art: An Approach to a Theory of Symbols*. London: Oxford University Press.
—— (1978) *Ways of Worldmaking*. Indianapolis, IN: Hackett.
Gottdiener, Mark and Alexandros Ph. Lagopoulos (eds) (1986) *The City and the Sign: An Introduction to Urban Semiotics*. New York: Columbia University Press.
Gray, Jonathan (2005) *Watching with the Simpsons*. London: Routledge.
Grayson, Kent (1998) 'The icons of consumer research: using signs to represent consumers' reality', in Stern (ed.) (1998), pp. 27–43.
Greenberg, J. H. (1966) *Language Universals*. The Hague: Mouton.
Greimas, Algirdas J. (1966/1983) *Structural Semantics*. Lincoln, NB: University of Nebraska Press.
—— (1970) *Du Sens*. Paris: Seuil.
—— (1987) *On Meaning: Selected Writings in Semiotic Theory* (trans. Paul J. Perron and Frank H. Collins). London: Frances Pinter.
Greimas, Algirdas J. and Joseph Courtés (1982) *Semiotics and Language: An Analytical Dictionary* (trans. L. Crist, D. Patte et al.). Bloomington, IN: Indiana University Press.
Grosz, Elizabeth (1993) 'Bodies and knowledges: feminism and the crisis of reason', in Alcoff and Potter (eds) (1993), pp. 187–215.
Guerrero, Laura K., Joseph A. DeVito and Michael L. Hecht (eds) (1990) *The Nonverbal Communication Reader*. Prospect Heights, IL: Waveland Press.

Guiraud, Pierre (1975) *Semiology* (trans. George Gross). London: Routledge & Kegan Paul.

Gumpert, Gary and Robert Cathcart (1985) 'Media grammars, generations and media gaps', *Critical Studies in Mass Communication* 2: 23–35.

Hall, Edward T. (1959) *The Silent Language*. Greenwich, CT: Fawcett.

—— (1966) *The Hidden Dimension*. New York: Doubleday.

Hall, Judith A. (1990) *Nonverbal Sex Differences: Accuracy of Communication and Expressive Style*. Baltimore, MD: Johns Hopkins University Press.

Hall, Stuart (1977) 'Culture, the media and the "ideological effect"', in James Curran, Michael Gurevitch and Janet Woollacott (eds) (1977) *Mass Communication and Society*. London: Edward Arnold, pp. 315–48.

—— (1973/1980) 'Encoding/decoding', in Centre for Contemporary Cultural Studies (ed.) *Culture, Media, Language: Working Papers in Cultural Studies, 1972–79*, London: Hutchinson, pp. 128–38.

—— (1981) 'The determinations of news photographs', in Cohen and Young (eds) (1981), pp. 226–43.

—— (1996) 'Cultural studies: two paradigms', in Storey (ed.) (1996), pp. 31–48.

Halle, Morris, Krystyna Pomorska, Ladislav Matejka and Boris Uspenskij (eds) (1984) *Semiosis: Semiotics and the History of Culture*. Michigan, OH: University of Michigan Press.

Halliday, Michael A. K. (1978) *Language as Social Semiotic*. London: Arnold.

Handa, Carolyn (ed.) (2004) *Visual Rhetoric in a Digital World*. Boston, MA: Bedford/St Martin's.

Harland, Richard (1987) *Superstructuralism: The Philosophy of Structuralism and Post-Structuralism*. London: Routledge.

Harris, Roy (1987) *Reading Saussure: A Critical Commentary on the 'Cours de linguistique générale'*. London: Duckworth.

—— (1995) *Signs of Writing*. London: Routledge.

—— (2001) 'Linguistics after Saussure', in Cobley (ed.) (2001), pp. 118–33.

—— (2003) *Saussure and His Interpreters* (2nd edn). Edinburgh: Edinburgh University Press.

Hartley, John (1982) *Understanding News*. London: Routledge.

Hatten, Robert S. (1994) *Musical Meaning in Beethoven: Markedness, Correlation, and Interpretation*. Bloomington, IN: Indiana University Press.

Hawkes, Terence (1972) *Metaphor*. London: Methuen.

—— (1977) *Structuralism and Semiotics*. London: Routledge.

Hayakawa, S. I. (1941) *Language in Action*. New York: Harcourt, Brace.

Hayes, E. Nelson and Tanya Hayes (eds) (1970) *Claude Lévi-Strauss: The Anthropologist as Hero*. Cambridge, MA: MIT Press.

Henley, Nancy M. (1977) *Body Politics: Power, Sex and Nonverbal Communication*. Englewood Cliffs, NJ: Prentice-Hall.

Hill, Charles A. and Marguerite Helmers (eds) (2004) *Defining Visual Rhetorics*. Mahwah, NJ: Lawrence Erlbaum.

Hinde, Robert A. (ed.) (1975) *Non-verbal Communication*. Cambridge: Cambridge University Press.

Hirsch, Julia (1981) *Family Photographs: Content, Meaning and Effect*. New York: Oxford University Press.

Hjelmslev, Louis (1961) *Prolegomena to a Theory of Language* (trans. Francis J. Whitfield). Madison: University of Wisconsin Press.

Hockett, Charles F. (1958) *A Course in Modern Linguistics*. New York: Macmillan.

Hodge, Robert and Gunther Kress (1988) *Social Semiotics*. Cambridge: Polity.

Hodge, Robert and David Tripp (1986) *Children and Television: A Semiotic Approach*. Cambridge: Polity Press.

Holbrook, Morris B. and Elizabeth C. Hirschman (1993) *The Semiotics of Consumption: Interpreting Symbolic Consumer Behavior in Popular Culture and Works of Art*. Berlin: Mouton de Gruyter.

Holdcroft, David (1991) *Saussure: Signs, Systems and Arbitrariness*. Cambridge: Cambridge University Press.

Holmqvist, Berit, Peter Bogh Andersen, Heinz Klein and Roland Posner (eds) (1996) *Signs of Work: Semiosis and Information Processing in Organizations*. Berlin: de Gruyter.

Howells, Richard (2003) *Visual Culture*. Cambridge: Polity.

Huxley, Aldous (1941) *Ends and Means: An Enquiry into the Nature of Ideals and into the Methods employed for their Realization*. London: Chatto & Windus.

Iampolski, Mikhail (1998) *The Memory of Tiresias: Intertextuality and Film* (trans. Harsha Ram). Berkeley, CA: University of California Press.

Innis, Robert E. (ed.) (1986) *Semiotics: An Introductory Reader*. London: Hutchinson.

Jablin, Frederic M. and Linda L. Putnam (eds) (2000) *The New Handbook of Organizational Communication: Advances in Theory, Research, and Methods*. Newbury Park, CA: Sage.

Jackson, Bernard S. (1985) *Semiotics and Legal Theory*. London: Routledge.

—— (1995) *Making Sense in Law Linguistic, Psychological and Semiotic Perspectives*. Liverpool: Charles.

Jakobson, Roman (1939) 'The Zero Sign', in Jakobson (1984a), pp. 151–60.

——— (1943) 'Franz Boas' Approach to Language', in Jakobson (1971b), pp. 477–88.

——— (1949a) 'Current Issues of General Linguistics', in Jakobson (1990), pp. 49–55.

——— (1949b) 'The Phonemic and Grammatical Aspects of Language in Their Interrelations', in Jakobson (1990), pp. 395–406; also in Jakobson (1971b), pp. 103–14.

——— (1949c) 'On the Identification of Phonemic Entities', in Jakobson (1971a), pp. 418–25.

——— (1952a) 'Patterns in Linguistics', in Jakobson (1971b), pp. 223–8.

——— (1952b) 'Results of a Joint Conference of Anthropologists and Linguists', in Jakobson (1971b), pp. 554–67.

——— (1953) 'Aphasia as a Linguistic Topic', in Jakobson (1971b), pp. 229–38.

——— (1956) 'Two Aspects of Language and Two Types of Aphasic Disturbances', in Jakobson and Halle (1956), pp. 67–96; also in Jakobson (1971b), pp. 239–59 and Jakobson (1990), pp. 115–33.

——— (1957) 'Shifters and Verbal Categories', in Jakobson (1990), pp. 386–92; extracted from 'Shifters, Verbal Categories, and the Russian Verb' in Jakobson (1971b), pp. 130–47.

——— (1958) 'On Linguistic Aspects of Translation', in Jakobson (1971b), pp. 260–6.

——— (1960) 'Closing Statement: Linguistics and Poetics', in Sebeok (ed.) (1960), pp. 350–77; first part reprinted as 'The Speech Event and the Functions of Language' in Jakobson (1990), pp. 69–79.

——— (1962) 'Results of the Ninth International Conference of Linguists', in Jakobson (1971b), pp. 593–602.

——— (1963a) 'Efforts Toward a Means–End Model of Language in Interwar Continental Linguistics', in Jakobson (1990), pp. 56–60; also in Jakobson (1971b), pp. 522–6.

——— (1963b) 'Parts and Wholes in Language', in Jakobson (1990), pp. 110–14; also in Jakobson (1971b), pp. 280–4.

——— (1963c) 'Linguistic Types of Aphasia', in Jakobson (1971b), pp. 307–33.

——— (1963d) 'Visual and Auditory Signs', in Jakobson (1971b), pp. 334–7.

——— (1963e) 'Towards a Linguistic Classification of Aphasic Impairments', in Jakobson (1971b), pp. 289–306.

——— (1966) 'Quest for the Essence of Language', in Jakobson (1990), pp. 407–21; also in Jakobson (1971b), pp. 345–59.

—— (1967) 'The Relation Between Visual and Auditory Signs', in Jakobson (1971b), pp. 338–44.

—— (1968) 'Language in Relation to Other Communication Systems', in Jakobson (1971b), pp. 697–708.

—— (1970) 'Linguistics in Relation to Other Sciences', in Jakobson (1990), pp. 451–88; also in Jakobson (1971b), pp. 655–96.

—— (1971a) *Selected Writings*, vol. 1, *Phonological Studies*. The Hague: Mouton.

—— (1971b) *Selected Writings*, vol. 2, *Word and Language*. The Hague: Mouton.

—— (1971c) 'Linguistics and Communication Theory'; in Jakobson (1990), pp. 489–97; also in Jakobson (1971b), pp. 570–9.

—— (1971d) 'Retrospect', in Jakobson (1971b), pp. 711–22.

—— (1972) 'Verbal Communication', in *Scientific American* (eds) *Communication*. San Francisco, CA: Freeman, pp. 39–44 (originally in a special issue of *Scientific American*, September 1972).

—— (1973) 'Some Questions of Meaning', in Jakobson (1990), pp. 315–23.

—— (1976) 'The Concept of Phoneme', in Jakobson (1990), pp. 217–41.

—— (1980a) 'The Concept of Mark', in Jakobson (1990), pp. 134–40.

—— (1980b) 'The Time Factor in Language', in Jakobson (1990), pp. 164–75.

—— (1981) 'My Favourite Topics', in Jakobson (1990), pp. 61–6.

—— (1984a) *Russian and Slavic Grammar: Studies 1931–1981* (eds Linda R. Waugh and Morris Halle). Berlin: Mouton.

—— (1984b) 'Language and Parole: Code and Message', in Jakobson (1990), pp. 80–109.

—— (1990) *On Language* (eds Linda R. Waugh and Monique Monville-Burston). Cambridge, MA: Harvard University Press.

Jakobson, Roman and Morris Halle (1956) *Fundamentals of Language*. The Hague: Mouton.

Jakobson, Roman and Claude Lévi-Strauss (1970) 'Charles Baudelaire's "Les Chats"', in Lane (ed.) (1970), pp. 202–21.

James, William (1890/1950) *The Principles of Psychology*, vol. 1. New York: Dover.

Jameson, Fredric (1972) *The Prison-House of Language*. Princeton, NJ: Princeton University Press.

Jencks, Charles (2002) *The New Paradigm in Architecture: The Language of Postmodernism*. New Haven, CT: Yale University Press.

Jensen, Klaus Bruhn (1995) *The Social Semiotics of Mass Communication*. London: Sage.

Jhally, Sut (1987) *The Codes of Advertising: Fetishism and the Political Economy of Meaning in the Consumer Society*. New York: Routledge.

Johnson, Richard (1996) 'What is cultural studies anyway?', in Storey (ed.) (1996), pp. 75–114.

Jones, Amelia (ed.) (2003) *The Feminism and Visual Culture Reader*. London: Routledge.

Katz, James E. and Mark Aakhus (eds) (2002) *Perpetual Contact: Mobile Communication, Private Talk, Public Performance*. Cambridge: Cambridge University Press.

Keller, Helen (1945) *The Story of My Life*. London: Hodder & Stoughton.

Keller, Rudi (1998) *A Theory of Linguistic Signs* (trans. Kimberley Duenwald). Oxford: Oxford University Press.

Kendon, Adam (ed.) (1981) *Nonverbal Communication, Interaction and Gesture*. The Hague: Mouton.

Kennedy, John (1974) *A Psychology of Picture Perception*. San Francisco, CA: Jossey-Bass.

Kevelson, Roberta (ed.) (1988a) *Law and Semiotics*. Dordrecht: Kluwer.

—— (1988b) *The Law As a System of Signs*. Dordrecht: Kluwer.

—— (1990) *Peirce, Paradox, Praxis: The Image, the Conflict and the Law*. Berlin: Mouton de Gruyter.

—— (ed.) (1991) *Peirce and Law: Issues in Pragmatism, Legal Realism and Semiotics*. New York: Lang.

—— (1999) *Peirce and the Mark of the Gryphon*. New York: St Martin's Press.

Kidwell, Claudia Brush and Valerie Steele (eds) (1989) *Men and Women: Dressing the Part*. Washington: Smithsonian Institution Press.

Kitses, Jim (1970) *Horizons West*. London: Secker & Warburg/BFI.

Knapp, Mark L. and Judith A. Hall (2002) *Nonverbal Communication in Human Interaction* (5th edn). Belmont, CA: Wadsworth.

Korzybski, Alfred (1933) *Science and Sanity: An Introduction to Non-Aristotelian Systems and General Semantics*. Lancaster, PA: Science Press.

Kostelnick, Charles and Michael Hassett (2003) *Shaping Information: The Rhetoric of Visual Conventions*. Carbondale, IL: Southern llinois University Press.

Krampen, Martin (1979) *Meaning in the Urban Environment*. London: Pion.

Kress, Gunther (1998) 'Front pages: (the critical) analysis of newspaper layout', in Allan Bell and Peter Garrett (eds) (1998) *Approaches to Media Discourse*. Oxford: Blackwell, pp. 186–219.

—— (2001) 'Sociolinguistics and Social Semiotics', in Cobley (ed.) (2001), pp. 66–82.

Kress, Gunther and Theo van Leeuwen (1996) *Reading Images: The Grammar of Visual Design*. London: Routledge.
—— (1998) 'Front pages: (the critical) analysis of newspaper layout', in Allan Bell and Peter Garrett (eds) (1998) *Approaches to Media Discourse*. Oxford: Blackwell, pp. 186–219.
—— (2001) *Multimodal Discourse: The Modes and Media of Contemporary Communication*. London: Arnold.
Kristeva, Julia (1970) *Le Texte du roman*. The Hague: Mouton.
—— (1973) 'The system and the speaking subject', *Times Literary Supplement* 12th October 1973: 1249.
—— (1974) *La Révolution du langage poétique*. Paris: Seuil.
—— (1980) *Desire in Language: A Semiotic Approach to Literature and Art*. New York: Columbia University Press.
—— (1997) *The Portable Kristeva* (ed. Kelly Oliver). New York: Columbia University Press.
Lacan, Jacques (1977) *Écrits* (trans. Alan Sheridan). London: Routledge.
LaFrance, Marianne and Clara Mayo (1978) *Moving Bodies: Nonverbal Communication in Social Relationships*. Monterey, CA: Brooks/Cole.
Lakoff, George and Mark Johnson (1980) *Metaphors We Live By*. Chicago: University of Chicago Press.
Lane, Michael (ed.) (1970) *Introduction to Structuralism*. New York: Basic Books.
Langer, Susanne K. (1951) *Philosophy in a New Key: A Study in the Symbolism of Reason, Rite and Art*. New York: Mentor.
Lanham, Richard A. (1969) *A Handlist of Rhetorical Terms*. Berkeley: University of California Press.
Lapsley, Robert and Michael Westlake (1988) *Film Theory: An Introduction*. Manchester: Manchester University Press.
Larrucia, Victor (1975) 'Little Red Riding-Hood's metacommentary: paradoxical injunction, semiotics and behaviour', *Modern Language Notes* 90(4): 517–34.
Lash, Scott (1990) *Sociology of Postmodernism*. London: Routledge.
Leach, Edmund (1970) *Lévi-Strauss*. London: Fontana.
—— (1976) *Culture and Communication: An Introduction to the Use of Structuralist Analysis in Social Anthropology*. Cambridge: Cambridge University Press.
—— (1982) *Social Anthropology*. London: Fontana.
Leeds-Hurwitz, Wendy (1993) *Semiotics and Communication: Signs, Codes, Cultures*. Hillsdale, NJ: Lawrence Erlbaum.
Leiss, William, Stephen Kline and Sut Jhally (1990) *Social Communication in Advertising: Persons, Products and Images of Well-Being* (2nd edn). London: Routledge.

Lemke, Jay (1995) *Textual Politics: Discourse and Social Dynamics*. London: Taylor & Francis.

Lévi-Strauss, Claude (1950/1987) *Introduction to the Work of Marcel Mauss* (trans. Felicity Baker). London: Routledge & Kegan Paul.

—— (1961) *Tristes Tropiques* (trans. John Russell). New York: Criterion.

—— (1962/1974) *The Savage Mind*. London: Weidenfeld and Nicolson.

—— (1964) *Totemism* (trans. Rodney Needham). Harmondsworth: Penguin.

—— (1968) 'The Culinary Triangle', in Counihan and van Esterik (eds) (1997), pp. 28–35.

—— (1969) *The Raw and the Cooked* (trans. John and Doreen Weightman). Chicago: University of Chicago Press.

—— (1972) *Structural Anthropology* (trans. Claire Jacobson and Brooke Grundfest Schoepf). Harmondsworth: Penguin.

Lewis, Justin (1991) *The Ideological Octopus: An Exploration of Television and its Audience*. New York: Routledge.

Leymore, Varda Langholz (1975) *Hidden Myth: Structure and Symbolism in Advertising*. New York: Basic Books.

Lidov, David (1999) *Elements of Semiotics*. New York: St Martin's Press.

Liszka, James Jakob (1996) *A General Introduction to the Semeiotic of Charles Sanders Peirce*. Bloomington, IN: Indiana University Press.

Liu, Kecheng (2000) *Semiotics in Information Systems Engineering*. Cambridge: Cambridge University Press.

—— (2004) *Virtual, Distributed and Flexible Organisations: Studies in Organisational Semiotics*. Berlin: Springer.

Liu, Kecheng and Rodney J. Clarke, Peter Bøgh Andersen and Ronald K. Stamper (eds) (2000) *Information, Organisation and Technology: Studies in Organisational Semiotics*. Berlin: Springer.

Liu, Kecheng and Rodney J. Clarke, Peter Bøgh Andersen, Ronald K. Stamper and El-Sayed Abou-Zeid (eds) (2002) *Organizational Semiotics: Evolving a Science of Information Systems*. Berlin: Springer.

Lodge, David (1977/1996) *The Modes of Modern Writing: Metaphor, Metonymy and the Typology of Modern Literature*. London: Arnold.

Lotman, Yuri (1976a) *Analysis of the Poetic Text*. Ann Arbor, MI: University of Michigan Press.

—— (1976b) *Semiotics of Cinema* (trans. Mark Suino). Ann Arbor, MI: University of Michigan Press.

—— (1990) *Universe of the Mind: A Semiotic Theory of Culture* (trans. Ann Shukman). Bloomington, IN: Indiana University Press.

Lovell, Terry (1983) *Pictures of Reality: Aesthetics, Politics and Pleasure*. London: BFI.

Lukken, Gerard and Mark Searle (1993) *Semiotics and Church Architecture: Applying the Semiotics of A.J. Greimas and the Paris School to the Analysis of Church Buildings*. Kampen: Kok Pharos.

Lyons, John (1977) *Semantics*, vol. 1. Cambridge: Cambridge University Press.

MacCabe, Colin (1974) 'Realism and the cinema', *Screen* 15 (2), pp. 7–27.

Macksey, Richard and Eugenia Donato (eds) (1972) *The Structuralist Controversy: The Languages of Criticism and the Sciences of Man*. Baltimore, MD: Johns Hopkins University Press.

Malandro, Loretta A., Larry Barker and Deborah Ann Barker (1989) *Nonverbal Communication* (2nd edn). New York: McGraw-Hill.

Malkiel, Yakov (1968) *Essays on Linguistic Themes*. Oxford: Blackwell.

Manovich, Lev (2001) *The Language of New Media*. Cambridge, MA: MIT Press.

Marion, Gilles (1994) 'L'apparence des individus: Une lecture socio-sémiotique de la mode', *Protée* 23(2): 113–19.

Martin, Bronwen and Felizitas Ringham (2000) *Dictionary of Semiotics*. London: Cassell.

Mayo, Clara and Nancy M. Henley (eds) (1981) *Gender and Nonverbal Behavior*. New York: Springer-Verlag.

McCracken, Grant (1987) 'Advertising: Meaning or Information', in Melanie Wallendorf and Paul Anderson (eds) *Advances in Consumer Research*, vol. 14. Provo, UT: Association for Consumer Research, pp. 121–4.

—— (1990) *Culture and Consumption: New Approaches to the Symbolic Character of Consumer Goods and Activities*. Bloomington, IN: Indiana University Press.

McFall, Liz (2004) *Advertising: A Cultural Economy* (Culture, Representation & Identity). London: Sage.

McKim, Robert H. (1972) *Experiences in Visual Thinking*. Monterey, CA: Brooks/Cole.

McKracken, Ellen (1993) *Decoding Women's Magazines: From 'Mademoiselle' to 'Ms.'* New York: St Martin's Press.

McLuhan, Marshall (1962) *The Gutenberg Galaxy*. Toronto: University of Toronto Press.

—— (1970) *Counterblast*. London: Rapp & Whiting.

McNeill, David (1995) *Hand and Mind: What Gestures Reveal about Thought*. Chicago: University of Chicago Press.

McQuarrie, Edward F. and David Glen Mick (1992) 'On resonance: a critical pluralistic inquiry into advertising rhetoric', *Journal of Consumer Research* 19: 180–97.

Meggs, Philip B. (1992) *Type and Image: The Language of Graphic Design.* New York: Wiley.

Melrose, Susan (1994) *A Semiotics of the Dramatic Text.* London: Palgrave Macmillan.

Merrell, Floyd (1991) *Signs Becoming Signs: Our Perfusive, Pervasive Universe.* Bloomington, IN: Indiana University Press.

—— (1995a) *Semiosis in the Postmodern Age.* West Lafayette, IN: Purdue University Press.

—— (1995b) *Peirce's Semiotics Now.* Toronto: Canadian Scholars' Press.

—— (1997) *Peirce, Signs, and Meaning.* Toronto: University of Toronto Press.

—— (2001) 'Charles Sanders Peirce's concept of the sign', in Cobley (ed.) (2001), pp. 28–39.

Messaris, Paul (1982) 'To what extent does one have to learn to interpret movies?' in Sari Thomas (ed.) (1982) *Film/Culture.* Metuchen, NJ: Scarecrow Press, pp. 168–83.

—— (1994) *Visual 'Literacy': Image, Mind and Reality.* Boulder, CO: Westview Press.

—— (1997) *Visual Persuasion: The Role of Images in Advertising.* London: Sage.

Metz, Christian (1968/1974) *Film Language: A Semiotics of the Cinema* (trans. Michael Taylor). New York: Oxford University Press.

—— (1971/1974) *Language and Cinema* (trans. Jean Umiker-Sebeok). The Hague: Mouton.

—— (1981) 'Methodological propositions for the analysis of film', in Eaton (ed.) (1981), pp. 86–98.

—— (1977/1982) *The Imaginary Signifier* (trans. Celia Britton, Annwyl Williams, Ben Brewster and Alfred Guzzetti). Bloomington: Indiana University Press.

Mick, David Glen and Claus Buhl (1992) 'A meaning-based model of advertising experiences', *Journal of Consumer Research* 19: 317–38.

Mick, David Glen and Laura G. Politi (1989) 'Consumers' interpretations of advertising imagery: a visit to the hell of connotation', in Elizabeth C. Hirschman (ed.) (1989) *Interpretive Consumer Research.* Provo, UT: Association for Consumer Research, pp. 85–96.

Middleton, Richard (1990) *Studying Popular Music.* Buckingham: Open University Press.

Miller, J. Hillis (1992) *Illustration.* London: Reaktion.

Minai, Asghar Talaye (1985) *Architecture As Environment Communication.* Berlin: Mouton De Gruyter.

Mitchell, W. J. T. (ed.) (1980) *The Language of Images.* Chicago: University of Chicago Press.

—— (1987) *Iconology: Image, Text, Ideology*. Chicago: University of Chicago Press.

—— (1994) *Picture Theory: Essays on Verbal and Visual Representation*. Chicago: University of Chicago Press.

Mitry, Jean (2000) *Semiotics and the Analysis of Film* (trans. Christopher King). Bloomington, IN: Indiana University Press.

Mollerup, Per (1997) *Marks of Excellence: The History and Taxonomy of Trademarks*. London: Phaidon.

Monaco, James (1981) *How to Read a Film*. New York: Oxford University Press.

Monelle, Raymond (1992) *Linguistics and Semiotics in Music*. London: Routledge.

—— (2000) *The Sense of Music*. Princeton, NJ: Princeton University Press.

Morley, David (1980) *The 'Nationwide' Audience: Structure and Decoding*. London: BFI.

—— (1981) '"The *Nationwide* Audience" – a critical postscript', *Screen Education* 39: 3–14.

—— (1983) 'Cultural transformations: the politics of resistance', in Davis and Walton (eds) (1983), pp. 104–17.

—— (1992) *Television, Audiences and Cultural Studies*. London: Routledge.

Morris, Charles W. (1938/1970) *Foundations of the Theory of Signs*. Chicago: Chicago University Press.

Morris, Pam (ed.) (1994) *The Bakhtin Reader: Selected Writings of Bakhtin, Medvedev, Voloshinov*. London: Arnold.

Muller, John P. (1995) *Beyond the Psychoanalytic Dyad: Developmental Semiotics in Freud, Peirce and Lacan*. London: Routledge.

Muller, John P. and Joseph Brent (eds) (2000) *Peirce, Semiotics and Psychoanalysis*. Baltimore, MD: Johns Hopkins University Press.

Myers, David (2003) *The Nature of Computer Games: Play As Semiosis*. New York: Lang.

Nadin, Mihai and Richard D. Zakia (1994) *Creating Effective Advertising Using Semiotics*. New York: Consultant Press.

Nattiez, Jean-Jacques (1977) 'The Contribution of Musical Semiotics to the Semiotic Discussion in General', in Sebeok (ed.) (1997), pp. 121–42.

—— (1992) *Music and Discourse: Toward a Semiology of Music* (trans. Carolyn Abbate). Princeton, NJ: Princeton University Press.

—— (2004) *The Battle of Chronos and Orpheus: Essays in Applied Musical Semiology* (trans. Jonathan Dunsby). Oxford: Oxford University Press.

Nava, Mica, Andrew Blake, Iain MacRury and Barry Richards (eds) (1997) *Buy This Book: Studies in Advertising and Consumption*. London: Routledge.

Needham, Rodney (ed.) (1973) *Right and Left: Essays on Dual Symbolic Classification*. Chicago, IL: University of Chicago Press.

Newcomb, Theodore M. (1952) *Social Psychology*. London: Tavistock.

Nichols, Bill (1981) *Ideology and the Image: Social Representation in the Cinema and Other Media*. Bloomington, IN: Indiana University Press.

—— (1991) *Representing Reality*. Bloomington, IN: Indiana University Press.

Nöth, Winfried (1990) *Handbook of Semiotics*. Bloomington, IN: Indiana University Press.

—— (ed.) (1998) *Semiotics of the Media: State of the Art, Projects and Perspectives*. Berlin: de Gruyter.

Ogden, Charles K. (1930/1944) *Basic English* (9th edn). London: Kegan Paul, Trench, Trubner & Co.

Ogden, Charles K. and Ivor A. Richards (1923) *The Meaning of Meaning*. London: Routledge & Kegan Paul.

Olson, David E. (ed.) (1994) *The World on Paper: The Conceptual and Cognitive Implications of Writing and Reading*. Cambridge: Cambridge University Press.

Osgood, Charles E., George J. Suci and Percy H. Tannenbaum (1957) *The Measurement of Meaning*. Urbana, IL: University of Illinois Press.

Ostwald, Peter F. (1973) *Semiotics of Human Sound*. Berlin: de Gruyter.

O'Toole, Michael (1994) *The Language of Displayed Art*. London: Leicester University Press.

Page, Adrian (2000) *Cracking Morse Code: Semiotics and Television Drama*. Luton: University of Luton Press.

Panofsky, Erwin (1970) *Meaning in the Visual Arts*. Harmondsworth: Penguin.

Paoletti, Jo B. and Carol L. Kregloh (1989) 'The Children's Department', in Kidwell and Steele (eds) (1989), pp. 22–41.

Parkin, Frank (1972) *Class Inequality and Political Order*. London: Granada.

Passmore, John (1985) *Recent Philosophers*. London: Duckworth.

Pavis, Patrice (1993) *Languages of the Stage: Essays in the Semiology of Theatre*. Baltimore, MD: Johns Hopkins University Press.

Peirce, Charles Sanders (1931–58) *Collected Papers* (8 vols: vol. 1, *Principles of Philosophy,* ed. Charles Hartshorne and Paul Weiss, 1931; vol. 2, *Elements of Logic*, ed. Charles Hartshorne and Paul Weiss, 1932; vol. 3, *Exact Logic (Published Papers)*, ed. Charles Hartshorne and Paul Weiss, 1933; vol. 4, *The Simplest Mathematics*; ed. Charles Hartshorne and Paul Weiss, 1933; vol. 5, *Pragmatism and Pragmaticism*, ed. Charles Hartshorne and Paul Weiss, 1934; vol. 6, *Scientific Metaphysics* ed. Charles Hartshorne and Paul Weiss, 1935; vol. 7, *Science and Philosophy*, ed. William A. Burks, 1958; vol. 8,

Reviews, Correspondence and Bibliography, ed. William A. Burks, 1958). Cambridge, MA: Harvard University Press.

—— (1966) *Selected Writings*. New York: Dover.

—— (1982–93) *The Writings of Charles S. Peirce: A Chronological Edition* (6 vols so far: vol. 1, *1857–1866*, ed. Max Fisch, 1982; vol. 2, *1867–1871*, ed. Edward C. Moore, 1984; vol. 3, *1872–1878*, ed. Christian Kloesel, 1986; vol. 4, *1879–1884* ed. Christian Kloesel, 1986; vol. 5, *1884–1886*, ed. Christian Kloesel, 1993; vol. 6, *1886–1890*, ed. Nathan Houser, 1993). Bloomington IN: Indiana University Press.

—— (1992) *The Essential Peirce: Selected Philosophical Writings* (2 vols: vol. 1, 1867–1893, ed. Nathan Houser and Christian Kloesel; vol. 2, 1893–1913, ed. Peirce Edition Project). Bloomington, IN: Indiana University Press.

Perron, Paul, Marcel Danesi, Jean Umiker-Sebeok and Anthony Watanabe (eds) (2003) *Semiotics and Information Sciences*. New York: Legas.

Peters, Jan M. (1981) *Pictorial Signs and the Language of Film*. Amsterdam: Rodopi.

Petrilli, Susan and Augusto Ponzio (2004) *Views In Literary Semiotics*. Ottawa: Legas.

Pharies, David (1985) *Charles S. Peirce and the Linguistic Sign*. Amsterdam: Benjamins.

Piaget, Jean (1929) *The Child's Conception of the World*. New York: Humanities Press.

—— (1971) *Structuralism* (trans. Chaninah Maschler). London: Routledge & Kegan Paul.

Plato (1973) *Phaedrus and Letters VII and VIII* (trans. Walter Hamilton). Harmondsworth: Penguin.

—— (1998) *Cratylus* (trans. C. D. C. Reeve). Indianapolis, IN: Hackett.

Polhemus, Ted (ed.) (1978) *Social Aspects of the Human Body*. Harmondsworth: Penguin.

Pollio, Howard, J. Barrow, H. Fine and M. Pollio (1977) *The Poetics of Growth: Figurative Language in Psychology, Psychotherapy and Education*. Hillsdale, NJ: Lawrence Erlbaum.

Preziosi, Donald (1979a) *The Semiotics of the Built Environment: An Introduction to Architectonic Analysis*. Bloomington, IN: Indiana University Press.

—— (1979b) *Architecture, Language and Meaning: The Origins of the Built World and Its Semiotic Organization*. Berlin: de Gruyter.

Propp, Vladimir I. (1928/1968) *Morphology of the Folktale* (trans. Laurence Scott, 2nd edn). Austin: University of Texas Press.

Quinn, Michael L. (1995) *The Semiotic Stage: Prague School Theater Theory*. New York: Lang.

Rapoport, Amos (1983) *The Meaning of the Built Environment: A Nonverbal Communication Approach*. Beverly Hills, CA: Sage.

Reddy, Michael J. (1979) 'The conduit metaphor – a case of frame conflict in our language about language', in Andrew Ortony (ed.) (1979) *Metaphor and Thought*. Cambridge: Cambridge University Press, pp. 284–324.

Reisz, Karel and Gavin Millar (1972) *The Technique of Film Editing*. London: Focal Press.

Remland, Martin S. (2000) *Nonverbal Communication in Everyday Life*. Boston, MA: Houghton Mifflin.

Richards, Barry, Iain MacRury and Jackie Botterill (2000) *The Dynamics of Advertising*. Amsterdam: Harwood.

Richards, Ivor A. (1932) *The Philosophy of Rhetoric*. London: Oxford University Press.

Rodowick, David N. (1994) *The Crisis of Political Modernism: Criticism and Ideology in Contemporary Film Theory*. Berkeley, CA: University of California Press.

Rosenblum, Ralph and Robert Karen (1979) *When the Shooting Stops . . . The Cutting Begins: A Film Editor's Story*. New York: Da Capo.

Ryan, T. A. and C. B. Schwartz (1956) 'Speed of perception as a function of mode of representation', *American Journal of Psychology* 96: 66–9.

Sagan, Carl (1977) *The Dragons of Eden: Speculations on the Evolution of Human Intelligence*. London: Hodder & Stoughton.

Saint-Martin, Fernande (1990) *Semiotics of Visual Language*. Bloomington, IN: Indiana University Press.

Sanders, Carol (ed.) (2004) *The Cambridge Companion to Saussure*. Cambridge: Cambridge University Press.

Sapir, Edward (1958) *Culture, Language and Personality* (ed. D. G. Mandelbaum). Berkeley, CA: University of California Press.

—— (1921/1971) *Language*. London: Rupert Hart-Davis.

Sarup, Madan (1993) *An Introductory Guide to Post-Structuralism and Postmodernism*. Athens, GA: University of Georgia Press.

Sassoon, Rosemary and Albertine Gaur (1997) *Signs, Symbols and Icons: Pre-History to the Computer Age*. Exeter: Intellect.

Saussure, Ferdinand de (1916/1967) *Cours de linguistique générale*. Paris: Payot.

—— (1916/1974) *Course in General Linguistics* (trans. Wade Baskin). London: Fontana/Collins.

—— (1916/1983) *Course in General Linguistics* (trans. Roy Harris). London: Duckworth.

Scanlon, Jennifer (ed.) (2000) *The Gender and Consumer Culture Reader.* New York: New York University Press.

Schapiro, Meyer (1996) *Words, Script and Pictures: Semiotics of Visual Language.* New York: George Braziller.

Schirato, Tony and Jen Webb (2004) *Understanding the Visual.* London: Sage.

Scholes, Robert (1983) *Semiotics and Interpretation.* New Haven, CT: Yale University Press.

Schroeder, Jonathan E. (2002) *Visual Consumption.* London: Routledge.

Scollon, Ron and Suzie Wong Scollon (2003) *Discourses in Place: Language in the Material World.* London: Routledge.

Scott, Clive (1999) *The Spoken Image: Photography and Language.* London: Reaktion.

Scribner, Sylvia and Michael Cole (1981) *The Psychology of Literacy.* Cambridge, MA: Harvard University Press.

Sebeok, Thomas A. (ed.) (1960) *Style in Language.* Cambridge, MA: MIT Press.

—— (1977) *A Perfusion of Signs.* Bloomington, IN: Indiana University Press.

—— (1994a) *Signs: An Introduction to Semiotics.* Toronto: University of Toronto Press.

—— (ed.) (1994b) *Encyclopedic Dictionary of Semiotics* (2nd edn), 3 vols. Berlin: Mouton de Gruyter.

Seiter, Ellen (1992) 'Semiotics, structuralism and television', in Allen (ed.) (1992), pp. 31–66.

Shannon, Claude E. and Warren Weaver (1949) *A Mathematical Model of Communication.* Urbana, IL: University of Illinois Press.

Shapiro, Michael (1983) *The Sense of Grammar: Language as Semeiotic.* Bloomington, IN: Indiana University Press.

—— (ed.) (1993) *The Peirce Seminar Papers: An Annual of Semiotic Analysis*, vol. 1. Providence, RI: Berg.

—— (ed.) (2003) *Essays in Semiotic Analysis* (Peirce Seminar Papers). Oxford: Berghahn.

Shepherd, John (1991) *Music as Social Text.* Cambridge: Polity Press.

Silverman, Kaja (1983) *The Subject of Semiotics.* New York: Oxford University Press.

Silverman, David and Brian Torode (1980) *The Material Word: Some Theories of Language and its Limits.* London: Routledge & Kegan Paul.

Slater, Don (1983) 'Marketing mass photography', in Davis and Walton (eds) (1983), pp. 245–63.

Smith, Frank (1988) *Understanding Reading.* Hillsdale, NJ: Erlbaum.

Sonesson, Göran (1989) *Pictorial Concepts*. Lund: Lund University Press.
—— (1998) 'Icon', 'Iconicity', 'Index', 'Indexicality' and 'Peirce', in Bouissac (ed.) (1998).
Sontag, Susan (1979) *On Photography*. London: Penguin.
Spence, Jo and Patricia Holland (eds) (1991) *Family Snaps: The Meanings of Domestic Photography*. London: Virago.
Stam, Robert (1992) *New Vocabularies in Film Semiotics: Structuralism, Poststructuralism and Beyond*. London: Routledge.
—— (2000) *Film Theory*. Oxford: Blackwell.
Steiner, Wendy (ed.) (1981a) *Image and Code*. Michigan: University of Michigan.
—— (ed.) (1981b) *The Sign in Music and Literature*. Austin, TX: University of Texas Press.
Stephens, Mitchell (1998) *The Rise of the Image, the Fall of the Word*. New York: Oxford University Press.
Stern, Barbara B. (ed.) (1998) *Representing Consumers: Voices, Views and Visions*. London: Routledge.
Storey, John (ed.) (1996) *What is Cultural Studies?* London: Arnold.
Sturrock, John (1979) (ed.) *Structuralism and Since: From Lévi-Strauss to Derrida*. Oxford: Oxford University Press.
—— (1986) *Structuralism*. London: Paladin.
Taft, Charles (1997) 'Color Meaning and Context: Comparisons of Semantic Ratings of Colors on Samples and Objects', *Color Research and Application* 22(1): 40–50.
Tagg, John (1988) *The Burden of Representation: Essays on Photographies and Histories*. Basingstoke: Macmillan.
Tamburri, Anthony Julian (2002) *Italian/American Short Films and Music Videos: A Semiotic Reading*. West Lafayette, IN: Purdue University Press.
Tapper, Richard (1994) 'Animality, Humanity, Morality, Society', in Tim Ingold (ed.) *What is an Animal?* London: Routledge, pp. 47–62.
Tarasti, Eero (1979) *Myth and Music: A Semiotic Approach to the Aesthetics of Myth in Music*. Berlin: de Gruyter.
—— (1994) *A Theory of Musical Semiotics*. Bloomington: Indiana University Press.
—— (1995) *Musical Signification: Essays in the Semiotic Theory and Analysis of Music*. Berlin: Mouton de Gruyter.
—— (2002) *Signs of Music: A Guide to Musical Semiotics*. Berlin: Mouton de Gruyter.
Thibault, Paul J. (1991) *Social Semiotics as Praxis*. Minneapolis, MN: University of Minnesota Press.

—— (1997) *Re-reading Saussure: The Dynamics of Signs in Social Life.* London: Routledge.

Thomas, Julia (ed.) (2000) *Reading Images.* Basingstoke: Palgrave.

Threadgold, Terry and Anne Cranny-Francis (eds) (1990) *Feminine, Masculine and Representation.* Sydney: Allen & Unwin.

Threadgold, Terry and Patricia Palmer Gillard (1990), 'Soap Opera as Gender Training: Teenage Girls and TV' in Threadgold and Cranny-Francis (eds) (1990), pp. 171–89.

Thwaites, Tony, Lloyd Davis and Warwick Mules (1994) *Tools for Cultural Studies: An Introduction.* South Melbourne: Macmillan.

Todorov, Tzvetan (1982) *Theories of the Symbol* (trans. Catherine Porter). Ithaca, NY: Cornell University Press.

Tomaselli, Keyan G. (1996) *Appropriating Images: The Semiotics of Visual Representation.* Højbjerg, Denmark: Intervention Press.

Tuchman, Gaye (1978) *Making News: A Study in the Construction of Reality.* New York: Free Press.

Tudor, Andrew (1974) *Image and Influence: Studies in the Sociology of Film.* London: George Allen & Unwin.

Ubersfeld, Anne (1999) *Reading Theatre* (trans. Frank H. Collins). Toronto: University of Toronto Press.

Umiker-Sebeok, Jean (ed.) (1987) *Marketing and Semiotics: New Directions in the Study of Signs for Sale.* Berlin: Mouton de Gruyter.

van Baest, Arjan (1995) *The Semiotics of C.S. Peirce Applied to Music: A Matter of Belief.* Tilburg: Tilburg University Press.

—— (2004) *A Semiotics of Opera.* Delft: Eburon.

van Leeuwen, Theo (1999) *Speech, Music, Sound.* London: Palgrave Macmillan.

—— (2005) *Introducing Social Semiotics.* London: Routledge.

van Leeuwen, Theo and Carey Jewitt (eds) (2001) *Handbook of Visual Analysis.* London: Sage.

Vestergaard, Torben and Kim Schrøder (1985) *The Language of Advertising.* Oxford: Blackwell.

Vico, Giambattista (1744/1968) *The New Science* (trans. Thomas Goddard Bergin and Max Harold Finch). Ithaca, NY: Cornell University Press.

Voloshinov, Valentin N. (1973) *Marxism and the Philosophy of Language* (trans. Ladislav Matejka and I. R. Titunik). New York: Seminar Press.

Wagner, Anne, Tracey Summerfield and Farid Samir Benavides Vanegas (eds) (2005) *Contemporary Issues of the Semiotics of Law: Cultural and Symbolic Analyses of Law in a Global Context.* Oxford: Hart.

Walker, John A. and Sarah Chaplin (1997) *Visual Culture: An Introduction.* Manchester: Manchester University Press.

Warner, Julian (1994) *From Writing to Computers*. London: Routledge.

Watney, Simon (1982) 'Making strange: the shattered mirror', in Burgin (ed.) (1982a), pp. 154–76.

White, Hayden (1973) *Metahistory: The Historical Imagination in Nineteenth-Century Europe*. Baltimore, MD: Johns Hopkins University Press.

Whittock, Trevor (1990) *Metaphor and Film*. Cambridge: Cambridge University Press.

Whorf, Benjamin Lee (1956) *Language, Thought and Reality* (ed. John B. Carroll). Cambridge, MA: MIT Press.

Wilden, Anthony (1987) *The Rules Are No Game: The Strategy of Communication*. London: Routledge & Kegan Paul.

Williams, Raymond (1974) *Television: Technology and Cultural Form*. London: Fontana.

Williamson, Judith (1978) *Decoding Advertisements*. London: Marion Boyars.

Wimsatt, William K. and Monroe C. Beardsley (1954) *The Verbal Icon: Studies in the Meaning of Poetry*. Lexington, KY: University of Kentucky Press.

Wollen, Peter (1969) *Signs and Meaning in the Cinema*. London: Secker & Warburg/BFI.

Worth, Sol (1981) *Studying Visual Communication*. Philadelphia, PA: University of Pennsylvania Press.

Yazdani, Masoud and Philip Barker (eds) (2000) *Iconic Communication*. Bristol: Intellect.

Yell, Susan (1990) 'Gender, class and power: text, process and production in Strindberg's *Miss Julie*', in Threadgold and Cranny-Francis (eds) (1990), pp. 190–210.

Young, Brian M. (1990) *Television Advertising and Children*. Oxford: Clarendon Press.

Zeman, J. Jay (1997) 'Peirce's Theory of Signs', in Sebeok (ed.) (1977), pp. 22–39.

INDEX

Language: the Basics

Second edition

R. L. Trask

Language: the Basics provides a concise introduction to the study of language. Written in an engaging and entertaining style, it encourages the reader to think about the way language works.

It features:

- chapters on 'Language in Use'; 'Attitudes to Language'; 'Children and Language' and 'Language, Mind and Brain'
- a section on sign language
- a glossary of key terms
- annotated guides to further reading.

Offering an accessible overview of a fascinating subject, this is an essential book for all students and anyone who's ever been accused of splitting an infinitive.

ISBN10: 0–415–20089–x (pbk)
ISBN13: 978–0–415–20089–9 (pbk)

Available at all good bookshops
For ordering and further information please visit
www.routledge.com